Power in the Changing Global Order

Power in the Changing Global Order

The US, Russia and China

MARTIN A. SMITH

polity

First published in 2012 by Polity Press
Reprinted in 2013

Polity Press
65 Bridge Street
Cambridge CB2 1UR, UK

Polity Press
350 Main Street
Malden, MA 02148, USA

ISBN-13: 978-0-7456-3471-5
ISBN-13: 978-0-7456-3472-2 (pb)

A catalogue record for this book is available from the British Library.

Typeset in 11.25 on 13 pt Dante
by Toppan Best-set Premedia Limited
Printed and bound in USA by Edwards Brothers, Inc.

For further information on Polity, visit our website: www.politybooks.com

Contents

Acknowledgements

Notwithstanding its many other virtues, Sandhurst is a place where institutional support for academic research remains in some respects rather qualified and uncertain. I am, therefore, especially grateful to the individuals from within my department who have provided feedback on drafts of this work, either in whole or on particular chapters. Chief amongst these is David Brown, who read the complete manuscript and – as usual – provided detailed and very helpful critique. Donette Murray and Alan Ward kindly read and offered useful comments on individual chapters. Dr Murray also provided the opportunity for me to present an early draft chapter on China to a meeting of the department's informal research group. I am, additionally, no less grateful for the very detailed and helpful comments and suggestions offered by the two anonymous readers commissioned by Polity. The book is substantially better as a result of their input.

One of the undoubted academic advantages of working at Sandhurst is the Central Library. Andrew Orgill and his team have been – as always – a source of immense help and support in obtaining books and other materials from a wide variety of sources. Grace Hudson of Bradford University's J. B. Priestley Library also kindly provided me with a reader's ticket, which enabled me to access her library's very useful holdings of materials on Russia. I am grateful, finally, to Louise Knight and David Winters at Polity for their patience and understanding over a project which took rather longer to complete than originally intended.

In the final analysis, this book is the product of the author's own research and thinking. Its contents and conclusions should not be taken to reflect the policy or views of the British government or Ministry of Defence, or the Royal Military Academy Sandhurst.

Martin A. Smith
Camberley, Surrey
September 2011

Introduction: Power in the Changing Global Order

The purpose and plan of this book

This book is about international power. The topic has been discussed extensively, but thus far with some significant limitations as far as the world politics and international relations literature is concerned. The main one has arisen from a noticeable disinclination on the part of international relations scholars to explore in depth what the idea of 'power' actually means. Analysts working in the field have often seemed more comfortable thinking and writing about who has power and what they do with it, rather than about the core issue of what it is.

The discussions that follow in this brief introduction will address this limitation in more detail. Chapters 1 and 2 will follow on from this by developing an approach to the understanding of power in the international arena. This will then form the conceptual basis for analysing the 'power' of the three states under consideration in this book. Because of the relative absence of relevant work in the world politics and international relations fields, much of the analysis in these opening chapters will draw upon the work of scholars working within the fields of sociology and philosophy.

Having developed a working understanding of power, in subsequent chapters of the book I will test and explore its utility in helping to construct and inform assessments of the 'power' of the contemporary United States, Russia and China. The overall aim here is not to offer a comprehensive introductory guide to power and power relations in the contemporary world *per se*. Hence, relatively little will be said about other states (or groupings of states), such as India, Japan or the European Union, that may be considered significant powers in their own right. By the same token, there will be little discussion of supposedly 'emerging' powers such as Brazil or South Africa.

The three states under consideration here have been chosen on the basis that they represent distinct and important case studies of key aspects of international power in the contemporary world (defined here as the period since the ending of the Cold War in 1989–91). Analysis of their particular characteristics, features and actions therefore affords the opportunity to develop a nuanced assessment of key distinctive features of power in the modern international arena.

After 1945, the United States became the central actor in an international system based on structures, norms and processes of what has been called 'liberal hegemony', which will be analysed in chapter 3. The US has remained, by common consent, a – if not indeed *the* – pivotal international power since the end of the Cold War. Accordingly, the post-Cold War US will receive substantial analytical attention in this book.

Analysts have generally defined the United States' status since the collapse of the Soviet Union at the end of 1991 with reference to the existence of a 'unipolar' world order. The premises of the unipolar concept will be introduced and examined in chapter 3. Chapter 4 will then assess the extent to which the 'real world' order of the 1990s was indeed marked by American unipolarity. During that decade, debates and controversies first arose (and have continued since) over whether the US was accumulating 'too much power' in the absence of an effective system balancer of the kind that the Soviet Union had been during the Cold War.

These debates reached a new intensity after the turn of the millennium. This was a development fuelled largely by the George W. Bush administration's alleged misuse of the US's unipolar status in ways that, according to some, ultimately damaged its international power. The controversies and debates surrounding the initial Bush approach to American power will be examined in chapter 5. There is strong evidence to suggest that the Bush administration recognized the damage that was being done by its early approach to the conduct of international relations, and that it learned from its mistakes and altered its course in significant ways during its second term in office from early 2005. In order to offer a fully rounded assessment of this controversial presidency, this evidence will be examined and discussed in chapter 6.

Russia occupies a unique place in post-Cold War power politics. During the 1990s, its leaders argued that the Russian state was the rightful and legal 'successor' to the defunct Soviet Union, and therefore a leading power in its own right. On the basis of this legal/ideational underpinning, coupled with efforts to consolidate the strength of the Russian state under Vladimir Putin, its leaders have made a claim that their state should be treated by others in the international arena – and most especially by the US – as an important centre of international power. The basis and substance of these Russian claims will be investigated in chapter 7.

Contemporary Russia's main contribution to the conceptual debates about international power has been the notion of 'multipolarity' as the most appropriate form of international relations and organization amongst leading states. Whilst multipolarity has remained largely ritualized rhetoric when used by leaders of states such as China and France, in Russia the debates about its meanings amongst officials and analysts have been, relatively speaking, quite sophisticated. Analysis of multipolarity should be an important component of any study of contemporary international power relations, and the Russian understandings of the concept will be explored here in chapter 8.

Since the 1990s, there has been much debate about the apparent 'rise of China' and the impact that this is having on the contemporary international order – in particular the position and role of the US. China's status differs from that of Russia because, whilst Sinologists sometimes argue that history suggests that it too is a 'natural' Great Power, contemporary Chinese leaders have cast its status clearly as that of a 'rising' power, suggesting that something new and unprecedented is emerging. At the same time, they have consistently stressed the non-threatening nature of this evolution, using phrases such as 'peaceful rise' and 'peaceful development'. The discussions in chapter 9 will focus on the bases and nature of China's rise. The analysis will focus in particular on the extent to which China's emergence can indeed fairly be assessed as a potentially threatening development.

As they have become increasingly confident in claiming the rise of their state, China's leaders have sought to develop the idea – inherent in their concepts of peaceful rise / development – that this will help to promote a 'more harmonious world'. The idea of 'harmony', borrowed from the Confucianist philosophical tradition, has featured prominently in what might be termed the official ideology of China's rise. In view of its importance in this context, its meaning and implications in the contemporary world will be discussed here in chapter 10.

The limitations of power analysis

As noted at the beginning of this introduction, international relations scholars have often shied away from detailed consideration of the question 'what is power?'. Defining it has indeed proved challenging. The noted French thinker Michel Foucault once described power as 'the most hidden, the most occulted, the most deeply invested experience in the history of our culture'.[1] Joseph Nye, a leading international relations scholar, suggested in similar vein that 'power in international politics is like the weather. Everybody talks about it, but few understand it.'[2]

In the related academic disciplines of history and international relations, the challenges of defining power have been especially evident. Broadly speaking, they have engendered three distinct responses. A first has been simply to ignore the challenge. This is a temptation that even eminent scholars have not always been able to resist. Thus, for example, in his 1980s bestseller *The Rise and Fall of the Great Powers*, Paul Kennedy offered nearly 700 pages of analysis without once clearly defining what he understood a Great Power actually to be. The closest Kennedy came in this book was with an oblique reference to France in the early twentieth century having slipped from Great Power status – 'if the mark of a Great Power is a country which is willing and able to take on any other'. Further clouding the picture, Kennedy then proceeded with the contention that this semi-definition was, in any event, 'too abstract' to be of much use in explaining actual French policy during the period in question![3]

A second response to the challenge of defining power has been to reduce it wholly or mainly to the possession of material resources, especially those of an economic or military kind. Indeed, these are often referred to by the shorthand terms 'economic power' and 'military power', respectively, as if power is produced naturally and automatically as a consequence of their existence and possession. This approach has held particular appeal for scholars working within the so-called realist tradition in international relations. Realist analysts tend to stress the competitive nature of international politics and the primary role played by states in shaping international relations, motivated largely by their leaders' desire to maximize relative security and power. Against this backdrop, John Mearsheimer, one of the best-known contemporary realist scholars, has identified military, and what he calls 'latent', power as being pivotal. Mearsheimer defines latent power as 'the socio-economic ingredients that go into building military power'.[4] For him, therefore, it is clear that military capacity constitutes the basis and indeed the essence of power *per se*.

A final and quite common response to the challenge of defining power has been to begin with a broad, simple and basic definition. Typically this suggests that power exists when actor 'A' gets actor 'B' to do something which 'B' might not otherwise have done. In this straightforward formulation, 'power' is effectively a commodity or resource which becomes tangible, quantifiable and effective when it is operationalized. This approach has the virtue of addressing definitional issues directly. An important limitation to it, however, is that it has proved prone to being used as a basis for the kind of reductionist analysis that equates 'power' simply with the possession of economic and military resources and capabilities.

It will be argued in the following chapters that this approach is, therefore, too narrow and limited and that it misses crucial *social* dimensions of power. Power is essentially social because it is always relative and a product of human relationships. If only one relevant actor existed, or if individual actors had no contact with one another, there would, by definition, be no opportunity (or need) for power. Thus, power, as John Rothgeb has put it, 'is found only when members of [a] system interact with one another'.[5] Therefore it is not solely or mainly a naturally occurring product of a given actor's material resources. Rather, power should be looked for mainly in the nature and outcomes of the actor's interactions with others.[6]

Summary of the argument

Power is mainly a social and relational construct, although it might well have a basis in the possession of resources. Such resources need not be material in nature, however, as the discussions in chapter 2 will make clear. It can also be argued that power is not a primordial phenomenon. That is to say, it is not something that exists simply as an inherent feature or product of the natural environment, and as a quality of certain actors within it. Power is created and operationalized as a consequence of social interaction. It requires conscious human endeavour and activity in order to assume tangible existence.

1

Understanding Power

As the discussions in the introduction here have indicated, there is relatively little for students of world politics and international relations to go on from within their own discipline in attempting to develop a deeper understanding of the nature of power. In order to do so it is, therefore, necessary to step outside disciplinary boundaries. It is worth considering, in particular, insights put forward by sociologists, who have argued that power is embodied in human relationships.

Power as relationships

Sociologists are, indeed, interested primarily in human relationships. Therefore, if it is accepted that power is essentially a social phenomenon, it is hardly surprising that notably detailed and sophisticated explorations of it should have been developed by them. Amongst the best known of those who have studied power has been the American sociologist Talcott Parsons. His distinctive insight was the suggestion that, in terms of its functionality, power can usefully be compared to money. In developing this metaphor, Parsons stressed that power is not primarily a material commodity or resource. Rather, he argued that it should be viewed as a vital – indeed *the* vital – medium of exchange in social and political relations, just as money is the vital medium of exchange in economic and commercial life.[1] In Parsons's analysis, if it is viewed as a medium of exchange, then power, like money, is worth very little in its own right. Its real value is found in the extent to which – and the effectiveness *with* which – it can be operationalized to obtain desired outcomes. Thus, in this view, power is essentially instrumental. Its worth lies in the extent to which it helps in achieving or advancing desired objectives.

In the world politics and international relations literature, the power/ money comparison has been quite widely criticized. Such criticisms have been made on the grounds that power resources, especially material ones, are less fungible than money. To speak of the fungibility of money means that it can be converted into something of equivalent worth and value in a variety of different transactions and contexts. With this in mind, it has been argued that, for example, a significant military capability will not necessarily convert into an effective power resource in the economic or commercial arenas. Traditional military capabilities might not even realize effective power in the face of certain types of armed threat, such as those involving the kinds of insurgency which occurred in Afghanistan after 2001 and Iraq after 2003.[2]

Yet, Parsons did not conceptualize power primarily in resource terms. The underlying point that he strove to make with his metaphor was that the operational utility and value of it are essentially interactive. Because it is relative, power can only be present in interactions amongst and between different actors. Power is therefore evident primarily in defined social processes and systems, rather than amongst essentially detached individual actors. This is an important core assumption of much of the sociological analysis.

Power is also more than just the sum total of the aggregate results of such interactions. Talcott Parsons rightly argued that it reflects, rather, 'the *capacity of a social system to get things done in its collective interest*. Hence power involves a special problem of the *integration* of the system, including the binding of its units, individual and collective, to the necessary commitments' [emphasis in the original].[3]

How might this view of power help us more usefully to understand it with particular reference to world politics and international relations? For realist scholars, the international system remains essentially anarchic, in the sense that there is as yet no established, reliable and embracing system of global governance, and therefore no ultimate global collective. Non-realists generally accept this, although they tend to be relatively more optimistic about the prospects for meaningful international cooperation and collaboration nonetheless.

Does the essentially anarchic nature of the international arena undermine the value of insights from those such as Parsons, who stress the importance of social systems? Not necessarily. A functioning social system does not have to be a *structural* entity, such as a state or government. Max Weber, perhaps the best-known sociologist of all, argued that a structured collective entity could not, in fact, exist. To that end, Weber wrote: 'Collectivities must be treated as *solely* the resultants and modes of organization of the particular acts of individual[s], since these alone can be treated as agents in a course of subjectively understandable action...there is no such thing as a collective personality which "acts'" [emphasis in the original].[4]

Thus individual actors *do* matter, although their importance in terms of power relations accrues mainly through their interactions with others. A viable and meaningful social system develops on the basis of a defined sense of shared interests and values amongst the individual actors. This, in turn, produces shared objectives and promotes common activity in pursuit of them. It does not mean that the constituent actors must always agree with each other on individual issues. It does, however, suggest that they must reach enduring agreement on some basic objectives and principles, which then condition their behaviour over a period of time.

This is important in order both to underwrite and to maintain the value of the shared exchanges amongst themselves. Individual actor-participants must be aware of, and willing to take into account, the prospective impact of their actions and activities on others when making decisions and contemplating action. This is the essence of what Max Weber termed 'social action'.[5]

Essential equivalence amongst actors

Bringing Parsons's power/money metaphor back into the picture at this point suggests that chief amongst the ground rules for social action should be acceptance that those participating enjoy in some meaningful way an equivalent status as actors, although this does not necessarily mean being regarded as equals across the board. This is important if power (or money) is to constitute a genuine and meaningful medium of exchange, given the mutuality and fungibility inherent in that.[6]

This argument can be illustrated by considering the hypothetical example of two individuals. If money is to retain its overall value and continue to be generally trusted as the key medium of economic exchange, then £100 spent by someone with nothing else left in the bank has to be worth as much at the point of transaction – and therefore be able to purchase as much in the transaction – as £100 proffered by a millionaire. In this particular context, therefore, the two would enjoy an essential equivalence, notwithstanding the basic material differences that exist between them. The latter of course are hardly irrelevant in the wider picture. The level of sacrifice and commitment required of the relatively impoverished individual in spending their last £100 is self-evidently significantly greater than that demanded of the millionaire. Context and the relative command of resources are therefore important conditioning – if not always determining – factors.

In international politics, what might be called essential equivalence is best reflected in what is known as the juridical equality of states. This is a legal construct. Its essential meaning is twofold. Firstly, in terms of the overall international system, states are legally identified as the most important individual actors. Secondly, all recognized states are legally entitled to the same core rights, entailed in their possession of legal sovereignty. The principal sovereign rights are recognition of bounded territory, formal protection from aggression by other states, and the right to participate in international diplomatic relations and processes. Legally speaking it is these, rather than the possession of military and economic capabilities, that constitute the foundation of what might be called a state's 'national power'.

This might in practice, as Stephen Krasner has argued, rest to a significant extent on 'organized hypocrisy' on the part of the states themselves, particularly the larger and more materially capable amongst them.[7] For Krasner, the 'hypocrisy' resides mainly in the extent to which the legal equality of all states is accepted as the basis for conducting international relations, notwithstanding the significant differences that exist amongst states in terms of size and material capabilities. States are clearly *not* equal in terms of their respective capabilities. Legally, however, they enjoy what is here called essential equivalence.

This is a very important 'hypocrisy'. A clear majority of states have evidently felt it important to maintain it as the basis of the international system since it was formalized in the mid-twentieth century, mainly through the United Nations Charter. For the argument being developed in this book, this matters because it provides the structural framework within which processes of international power, as understood here, can and do operate.

Evidence for the enduring hold of the idea of juridical equality (enshrined since 1945 mainly in Article 2 of the UN Charter)[8] can be seen in the intense controversies and hostile reactions engendered on the occasions when it can be seen to have been violated. Often this has occurred as a result of external military interventions. The North Korean attack on its southern neighbour in June 1950 and Iraq's invasion of Kuwait in August 1990 are obvious examples. Perhaps more revealing are the controversies generated by proclaimed 'policing actions' designed to prevent or halt human rights abuses or attacks on civilians taking place within states. These declared 'humanitarian interventions' can themselves give rise to concerns about interference in a state's 'sovereign affairs'. The NATO bombing of Serbia over Kosovo from March to June 1999 is a well-known case in this context.

Possibly mindful of the controversies generated by that action, NATO members in early 2011 accepted significant constraints on the military operations which they conducted over Libya, under a UN resolution calling for the protection of civilians from attack in the context of that state's degeneration into a *de facto* civil war.

Overall, juridical equality has helped both to shape and to constrain the ways in which power is conceived and operationalized in the international system. This does not mean that Hans Morgenthau was wrong in his classic realist assertion that 'international politics, like all politics, is a struggle for power'.[9] What matters is how that 'struggle' is conducted. Many individuals might wish to make more money. It would make no sense, however, for them to 'struggle for money' in ways that risk destabilizing and beggaring their local, regional or national economies, and thereby impoverishing everybody, including themselves. By the same token, a 'struggle for power' can take place in ways and with means that do not presuppose that an international system based on the juridical equality of states will become seriously or terminally degraded. This does not, of course, *guarantee* that this will necessarily happen in practice. The situation outlined here assumes that the actors involved will proceed on the basis of a rational calculation that individual and collective gains are closely bound together, if not, indeed, inseparable.

Notwithstanding his contention that power is an 'existential necessity',[10] Morgenthau did accept that, in international practice, states have devised means to ensure that it is channelled and constrained – imperfectly but nonetheless significantly – by a body of international law. This has been developed amongst states in relation to such fundamentally important matters as their own juridical equality, mutual recognition and territorial jurisdiction, and the use of armed force. These are the essential accoutrements of the legal concept of sovereignty.[11] As one analyst observed at the end of the twentieth century: 'Although all states do not obey international law all the time, they obey it often enough for law to constitute an important formative fact in modern international relations.'[12] Analysts have further noted that formal international law has been buttressed by the evolution of more informal but nonetheless significant 'international regimes'. These are principles, norms and patterns of accepted behaviour, which also help to shape the expectations and behaviour of state actors in the international system.[13]

Reflecting on the points made above, it can be said that the underlying nature of contemporary international relations is perhaps best represented as approximating to the 'anarchical society' depicted most famously in academic terms by Hedley Bull.[14] There remain no overarching system or structures of global governance. Yet a significant and influential system of law, norms and rules has been constructed by and around the constituent state actors. Taken together, these serve significantly to shape and regulate the behaviour of most states for much of the time. As suggested earlier, they also provide the framework for the operationalization of international power.

'Networked power'

Since the end of the Cold War, some analysts have been suggesting that, as a result of advances in communication and information technologies, a new dimension to the evolving 'international society' has been increasingly in evidence. The voguish concept of 'networks' has often been used to try to capture and explain this development.

As with many 'in' terms, this one has been used rather loosely and with reference to different phenomena. The notion of 'networked power' has been employed by some in specific reference to the role played by new and accessible information and communication technologies, such as Facebook, Google and Twitter, in helping to facilitate the mobilization of popular movements seeking change against established political regimes. The dramatic upsurge of mass protest in the Arab world in the early months of 2011 was attributed in part to the increasing availability of such tools amongst general populations. The historian Dan Snow, for example, argued that the rise of the protest movements showed that '"connectivity" [via popular access to new technologies] is a precondition of turning discontent into revolution'.[15]

The significance of the impact of new technologies in this context can be exaggerated. After all, the rapid and largely peaceful collapse of communist governments throughout Eastern Europe in the autumn of 1989 – the events that triggered the ending of the Cold War – was at least as dramatic as the events of the 'Arab spring' twenty-one years later. The former events took place in an era *before* internet and mobile telecommunications technologies were widely available to the general public.

Notwithstanding this, it would be foolish to write off the emerging technological networks as having no potential effect on power relationships. Robert Keohane and Joseph Nye have suggested that the growing significance of the new technologies places an increasing premium on information. For Keohane and Nye, the key for states seeking to retain or develop power in the current 'information age' is credibility. They see power as emanating increasingly from the reliability and honesty of the information that actors provide. On this basis, they predict that 'geographically based states will continue to structure politics in an information age, but they will rely less on material resources and more on their ability to remain credible to a public with increasingly diverse sources of information'.[16] Keohane and Nye's argument is based on the notion that the key to power resides in the extent to which actors can make themselves attractive to others on the basis of information provided by and about themselves. This has clear links with Nye's earlier concept of 'soft power', which will be discussed further in chapter 2.

In their argument, Keohane and Nye perhaps overestimate the extent to which the availability of technologies is creating a more level playing field between state and non-state actors with regard to controlling, distributing and accessing information. The former have shown that they can take effective action to curtail the availability of information if they are determined to do so. A well-known example of this in recent years has been the creation and maintenance of the so-called great firewall of China. This term has been used to describe the restrictions imposed by the Chinese government on internet service providers and search engines seeking to link up Chinese users. Using the threat of denying or rescinding licences to operate in the vast Chinese services market, the government has thus far been largely successful in compelling the providers, in effect, to self-censor the information available on their sites, by filtering out links containing information which the Chinese government considers to be detrimental to its interests. In another example, the government of Hosni Mubarak in Egypt, battling to resist popular protests in January and February 2011, compelled the major mobile-phone networks operating in the country to turn off their signals, using threats to revoke licences in order to ensure compliance.

Overall, the significance of networked power, in the sense in which that concept has been understood in the popular media and by academic analysts such as Keohane and Nye, is still open to doubt. It is therefore an area that would benefit from further research. The relative influence and significance of technology-based networks has not yet been systematically proven. All too often, it appears that its importance and significance is simply asserted and assumed. Did Mubarak's attack on the Egyptian mobile-phone networks in 2011 reflect an appropriate evaluation of the impact of such technologies in mobilizing opposition against his regime, or does the fact that it did not ultimately prevent a successful revolution against him suggest that the key drivers for change lay elsewhere? Intuitive common sense suggests that mass popular movements of the kind that sprang up in Egypt and elsewhere in the Arab world in early 2011 were likely spurred into existence by a complex and disparate interplay of factors and facilitators. Ready access to communication and information networks was likely to be one, but its *relative* importance is difficult to determine. It also remains thus far somewhat unquantified and under-analysed.

Of rather more direct relevance and consequence for the discussions in this book is the broader understanding of networks suggested by Anne-Marie Slaughter, an American academic and former senior official in the Obama administration. The approaches discussed so far in this section basically see networks as being technology-based phenomena. In Slaughter's view, the term appropriately describes a broader and more complex array of means and channels for interaction, coordination and discussion amongst actors. Of course many of these can be and doubtless are facilitated and enhanced by modern technological innovations. However, networks in this broader view are in essence *socially*, rather than technologically, based.

Slaughter argues that, in the modern world, the principal 'measure of power is connectedness'. As with other 'network theorists', it is apparent that, for her, states remain major, but by no means the only, actors of significance on the world stage. She suggests that, 'in this world, the state with the most connections will be the central player'. Unsurprisingly perhaps, this former State Department official also believes that, of the major world states, the United States is currently best placed to be that central player.[17]

Slaughter's specific arguments about the US will be explored further later in this book, particularly with regard to the approaches adopted by the administrations led by George W. Bush and Barack Obama, respectively. In the context of the unfolding discussions here, her notion of international networks reinforces the core point that power is fundamentally about interactions and relationships. It is also, simultaneously, about *process*, and it is to this second aspect that attention will turn for the remainder of this chapter.

Power as process

Reflecting their view that power is at bottom about human relations, sociologists in particular have long argued that it should be viewed as being a process rather than a 'thing'. In this context Dennis Wrong, for example, has argued that: 'power . . . is not a separate resource possessed by individuals or groups additional to the resources of wealth, status, skill. . . . Power is, rather, the activation of these resources in order to pursue goals or outcomes.'[18] This helps us to identify an essential link with what are frequently referred to as 'power resources'. For many working within the fields of world politics and international relations, power resources are to be found chiefly in the population size, military capability and basic economic measurements of individual states. It is, however, an oversimplification to suggest that power resides *innately* in such resources and therefore is itself some kind of commodity that can be possessed in a reliable and tangible way. These resources in themselves are effectively inert. What matters in converting them into factors of power is their 'activation', to use Wrong's term. This occurs through human agency and is most reliably effected through social interactions and processes.

State actors can thus in practice be less – or indeed more – 'powerful' than their possession of material resources might on paper suggest. The key is the effectiveness and skill with which their leaders can harness their possession of relevant resources to achieve desired ends through interactions with others. Some have referred to the *de facto* 'space' between material base and potential operationalized effects as constituting the essence of an actor's 'latent' power.[19] This broader understanding of latent power has become more generally used and accepted than the narrower one developed by John Mearsheimer, and briefly discussed in the introduction to this book.

Resources, therefore, do have an important role to play, as suggested by Wrong. Money, for example, cannot just be *assumed* to exist. Its value must be represented in a tangible form (most commonly of course in the shape of notes and coins) in order for it to be operationalized. This is also the case with power. A key difference is that, unlike notes and coins, which carry a set, ascribed and accepted denomination, the value and hence effectiveness ascribed to power resources is often far more subjective and conditional. It is dependent substantially upon how they are used, in what context, and by whom. Nevertheless, resources do play an important – if essentially supporting – role in giving power a tangible form and hence also value and effect in practice.

Political will

If power is a process, it is certainly not a depersonalized one. Its operationalization occurs, as noted, as a result of conscious and deliberate human initiative and activity. In this context, the sociologist Steven Lukes has rightly argued that 'observing the exercise of power can give evidence of its possession, and counting power resources can be a clue to its distribution, *but power is a capacity, and not the exercise or the vehicle of that capacity*' [emphasis added].[20]

This raises the question of the role and importance of what is often called 'political will'. This has historically proved relatively straightforward for observers to identify as a key power factor. Antonio Gramsci, one of the leading Marxist thinkers of the early twentieth century, wrote extensively about both collective and individual will. He argued that 'reality is a product of the application of human will to the society of things'.[21] In similar vein, the controversial American sociologist C. Wright Mills defined 'the powerful', in American society, as being, 'of course, those who are able to realize their will, even if others resist it'.[22]

In debates about world politics, 'will' has often been ascribed an important role as well. This has sometimes been done explicitly. Hans Morgenthau, for example, defined a Great Power as being 'a state which is able to have its will against a small state, which in turn is not able to have its will against a Great Power'.[23] On other occasions the notion of will has been an implicit – but nonetheless important – element in attempts to conceptualize international power. Another well-known international relations scholar, Klaus Knorr, introduced into the debate the notion of what he called 'actualized' power. This represented Knorr's attempt to get to grips with the idea that material resources do not in themselves constitute the essence of power. Knorr concurred with the view that resources become important to the extent that they are consciously employed as a result of human decision in order to try and produce particular desired effects. In this way, he argued, the 'putative' power of resources becomes 'actualized'.[24] More recently, Michael Barnett and Raymond Duvall have drawn a similar distinction between what they have rather grandiloquently called 'social relations of constitution' and 'social relations of interaction'.[25]

These formulations basically correspond to what here may be called, respectively, *asserted* and *ascribed* power. In the case of the former, an actor consciously and deliberately seeks to control the decisions and actions of others, whilst, in the latter, its role, position and status – along with that of the others – to a significant extent emerges from, and is effectively determined by, the social relations amongst them. This implies a markedly more consensual arrangement. Put in everyday English, this is essentially the distinction between possessing power *over* somebody or something and power *to* achieve some desired result or effect. In reality, both forms may be present simultaneously – though probably to different degrees – in any given social relationship.

'Superior' and 'inferior' power

Although easy to identify theoretically as an important element of the debates, the notion of will has long proved to be difficult to pin down in terms of how best to understand it, and the role it plays as a power factor, in practice.[26] In an oft quoted definition of power, the philosopher Bertrand Russell suggested that it involves 'the production of *intended* effects' [emphasis added].[27] Similarly, in his recent work on power, Joseph Nye has argued that 'from a policy point of view we are interested in the ability to produce *preferred* outcomes' [emphasis added].[28] For Russell and Nye, therefore, it is clear that power is not simply about the ability to produce outcomes *per se*. This is a vital point. In summary here, therefore, it may be said that, on the basis of the discussions in this section, a working definition of 'will' is that the term denotes deliberate human action with predictable and controllable consequences and outcomes.

The extent to which power is apparent only if it is clear that an intended effect or preferred outcome has been achieved is open to debate.[29] The obvious question suggested by such formulations is whether power is apparent if an action results in the production of *unintended* effects or an outcome ensues that does not accord with the initiators' preferences. This is an important question in the real world. The Soviet Union, for example, surely did not intend the brutal and costly consequences that followed from its invasion of Afghanistan in 1979. These arguably included setting in train some of the processes and forces which ultimately led to its own collapse twelve years later. Similarly, it cannot convincingly be claimed that the US intended to plunge Iraq into bloody chaos following its invasion in 2003. Does this mean, therefore, that in these cases the actors concerned did not really operationalize power, as the effects of their policies and actions were neither desired nor, presumably, foreseen?

Russell did not really clarify his thinking on this important question. Nye is also somewhat fuzzy, writing that, 'if the effects are unintended, then there is power to harm (or benefit), but it is not power to achieve preferred outcomes'. This is self-evident, but it still leaves unclear whether Nye thinks that the former is somehow a lesser kind of power.[30] Dennis Wrong, meanwhile, has suggested that motivation is irrelevant.[31] What ultimately counts for him are *outcomes* rather than intentions. The possession of a 'will to power' in itself does not guarantee that the outcomes produced by the operationalization of that will can be reliably predicted or controlled. What matters is the fact that effects clearly occurred that would not have happened otherwise. Therefore power has been produced at the point that those effects were generated, although the impact of this process on the producer may not be as intended, and may in fact be negative.

The progressively diminishing ability of the states concerned to generate intended or preferred outcomes in the cases cited above – evident for the Soviet Union in Afghanistan during the 1980s and the US in Iraq from mid-2003 – showed limitations on their ability to produce effective power *from their own perspectives*. This does not mean of course that power was *objectively* absent in these contexts. Rather, it was increasingly being produced by other actors *against* the Soviet Union and the United States, respectively. This reminds us, once again, that power is generated as a result of interactions within a social process – which can of course be an essentially violent one. It can therefore be produced by the 'targets' of the original actor against that actor, and in ways that are neither anticipated nor desired by the latter.

Taking into account the views of those such as Russell and Nye, it is useful here to suggest the existence of a qualitative distinction between power that produces intended or preferred effects and the kind that leads to effects that do not correspond to the power producer's wishes. In both cases it is apparent that a type of power has in fact been operationalized. In the case of the former, however, the power produced may be described as qualitatively *superior*, because its effects had been demonstrably intended and outcomes have proven to be controllable by the initiating actor. The type of power that does not meet these criteria may, conversely, be described as *inferior*.

In order to achieve effects, whether intended or not, most analysts would agree that 'power resources' are required. These may be material or non-material in nature. In order to complete this overall evaluation of the essentials of power, the nature and importance of major resources will be examined and assessed in the next chapter.

2

Power Resources

In a classic study of power and governance in an American city, first published in the early 1960s, Robert Dahl succinctly defined a resource as 'anything that can be used to sway the specific choices or the strategies of another'.[1] Resources in the sense in which Dahl understood them do not necessarily have to be material. The term can apply equally to less tangible, but nonetheless vital, attributes such as legitimacy and authority. Dahl also argued that resources are not directly a form of power itself. Rather, they are a potential means by which power can be produced, depending upon whether and in what way actors with resources seek to use them.[2] These insights provide the basis for the understanding of the utility of 'power resources' which will be developed and used in this book.

'Hard power' and material resources

To restate a core point: the possession of significant resources will not *automatically* give those who hold them the ability to achieve intended or preferred effects – i.e., superior power. In 1972, Hans Morgenthau captured the essence of this argument in a pithy metaphor, which he used to describe American military impotence during the Vietnam War. Morgenthau compared the US to a man 'who is attacked by a swarm of bees and has a sub-machine gun with which to defend himself'. He argued: 'It is exactly the discrepancy between the primitive nature of the attack…and the high sophistication and potency of [his] weapon…which makes him helpless in the face of this particular challenge.'[3]

Material resources (or 'hard power', as they are often generically termed) are still important, however. To return momentarily to the metaphor of the poor man and the millionaire discussed in chapter 1: each of these individuals is both formally and actually equal *for as long as they both wish to spend just £100*. However, the latter of course has vastly greater monetary capacity, which he can additionally choose to employ if he wishes. Thus there *is* an essential difference between the two. It is the resource discrepancy that endows the latter with potentially significantly greater actualized power capacity. On the other hand, the real-world impact of this will very likely be context dependent, as Morgenthau's metaphor of the bees illustrates. It is, therefore, by no means guaranteed that the power realized by the use of greater material resources will always be of the superior kind.

In international politics, two kinds of material resource are almost always identified as being especially relevant in the power-producing context. These are military and economic. Inis Claude, in an early definition of power by an international relations scholar, suggested that it was 'essentially military capability – the elements which contribute directly or indirectly to the capacity to coerce, kill and destroy'. Claude acknowledged that this did not constitute the totality of power, although in the Cold War context in which he was writing: 'The capacity to do physical violence...[was] the variety of power which most urgently requires effective management.'[4]

Neither the end of the Cold War nor arguments that the destructiveness of modern military technologies had been making major war effectively obsolete even before then[5] have prevented realist scholars from continuing to assert that military capabilities remain the *sine qua non* of international power. As noted in the introduction, John Mearsheimer has argued for the near absolute primacy of the military element. Paul Kennedy, meanwhile, in *The Rise and Fall of the Great Powers*, argued that economic resources are of prime importance. His argument rests on the premise that, without a strong economic, commercial and financial base, a state will not be able to develop and sustain a significant military capability. Kennedy, therefore, by no means ignored the importance of military capabilities. Rather, he believed, quite reasonably, that economic capability is of vital instrumental importance in underpinning them.

The size of a state's population has also been cited as a key power resource,[6] although the rationale behind this is often simply asserted rather than justified or explained. Power should not be reduced merely to a numbers game, however, and the significance of population size is perhaps best comprehended as one element in a state's overall *economic* resources. What counts, as Kennedy and others have noted, is not population size *per se*, but rather the extent and effectiveness with which a population can be mobilized by a government in the service of industrial production, wealth creation and the consequent generation of military capability.[7] The demands placed by population size and growth on a state's economic, political and social welfare structures can also have a significant impact on its power capacity. This has become a particularly salient issue in China, as will be discussed further in chapter 9.

In recent years, an increasingly popular view has been that economic assets are becoming more effective than their military counterparts as a form of hard power. In part, this is because the military tool, at least in its traditionally understood sense of regular battlefield armies fighting wars under effective state direction and control, has arguably been of declining utility following the end of the Cold War and the events of September 11, 2001. This prevailing wisdom has been contested.[8] Nevertheless, the frustrations and obstacles encountered by the US armed forces in post-invasion Iraq from 2003, and by NATO's in Afghanistan in the years since the removal of the Taliban regime in autumn 2001, do lend it substantial empirical support.

It has also been argued that possession of significant economic capabilities can produce what has been called 'structural power'. Susan Strange was perhaps the best-known exponent of this concept. She used the term to suggest that states that possess significant economic, commercial and financial capacity[9] are particularly well placed to affect the behaviour of others. Consistent with the argument being developed in this book, Strange's idea located power itself in the interactions and transactions that take place amongst actors, rather than seeing it as being a property inherent *per se* in the material resources that they possess. She argued that 'power...is to be gauged by influence over outcomes rather than mere possession of capabilities or control over institutions.'[10]

Overall, it is clear that an appreciation of the nature of power should include an understanding of the importance of key material resources. There are drawbacks, however, with using a limited resource-based analysis to try and define the essentials of the concept. Although the resource holdings of individual actors can and do change over time, an analysis premised mainly on material capabilities is still likely to be too rigid and static to account adequately for 'the dynamics of power change', as Ronald Tammen and his colleagues have put it.[11] Material resources undoubtedly have a role to play in helping us to understand what power is. However, as the arguments developed thus far are further unfolded in the context of the three major state case studies in this book, it will be suggested that they are not the *key* determinants of effective international power in the post-Cold War world.

'Soft power' and influence

As is well known, Joseph Nye's major contribution to the field of academic power studies has been through the development of the concept
of what he has called 'soft power'. Nye defines soft power as 'the ability
to get what you want through attraction rather than coercion or pay-
ments. It arises from the attractiveness of a country's culture, political
ideals, and policies.' Being viewed as a *legitimate* actor is an important
source of soft power, according to Nye. Writing of the US, he asserts that,
'when our policies are seen as legitimate in the eyes of others, our soft
power is enhanced.'[12]

Soft power is still relatively new as a tool of analysis in the study of
world politics and international relations. Indeed, Nye explicitly claims to
have invented it.[13] However, the thinking underlying the concept is not so
new. During the 1970s, for example, Jeffrey Hart put forward a similar idea,
which he called 'noncoercive power'.[14] Notions comparable to soft power
have also long found expression in academic debates over the distinction
between 'power' and 'influence'. Talcott Parsons, for example, defined
influence in a manner which bears comparison to Nye's later definition of
soft power. According to Parsons, 'Influence operates entirely on the intentions of the object of persuasion and through positive channels. It tries to
convince him that acting as the persuader desires is in his own and the
collective interest.'[15] Steven Lukes has suggested that it is 'the supreme
exercise of power to get another or others to have the desires you want
them to have – that is, to secure their compliance by controlling their
thoughts and desires'.[16] This raises the question of the extent to which this
kind of manipulation in itself constitutes a distinctive process of power.
Lukes argues that it does, and that power is only really apparent in a situation of conflict of interest, in which one side gains the upper hand
through effective manipulation.[17] Manipulation can, therefore, be an exercise of will.

Influence has been examined and discussed by world politics and
international relations specialists as well as by sociologists. In debates
amongst the former, it is sometimes referred to in a somewhat derogatory
manner. It has been seen as softer (in a negative sense), less defined and
more difficult to direct and control than power itself, and therefore as being
of less potential benefit and utility to actors. The well-known British international relations scholar Martin Wight encapsulated this sceptical view
when he wrote: 'Just as in domestic politics influence is not government,

so in international politics influence is not power. It is concrete power in the end that settles great international issues.'[18]

Joseph Nye's articulation of soft power can be seen, in this context, as partly an attempt to rescue the traditional and somewhat tarnished notion of influence, and to make the case for its being both a distinct and an effective component of power in its own right. First articulating his idea publicly in 1990 – as the Cold War order was clearly unravelling – Nye caught the mood of the times, as debates began about the possibility of moving to a less militarized and more cooperative international system. He should also be commended as one of the relatively few international relations specialists to grapple with the task of defining power, in a profession where many others have shied away from it.

Nye's soft power has a narrower focus than many earlier articulations of influence. As noted above, Nye's focus is specifically on the notion of attraction. Many concepts of influence are somewhat broader and embrace other forms of inducement, such as the offer of economic incentives (what David Baldwin called 'positive sanctions').[19] Unfortunately for Nye, the very popularity of his concept over the last two decades has contributed to its becoming somewhat distorted. As he himself has lamented, soft power has sometimes been used as 'a synonym for culture, economics or anything other than military force'.[20] As one might expect, therefore, soft power has been subject to similar criticisms to those directed at broader notions of influence. These boil down to the argument that it is 'soft' in the negative sense, and therefore of limited utility in generating intended effects and thus forming the basis of a viable and effective operationalization of power.

Such criticisms are substantially justified. Soft power does seem – almost by definition – to be difficult for an actor to operationalize consciously and deliberately. It is not clear from Nye's various publications whether or how attraction can be made to 'work', through a social process or relationship, as a means of affecting behaviour in order to achieve or advance – in Nye's own words – 'preferred outcomes'. This is not to deny the existence of soft power *per se*. It is, however, to suggest that it is more innate than instrumental. To the extent that it does exist, soft power is *conferred* by others, rather than *created* by oneself. This makes it relatively less susceptible to deliberate and reliable direction and operationalization on the part of individual actors.[21]

An important related question here concerns how the impact of soft power can and should be quantified and measured.[22] Often, polling evidence is cited, showing how a state is perceived by peoples living in other states and societies. In the case of the United States, some point to the global popularity of American brands of fast food, soft drinks and sports-wear. Such analysis seldom if ever identifies or suggests causal links between expressing admiration for another society, or consuming its products, and altering or amending attitudes and behaviour in a favourable direction as far as the 'other' is concerned. Indeed, such analysis as there is in this area often argues that, if perceptions develop of aggressive 'Americanization' or Western 'cultural imperialism', there is a danger of *repelling*, rather than attracting, other societies and states.[23]

In reality, therefore, apparent instances of soft power 'working' might more accurately be seen as cases in which rather broader techniques of influence have been successfully brought to bear. A good example of this can be seen with regard to the short-lived crisis between the UK and Iran in spring 2007, over the latter's detention of British sailors and marines, who had allegedly been caught trespassing in Iranian waters in the Persian Gulf. In fact, it was soon established beyond reasonable doubt that the British personnel had been patrolling in *Iraqi* territorial waters, at the request of the elected Iraqi government. Once this became apparent, the Iranians began looking for a way to defuse the stand-off. This was accomplished when the British personnel were unconditionally released. The prominent British media commentator Will Hutton lauded the outcome as an excellent example of soft power in action. In fact, Hutton's analysis made it clear that it was nothing of the kind. There was no sense of the Iranians responding to the appeal or attractiveness of either British society generally or the UK government's specific political ideas. Rather, according to Hutton, it was the potential for significant loss of face in the international arena, coupled with the prospect that the European Union might impose economic and commercial sanctions if the crisis dragged on, that ultimately persuaded the Iranian government to release the British personnel and so end the crisis.[24]

The thrust of the discussions here is not designed to suggest that Nye's concept has no value as a tool for analysing power. It is, however, important to bear in mind its inherent limitations when using it for these purposes. Soft power has been in fashion for nearly two decades and, as Nye himself has acknowledged, its popularity has not had wholly positive effects. It has too often uncritically been assumed to be 'a good thing', and it has not, therefore, always been subject to rigorous definition and analytical use. Largely as a consequence of this, the concept has – as Nye has also acknowledged – been stretched too far. With this in mind, it will be used with due care and attention in the analysis that follows in subsequent chapters of this book.

Ideas and ideologies

At the heart of Nye's notion of soft power is the belief that an actor's social and political values and ideas can have significant appeal and, further, can influence the thinking and actions of others. This links soft power to what is called the 'social constructivist' school of international relations theory. Analysts working within this tradition have offered insights that are often overlooked by those who approach power mainly from a consideration of the impact of material resources. They argue that shared ideas about what is 'right' and 'wrong' in themselves can be a potent force in shaping and motivating the operationalization of power, and also in helping to ensure that its effects are successful and sustainable. As with Nye's soft power, this is hardly a wholly new insight. It was articulated in the 1950s by C. Wright Mills, for example.[25] In the contemporary world politics and international relations context, however, it is undoubtedly the work of the social constructivists, spearheaded by Alexander Wendt, which has been instrumental in ensuring that the role and importance of ideas has been placed squarely on the analytical agenda.

The central proposition put forward by Wendt is that shared ideas, rather than material resources, form the key influencing factor that shapes the structure and processes of human interaction and association. Therefore, the structure of international relations is essentially socially, rather than materially, determined. For social constructivists ideas play a key role in helping to create and motivate social systems and social action. Ideas can be religious in nature, such as 'fundamentalist' understandings of Islamic teaching; they can be quasi-religious, such as Confucianism in imperial (and modern) China; or they can be secular, such as Marxism or 'Western-style' liberal democracy.

In the international context, Wendt argues that, overall, ideas motivate the formulation and articulation of actors' interests, and these interests in turn motivate and condition both the existence and the operationalization of their power. As Wendt summarizes: 'Power and interest have the effects they do in virtue of the ideas that make them up.'[26] With this in mind, ideas are most likely to function as a power resource when they are incorporated into political ideologies. Ideologies in this context are defined sets of beliefs (religious or secular) about the basis upon which a state's governance and political, social and economic affairs should be organized and regulated. Ideologies may evolve in ways specific to the state and society concerned, or they may be viewed as having more general applicability to other states and societies, perhaps even on a global basis.

Torbjørn Knutsen has argued persuasively that, historically, many analysts in the world politics and international relations fields have overly neglected the importance of ideas and ideologies as a power resource in their own right. Reflecting on historical developments, Knutsen suggests that they matter not only in underpinning an international order (in the sense defined by Hedley Bull) but also at the domestic level in underpinning social cohesion within individual states and societies. This latter can, in itself, provide an essential part of the overall 'resource' base of states. This argument suggests, in summary, that domestic social cohesion, and the normative consensus necessary to create and maintain it, is effectively a power resource in its own right – as important, indeed, as 'hard' military and economic resources.[27]

Legitimacy

Legitimacy is a 'soft' resource in the sense of being important but essentially intangible. It can be defined straightforwardly as the perceived right to use power.[28] The concept of legitimacy has long been an important component in the development of thinking about power overall. In a helpful review, Barry Hindess traces concerns about it back to the English political philosophers Thomas Hobbes and John Locke in the seventeenth century.[29] The sociologist Dennis Wrong goes further and suggests that the need for humans using power to be regarded as doing so legitimately is an almost primordial element of human nature. Wrong argues that this 'has roots in the infantile experience of dependence as understood by psychoanalysis'.[30]

Sociologists and philosophers have argued that the presence or absence of legitimacy is a pivotal factor in differentiating between distinct types of power – or indeed in differentiating power from some other kind of process and effect. To illustrate this point, reference can usefully be made to the distinction drawn by Max Weber in the early twentieth century between 'power' and 'domination'. This rested on the presence or absence of an element of voluntary compliance. 'Power', wrote Weber, described 'the probability that one actor within a social relationship will be in a position to carry out his own will despite resistance'. 'Domination', meanwhile, 'is the probability that a command with a given specific content will be obeyed by a given group of persons.'[31]

Weber's basic distinction thus rested upon the difference between an inherently conflictual relationship – or at least one with the potential for conflict – and one based upon consent, with the consequent willingness of others to be persuaded into compliance with an actor's wishes. Weber also made clear that domination, in his sense of the term, cannot exist without legitimacy: 'The continued exercise of every domination...always has the strongest need of self-justification through appealing to the principles of its legitimation.'[32] He famously identified three principal sources of legitimation in this context, which he called the 'rational' (based on legal rules), 'traditional' (based on custom) and 'charismatic' (based on the personal authority of an individual).[33] Weber's typology here stands comparison with Joseph Nye's contemporary notion of soft power. This is because it is apparent from Weber's writings that he envisaged the utility of the latter two sources in particular as relying primarily on their ability to attract, based, respectively, on a sense of cultural affiliation and tradition and on the personal qualities of individual leaders.

Max Weber's particular understanding of the terms 'power' and 'domination' has not been widely adopted and used by others. Nevertheless, a similar distinction to the one that he drew between them, based on legitimacy, was reflected in the work of later sociologists and philosophers. Bertrand Russell, for example, developed the notion of what he called 'naked' power. Power became 'naked', in Russell's view, when it lost or was deprived of the legitimation provided by tradition and custom. This, in turn, ensured that this form of power could not be formulated or utilized in a consensual context.[34] Often, analysts settled upon the word 'authority' to distinguish what Weber called 'domination' from forms of power based on coercion. Talcott Parsons and C. Wright Mills both used 'authority' in this way, for example.[35]

Comparable views have been evident in thinking about world politics and international relations, with 'authority' frequently being distinguished from 'power' by analysts and commentators. Martin Wight, for example, argued that, in the international context, 'Power is not self-justifying; it must be justified by reference to some source outside or beyond itself, and thus be transformed into "authority".'[36] In his work on the importance of the ideational dimension of international politics, Alexander Wendt developed a similar argument, writing that the key to success for states in advancing their agendas lies in achieving legitimate authority and not 'mere influence or power'.[37] In a 2005 lecture, a leading American scholar, Stanley Hoffmann, reflected the thinking of many critics of the George W. Bush administration when he argued that effective American power 'depends not just on force but also largely on the authority of the

United States, of which legitimacy is a major component'. Hoffmann further asserted that, in order to be considered legitimate, a militarily dominant state, such as the US, 'has to be limited[,] contained[,] and [its actions] authorized by an authority which may be debatable but widely accepted'.[38]

Debates about legitimacy have hardly ever taken place over whether it is desirable, if not indeed essential, *per se*. As with soft power, it is widely assumed that legitimacy is a good thing, and inherently a positive and necessary prerequisite for the effective operationalization of power – as the views outlined above illustrate. The issues which have attracted most debate have been, firstly, whether legitimacy, as defined by Weber and others, is too subjective a concept to be of much positive value, either analytically or in the real world. This has been related in turn to debates over sources and types of legitimacy.

Political theorist David Beetham has caustically described Max Weber's influence on thinking about legitimacy as being 'an almost unqualified disaster'.[39] Beetham especially deplores the subjectivity which he argues is inherent in Weber's notion of domination – that is, the idea that an operationalization of power becomes legitimate simply because people believe it to be so. Beetham's concern is with the existence of manipulation, not merely as a technique but potentially as a distinctive type of power in its own right. In this context, C. Wright Mills had earlier argued that: 'Among the means of power which now prevail is the power to manage and to manipulate the consent of men…much power today is successfully employed without the sanction of the reason or the conscience of the obedient.'[40] This raises fundamental questions about the sources of legitimacy. Can it simply be generated – or manipulated into being – by those seeking to operationalize power?

Debates over sources of legitimacy have produced a substantial academic literature and precious little underlying agreement. In the international context, Ian Clark has nevertheless managed to distil the essence of the debates succinctly. Clark identifies two basic views of legitimacy:

> One postulates legitimacy as a product of 'domestic' political values; the other sees it as something conferred by international norms…In the former, international institutions derive their legitimacy from the democratic credentials of the individual states; in the latter, the actions of individual states derive their legitimacy from international society.[41]

The second of these approaches offers a better prospect of some kind of international system of checks and balances on the use of power than the former, with its emphasis on the prerogatives of individual state actors. The danger with the former is that it does not seem – at least on first inspection – to offer any real safeguard or disincentive to pursuing actions and policies based upon the idea that 'might equals right'. It suggests that *self*-legitimation is indeed possible for those actors that feel strong and confident enough to proclaim it.

This approach was evident in the attitude of Soviet leaders to the preservation of communist systems in Eastern Europe during the Cold War. It was made explicit in the form of the so-called Brezhnev Doctrine, publicized in the wake of the Soviet-led Warsaw Pact military intervention to reimpose orthodox communist control in Czechoslovakia in August 1968. This *post facto* justification for that action asserted that it was justified on the basis of 'socialist legitimacy'. This meant that the policies pursued by governments within established communist states must 'damage neither socialism in their own country nor the fundamental interests of the other socialist countries nor the worldwide workers' movement, which is waging a struggle for socialism'. Essentially, therefore, the Brezhnev Doctrine asserted that there was a legitimate basis for the Soviet Union to place restrictions on the sovereign prerogatives of the other 'socialist states' in Europe.[42]

Despite their differences, and the potential for its misuse in practice as in the example discussed above, analysts of legitimacy are in general agreement in seeing it as an important and desirable restraint on the operationalization of power, especially in potentially coercive forms. There is also evidence that political leaders sometimes think in similar ways. In the spring of 1999, for example, the US and its NATO allies strove to convince the leaders and peoples of other states that their military action against Serbia over the situation in Kosovo was legitimate. They could not do this by reference to a legal mandate in the form of a resolution passed by the United Nations Security Council, as the Russian government had clearly stated its intention to block any such authorization. The best available mechanism, therefore, was NATO itself. The argument was made that action under the auspices of an international security institution made up of (then) nineteen democratic states was, *de facto*, legitimate. To bolster this claim in practice, the leaders of the NATO member states participating in the Kosovo air campaign accepted the need for practical limitations on the way in which it was being conducted, principally in terms of bombing intensity and targeting strategy.[43]

Hegemony

Legitimacy is not an alternative to power, or distinct from it. It is – or should be – an essential component part. Its major function is to guide, condition and sometimes constrain the power operationalizing process. David Beetham made this point succinctly when he argued that 'legitimate power . . . is limited power'.[44] This thinking has deep roots and can be traced back to the ancient notion of hegemony. Today, 'hegemony' is often used to describe coercive and illegitimate forms of power. The original concept was, however, significantly different – and legitimacy was central to it. The word comes from the Greek *hegemonia*, meaning 'leadership'. Richard Ned Lebow, a leading contemporary scholar of the concept in its original form, has noted that the ancient Greeks deliberately distinguished between *hegemonia*, which had clear connotations of *legitimate* leadership, and *arkhe*, denoting coercive control. *Arkhe* approximates to the notion of 'power' as Weber used it, and it was based on possession of material resources.[45] According to Lebow, *hegemonia* 'is only possible within a community whose members share core values and is limited to activities that are understood to support common identities.'[46]

A reading of Thucydides' *History of the Peloponnesian War*, one of the most noteworthy writings to have survived from ancient Greece, helps to amplify this. On first reading, it might appear that Thucydides made the case that hard power – rather than legitimate leadership – is what ultimately counts in human affairs. Probably the best-known part of the *History* is the so-called Melian Dialogue, in which the Athenians demanded that Melos – a smaller and materially weaker state – submit to their control. According to Thucydides' narrative, the Athenians based their demand on the proposition: 'Right, as the world goes, is only in question between equals in power, while the strong do what they can and the weak suffer what they must.'[47] Yet, the *History* can be read and understood in rather more subtle and nuanced ways: as a warning *against* the abandonment of legitimated leadership and a consequent move towards a form of power based on coercive control.

Overall, Thucydides tells the story of the failure of the Athenians to force a definitive victory in the series of military campaigns that made up the Peloponnesian wars, and their consequent entanglement in endless conflicts. Thus, hard power, or *arkhe*, does *not* prove itself to be ultimately successful or effective.[48] At various points in his narrative, Thucydides makes clear – usually through the speeches of the principal characters in his drama[49] – that the notion of the domination of the weaker by the stronger could only be justified, and was only likely to endure, if the latter's actions were founded upon a legitimate basis, which in turn inspired loyalty and trust. Thus, for example, Thucydides has a group of Corinthian envoys argue that 'supremacy has its duties. With equitable administration, where the private interest of the leaders is concerned, there must be a care for the common welfare as special as the honours for which they are selected in other matters.'[50] Elsewhere, envoys from Mitylene explain their reasons for revolting against Athens: 'As long as the Athenians led us fairly we followed them loyally; but when we saw them...try to compass the subjection of the allies, then our apprehensions began...trust in Athens as a leader,...we could no longer feel,...it being unlikely that she would reduce our fellow confederates, and not do the same by the rest, if ever she had the power.'[51]

Given the fractured geographic and demographic nature of the ancient Greek world, allies were important – indeed, essential. It was unlikely that any single state would be able to develop sufficient material strength so as to be able to win a major war decisively on its own. This is reflected in the space that Thucydides devotes in the *History* to events, speeches and dialogues that are focused on issues and problems affecting alliances. A shift in allegiance by one of the smaller states could have significant consequences, in that it could result in overall leadership – or 'supremacy' – passing from one of the dominant states to another.[52] Even neutrality on the part of one of the smaller states could be seen as a source of potential danger to the leaders. This is one of the underlying themes in the Melian Dialogue. Thucydides has the Athenian representatives respond to the Melian suggestion that their state adopt a neutral stance by saying that, in such circumstances: 'Your hostility cannot so much hurt us as your friendship will be an argument to our subjects of our weakness, and your enmity of our power.'[53]

Overall, Thucydides' writing makes a clear argument for the desirability and, indeed, importance of *hegemonia*. This is the case, firstly, for the smaller states. They could hope to gain military protection and derive economic benefits from being part of an international system led by what today might be termed (tautologically to the ancient Greeks) a 'benign hegemon'. Strong states in turn gained military allies. As importantly, they also acquired and retained the legitimacy that was considered essential to the maintenance of their leadership. In short, two core messages emerge from Thucydides' *History of the Peloponnesian War*. Firstly, hegemony, as understood by ancient Greeks, is essential for sustainable international leadership. Secondly, and echoing David Beetham's point quoted earlier: 'hegemony requires the prudent exercise of power'.[54]

The fact that debates about the concept and importance of hegemony have continued into the contemporary era is due in no small measure to the influence of the writings of Antonio Gramsci in the early twentieth century. He wrote little about international relations directly, considering them to be a second-order product of class-based relations within societies.[55] Nevertheless, Gramsci's ideas have attracted the interest of some international relations scholars, who have argued that they can profitably be adapted and used as a tool for analysing power in the international arena.[56] They are, therefore, worth briefly considering here.

Gramsci articulated his basic concept of hegemony thus:

> Hegemony presupposes that account be taken of the interests... of the groups over which [it] is to be exercised, and that a certain compromise equilibrium should be formed... But there is also no doubt that... such a compromise cannot touch the essential; for though hegemony is ethical-political, it must also be economic.[57]

Taking into account the Marxist focus on economic relations, and also his focus on the domestic context, Gramsci's concept of hegemony shares with the original ancient Greek notion the idea of legitimated leadership. For Gramsci, legitimacy derived from the extent to which 'subaltern groups' (as he often called them) consented to being led. This did not eliminate the possibility (and, indeed, on occasion desirability) of coercive elements being employed. Rather, the key to effective leadership – and hence progress – lay in achieving 'equilibrium' – a core concept in Gramsci's thought – between coercion and consent.[58] Gramsci called this the 'dual perspective' – embracing 'the levels of force and of consent, authority and hegemony, violence and civilisation'.[59]

Thus, Gramsci's concept of hegemony embraces a clear coercive element. The notion of consent is an essential element of it as well, and it is this that is usually cited when Gramsci's work is discussed in the international relations context.[60] Nevertheless, it can be argued that the dual perspective in Gramsci's thinking elevates the coercive element of hegemony above that judged prudent in ancient Greek thought, as reflected by Thucydides.

It is instructive here to touch briefly upon the thinking of Michel Foucault. Although he did not deal with the notion of hegemony directly, much of Foucault's work on power suggests that he conceived of it in ways that bear comparison with the ideas discussed above. He wrote: 'Power is less a confrontation between two adversaries or their mutual engagement than a question of "government".'[61] He also argued strongly that power should be seen as essentially a positive, rather than a repressive or prohibitive, process or force. In his book *Discipline and Punish*, Foucault asserted: 'We must cease once and for all to describe the effects of power in negative terms: it "excludes", it "represses", it "censors", it "abstracts", it "masks", it "conceals". In fact, power produces; it produces reality, it produces domains of objects and rituals of truth.'[62]

Foucault's essentially positive view of power, resting on a system of mutual and consensual obligation, is evident from the extended metaphors which he developed to try to capture its essence. For example, he wrote that the power relations suggested by his broad concept of 'government' could be compared to those between a father and his wife and children in a functioning family unit.[63] This suggested a paternalistic view of the particular obligations of the stronger parties in a power relationship – to take the lead in looking after the basic security and other needs of the less materially well equipped or altogether dependent. The same supposition is inherent in another metaphorical discussion which Foucault developed. This set forth the notion of 'pastoral power', which he conceptualized as the kind of relationship maintained between a shepherd and his flock.[64]

The key shared perspective uniting the work of Thucydides, Gramsci and Foucault is the idea that effective power rests significantly upon a sense of mutual and shared responsibilities on the part of all the actors involved. Leading or dominant actors have particular responsibilities. The main one, evident explicitly in the work of both Thucydides and Gramsci, is for leaders to take into account – and be seen to be doing so – the interests and concerns of subordinates. This is also implicit in Foucault's broad notion of 'government'. Additionally, Thucydides and Gramsci embraced the notion that the appropriate and effective discharging of leadership responsibilities should be reciprocated by the followers accepting responsibilities of their own. In his prison notebooks, Gramsci often referred to non-hegemonic classes or groups as 'subalterns'. In military life subalterns are junior officers. Nevertheless, their views and interests should be considered and taken into account by their superiors if the authority system upon which armed forces are based is to function in a fully effective manner. On the other hand, subalterns have a duty to obey their superiors once the latter have arrived at a duly constituted and informed decision. The underpinning sense of *shared mutual obligation* essential to the effective operation of this kind of relationship both reflects and embodies the system's legitimacy. It is the essence of hegemony.

What is power?

As should be apparent from the discussions in this and the preceding chapter, power is – to paraphrase Michel Foucault – an especially hidden and occulted concept. Foucault also rightly observed, however, that it is integral to the human experience – and most especially human relationships. We need to understand it better, therefore. Specifically, it would make little sense to proceed to the analysis of the US, Russia and China in this book without establishing an analytical framework to help measure and quantify their respective 'power' in the post-Cold War world. With this objective in mind, it is possible to draw out three key elements from the discussions so far.

Firstly, drawing primarily from the approach adopted by sociologists, it can be argued that power is to be found working in and through *social interactions and relationships, bounded by formally or informally regulated processes and institutions.* The latter can be termed 'networks' in the sense articulated by Anne-Marie Slaughter. Such networks form the basis of international 'structures', in the sense in which that concept will be used in this book.

Secondly, and drawing on the insights provided by Bertrand Russell and Joseph Nye, amongst others, it can be seen that power is not simply about making things happen. Rather, as Russell suggested, it is fundamentally about *the production of intended effects.* It is accepted that, if effects of any kind are produced – whether they conform to the originator's intention or not – it can reasonably be inferred that some kind of power has been operationalized. Nevertheless, there is a qualitative distinction between this and the production of intended or preferred effects. It was suggested in chapter 1 that the descriptors 'inferior' and 'superior' power can serve in helping to delineate this distinction.

Finally, it can be argued that a healthy and effective structure of power relations amongst leading states, of which three in particular are to be analysed in this book, should be based on a *viable and effective system of international 'hegemony'*, as that term was defined above. The key to this kind of hegemony is, as noted, an accepted sense of *mutuality* (although this need not mean *equality*) in terms of responsibilities and obligations.

3

Hegemony, Unipolarity and the US

As is well known, the United States is often described as a hegemon (or *the* hegemon) in the contemporary international system. Building on the analysis of the concept of hegemony in chapter 2, the discussions in this chapter will open with a consideration of how the term has been understood with specific reference to world politics and international relations. Subsequently, the analysis here will proceed to consider how the US acted as an international hegemon during the Cold War years, using a case study of relations with its core NATO allies in Europe.

This brief case study will help us to contextualize the analysis of post-Cold War American approaches in chapters 4, 5 and 6. With this in mind, the discussions in this chapter will, finally, explore the post-Cold War concept of American 'unipolarity'. They will ask whether a unipolar international system can be compatible with one also based on hegemony, as that concept is understood here.

Hegemony in the international arena

In his 1973 book *The World in Depression*, the economist Charles Kindleberger developed the argument that global economic and financial stability, and hence prosperity, could most effectively be maintained when a single state is able and willing to underwrite the structures and processes of the international economic system by, for example, acting as 'lender of last resort'. This constituted Kindleberger's definition of a 'hegemonic power'. His basic argument about the causes of the economic depression of the 1930s – the main focus of his analysis – was that it occurred mainly because there was no state then available that was both able and willing to play this kind of hegemonic role.[1] As the discussions in chapter 2 here have shown, Kindleberger certainly did not invent the notion of international hegemony. Nevertheless, he can fairly be credited with reintroducing it as a term of reference into debates specifically about world politics and international relations.

Kindleberger's concept of hegemony rested, as noted, on the notion of a single leading state – what many today would call a 'unipole' – but one that had a clear sense of the importance of maintaining the international economic system as a whole, and was thus prepared to act on this basis. There is an evident echo of Gramsci's thinking about hegemony in this notion. The hegemon's leading role, in Kindleberger's view, should be undertaken not via compulsion or coercion, but with the voluntary and willing support and cooperation of other, less materially capable actors in the system. These could in turn expect to share in the benefits – or 'public goods' – safeguarded and made available by the leading state's underwriting of the system. Thus they had a direct stake in supporting and maintaining this kind of hegemony.

As is apparent from this brief summary, Kindleberger portrayed hegemony in essentially positive terms, but this view was by no means universally shared at the time he was writing. The Maoist government in China, which was developing its presence in the international system via an emerging *rapprochement* with the US, and taking over the Chinese seat on the UN Security Council, repeatedly railed against 'hegemonism' in international relations (as will be discussed further in chapter 10). Indeed, a recurring theme of China's foreign policy statements since Mao's time has been a hostile attitude to international hegemony – whether associated with the Soviet Union, the United States or any other state. 'Hegemony' in official Chinese statements has been consistently equated with aggressive attempts at subjugation of the weak by the strong. This critique has found a place in the wider ongoing debates about international hegemony, especially amongst those critical of the role played by the United States.

In academic terms, Kindleberger's work has become important not just for economists, but more widely too. This is because it is often seen as forming the foundation for what has come to be known as 'hegemonic stability theory'. Those who have developed this school of thought within international relations have generally focused on how peace, security and order (including, but not limited to, the economic realm) are best maintained in a world which incorporates the existence of hegemonic states of the kind suggested by Kindleberger.

These analysts have often been concerned with the potential impact of the decline of established hegemons and/or the rise of new ones. A distinctive subset of hegemonic stability theory has therefore become apparent: what might be called hegemonic *transition* theory.[2] A specific debate has developed over the possibility of 'hegemonic war' breaking out. This would be armed conflict occurring when an established hegemon was confronted by a rising challenger which was determined to displace it at the pinnacle of the international system. Robert Gilpin described hegemonic wars as thus being conflicts over 'the fundamental issues [of] leadership and structure of the international system'. This way of thinking suggests a 'zero sum' view of international hegemony – i.e., it is not something that can or will be shared. In this view, if a serious challenger appears, its objective (presumed to be gaining hegemonic status for itself) could only be achieved at the expense of an established hegemon.[3]

How might international hegemons decline? In *The Rise and Fall of the Great Powers*, Paul Kennedy famously argued that, historically, Great Powers go into decline because of 'imperial overstretch'. This was not a new idea. The suggestion that, materially, the relatively best equipped states tend to allow an unsustainable gap to develop over time between the territorial and military ambitions of their leaders (and sometimes wider populations) and their ability to produce economic and financial resources can be traced back to at least 1943. In that year, Walter Lippmann's famous book on *US Foreign Policy* first appeared. In this work, Lippmann argued that effective foreign policy 'consists in bringing into balance, with a comfortable surplus of power in reserve, the nation's commitments and the nation's power'.[4]

Hegemonic responsibility

Achieving and maintaining this balance is likely to be especially difficult for hegemons, at least in the kind of international arrangement suggested by Charles Kindleberger. This is because such states must take on and maintain the greatest international responsibilities and commitments. These included, in Lippmann's analysis, 'obligations' beyond their territorial boundaries that 'may in the last analysis have to be met by waging war'. This has become an important element in international relations thinking.

Contemporaneously with Lippmann (and three decades before Kindleberger published *The World in Depression*), a similar notion of great power bringing great responsibility was a core feature of the analysis in a book by an international relations scholar named William Fox. His work is of particular interest and importance here because, in it, he introduced the notion of 'superpower'. This, of course, quickly became the international term of choice to describe the Cold War status of the United States and the Soviet Union. In *The Super-Powers*, Fox argued that not only is superpowerdom characterized by 'great power plus great mobility of power', but also that superpowers should be expected to play the key role in underwriting international arrangements designed to provide peace and security throughout the global system.[5]

Thus, it can be seen that international relations thinkers were already developing ideas about hegemonic responsibility and hegemonic stability well before Kindleberger, even though the latter has been – as noted – widely viewed as the father of hegemonic stability theory. Further, there is evidence to suggest that similar thinking to that being developed by scholars such as William Fox in the final years of the Second World War influenced the designs of governments, diplomats and officials who were seeking to put in place an international system designed to prevent any future relapse into general war amongst major states. It was reflected most clearly in the negotiations that produced the United Nations in 1945, and in particular in the composition and working procedures of the UN Security Council.

As is well known, the Security Council's membership consists of five *de facto* 'Great Powers', whose status is formalized within it by permanency of tenure and also by possession of the right of veto over most decisions and draft resolutions. The other ten members have no permanent seat (rotating through on two-year cycles) and no formal veto rights. Under the terms of the UN Charter, however, it is made clear that Security Council members, and by definition the so-called P5 states in particular, are, in return for their exalted status, expected to take on, through their membership of the Council, the 'primary responsibility' for maintaining international peace and security.[6] Undertaken competently and diligently, this role would provide – in the eyes of the international community (i.e., UN members generally) – the means for legitimizing the enduring role and status of the P5.

Walter Lippmann's argument about the potentially debilitating gap between capabilities and commitments has also proved to be of durable interest and relevance, as evidenced by the fact that the phrase 'Lippmann gap' remains in use as a means of describing a situation where a state's commitments are judged to be running ahead of its material resources and capabilities.[7] Its influence is certainly apparent in Paul Kennedy's work, particularly in his assertion that, for hegemonic states to maintain their position, it is 'vital to preserve the proper balance between the country's military and naval effort on the one hand and the encouragement of the national wealth on the other'.[8]

Kennedy's emphasis is on material capabilities as the core measurement of power. To that end, he argues that economic and financial resources constitute the most important material underpinnings. It is significant that the actual term 'hegemon' is not used by Kennedy to describe any state before newly industrialized Great Britain in the nineteenth century. 'What the Industrial Revolution did', Kennedy argues in relation to Britain, 'was to enhance the position of a country already supremely successful in the pre-industrial, mercantilist struggles of the eighteenth century, and then to transform it into a different sort of power.'[9] A hegemon, for Kennedy, is clearly therefore this 'different sort of power', which emerges on the basis of pre-eminent economic and industrial strengths.

Like Kindleberger, Kennedy had very little to say about power in social terms. Hence, there is not much about public goods in his work either. For Kennedy, it is apparent that states strive for hegemony for reasons of self-interest, and indeed self-preservation, in a competitive international environment. Reflecting this essentially realist view, Kennedy and other diplomatic historians have displayed an enduring interest in debating ideas about the 'balance of power'. This is a generic term for which one analyst has identified no fewer than eight distinct meanings.[10] As with many international relations scholars, historians generally have tended to be less interested in discussing the *nature* of international power than in the debates about its *distribution*. The relative emphasis on the catch-all (and therefore not analytically very useful) concept of the balance of power is one significant reflection of this.

'Liberal' hegemony

The notion of 'hegemony', as it is widely used and understood in contemporary academic writing and everyday speech, has become noticeably 'hardened' in comparison with its origins in ancient Greek thought. In chapter 2 it was noted that Thucydides stressed the efficacy of a prudent and collegial process of leadership, and also that Gramsci argued for the importance of achieving and maintaining 'equilibrium' in a hegemonic relationship. In contrast, one more recent observer pithily and accurately described hegemony in much contemporary debate as being used simply to denote 'imperialism with good manners'.[11]

It should be noted in this context that some have questioned whether the practice (as opposed to what might be called Thucydides' theory) of hegemony in the ancient Greek world was actually that much softer. Eric Robinson, for example, has written that the kind of behaviour by allies routinely tolerated today (such as refusal to host bases and participate in combined military operations) would, if displayed by an ally of Athens in Thucydides' time, almost certainly have provoked 'military assault in response'.[12] Charles Maier, meanwhile, has argued that his reading of

Thucydides does in fact suggest that hegemonic states permit significant autonomy to smaller allies only when they are sure that the governance of the latter 'is in safe hands'. Overall, Maier paints a picture of recognizably imperialistic relationships in the ancient Greek world.[13]

Returning to the debates about contemporary international relations, John Mearsheimer has provided what may be termed a classic definition of 'hard' hegemony. In this context, Mearsheimer has argued that 'a hegemon is a state that is so powerful that it dominates all the other states in the system. In essence, a hegemon is the only great power in the system.'[14] Having said that, he then asserts that no genuinely global hegemon of this kind has ever actually existed. This is due mainly to 'the stopping power of water'. Even in the modern technological age, it is still difficult for any state to project substantial and sustainable military force across oceans and seas – Mearsheimer's critical test for effective hegemons.[15] He argues that the US is the most significant contemporary state, but that even it qualifies only as a 'regional hegemon' – that is, a state with the military capacity to dominate a continental landmass (the Americas), but not genuinely to dominate on a global basis.[16]

As should be apparent from the discussions thus far, there is no general consensus on the meaning of 'hegemony' in the international context. With this in mind, John Ikenberry has helpfully clarified the two most important strands in the contemporary debates: between what he calls the 'liberal' and 'imperial' variants of hegemony. It is apparent that, in Ikenberry's conceptualization, liberal hegemony corresponds closely to the hegemonic thinking evident in the writings of Thucydides, although Ikenberry does not make that comparison explicit. It may be recalled that the Greek historian argued that significant material power should bring with it 'a care for the common welfare' and a defined sense of mutual responsibility and obligation.[17] For Thucydides, this was based not on altruism, but on recognition by the hegemon of the indispensability of allies for advancing its own interests and maintaining its leading status in the world. Ikenberry's concept of imperial hegemony, on the other hand, corresponds to the essentially domineering understanding evident at the core of Mearsheimer's work.[18]

At first sight, it appears that Mearsheimer portrays a world corresponding closely to Thucydides' much quoted aphorism that 'the strong do what they can and the weak suffer what they must'.[19] It should be recalled, however, that, according to Mearsheimer's worldview, the power of even the materially strongest states today is crucially limited by the stopping power of water. This prevents even the United States from assuming true global hegemony, as Mearsheimer defines it. This argument has been challenged by Christopher Layne, amongst others. Layne argues convincingly that, in the years since the mid-twentieth century, the United States *has* successfully overcome the limitations imposed by the stopping power of water. It has done this by constructing and maintaining an extensive network of hundreds of permanent military bases and support installations around the world.[20]

The maintenance of this 'empire of bases' in peacetime obviously requires the support of the overseas host states. In other words, it depends upon allies, both formal and informal. Critics, such as Chalmers Johnson, have argued that these allies have little real choice, given the material preponderance of the US and its consequent ability to coerce them if resistance were to be encountered.[21] Yet the picture, in reality, is more nuanced than Johnson suggests.

There is no doubt that the US can offer security and economic and financial inducements to established or prospective hosts, always with the proviso that these could be withdrawn in response to obstructive or uncooperative behaviour.[22] At the same time, if there has been a clear and sustained demand for it to close its bases, as was the case in France in the mid-1960s or the Philippines in the early 1990s, then the US in practice has acquiesced. Host states can also induce changes in, or modifications to, American attitudes and policy in return for continuing to play host. This has been apparent with regard to the willingness of successive US administrations to mute official criticism of the government of Uzbekistan's human rights record, in return for continuing to maintain important military basing and transit rights in that country since September 11, 2001. It could also be seen in the Obama administration's comparatively very constrained response to the violent suppression of popular protest movements in Bahrain – host to an important US naval base – during the 2011 Arab uprisings.

Mearsheimer's conception of hegemony is ultimately limited. It does not account for the extent to which power is reflected in processes of social interaction, rather than being based solely or mainly on material capabilities. American power (and, indeed, that of other important states) in the contemporary world has come to depend upon an international structure embracing military, economic, commercial and diplomatic collaboration to a far greater extent than analysts such as Mearsheimer and Paul Kennedy appear to allow for.

In its contemporary form, this structure was substantially created in the aftermath of the Second World War. It is often analysed primarily in terms of international organization. In these terms its core elements are, firstly, the United Nations 'system', consisting of the key UN organizations based in New York, and forty plus specialized UN agencies with headquarters around the world. Also important are the so-called Bretton Woods economic, financial and commercial organizations. The main Bretton Woods organizations today are the International Monetary Fund, the World Bank and the World Trade Organization.

The organizational features of this international structure are evidently an important part of its overall framework. The structure has been effectively analysed by John Ikenberry in a way that captures its equally important *social* characteristics as well. In Ikenberry's words:

> East Asian and European states agree to accept American leadership...In return, the United States...reinforces the stability of these long-term mutually beneficial relations by making itself more 'user friendly'...playing by the rules and creating ongoing political processes with these other states that facilitate consultation and joint decision-making.[23]

This is the essence of liberal hegemony. 'Liberal', in this context, essentially means 'open', in the sense that all participating states, including the US, are open to influence from other participants in the system. This view resonates with the idea of social power being essentially an enabling rather than a prohibiting process, as argued by Michel Foucault.

During the Cold War period, political consultations with allies were a key component element of the 'lubrication' identified as key to the whole US-led alliance system by the eminent diplomatic historian John Lewis Gaddis (discussed in more detail later). They were most evident in relations between the US and its NATO allies in Western Europe. This example will, therefore, be the main focus of analysis in the next section. These discussions offer a brief illustrative case study of a liberal hegemonic order operating in practice.

Liberal hegemony in practice: the US and Europe in the Cold War years

In the years immediately following the Second World War, the US was at its strongest in material terms, producing nearly half the world's economic product and with an (albeit brief) monopoly over atomic weapons capability during the 1940s. Despite this, American leaders displayed little evident interest in turning Western Europe into some kind of military protectorate, or economic dependency, and acting thereby as an 'imperial hegemon'.

The story of how American troops came to be stationed in Europe on a permanent peacetime basis from the early 1950s has appropriately been described as representing the creation of an American 'empire by invitation'.[24] The main political pressures driving the deployment and maintenance of a substantial American military presence in Europe were 'pull' factors coming from European governments themselves, rather than 'push' factors emanating from the American side. Indeed, there was active debate within the American government – most especially in the State Department – about whether the US should avoid deploying a sizeable military presence and focus instead on encouraging the emergence of Western Europe as an essentially self-sufficient 'third force' in military terms, alongside the United States and the Soviet Union.[25] Particular hopes were, for a time, invested in the United Kingdom being able and willing to lead in galvanizing an indigenous effort along these lines.[26]

Once the US was committed militarily to Western Europe, and as its wider international role and status came to depend increasingly – if not decisively – on its role there, American leaders felt obliged to bear significant burdens and costs in order to maintain its presence. The most obvious were the financial ones. In 1985, it was calculated that, out of a total US general purpose defence budget of $241 billion, no less than $134 billion was taken up by European commitments, with another $42 billion allocated to support the US military presence in Asia.[27]

Most important in the context of the discussions here, however, was the *political* price which US leaders felt they had to pay in order to ensure that their allies were kept solidly on side. The 'cost' in this sense was a continuous and frequently time-consuming process of political consultation and negotiation, with American leaders constantly having to win the support of allies 'issue by issue', rather than being able to assume that such support could ever be taken for granted.[28] American leaders could not be sure, even at times of dire international crisis, that their allies would automatically support the US, at least in active and practical ways. Even in October 1962, at the height of the Cuban missile crisis – perhaps the most serious crisis of the whole Cold War period – allied support for the US position was less than complete, notwithstanding intense American diplomatic lobbying. Thus, for example, Canada refused to allow American bomber aircraft to use its airfields, and NATO members as a whole rejected an American suggestion that their NATO assigned forces should be placed on a state of heightened alert, as a warning to the Soviet Union not to escalate the crisis with a possible military probe against West Berlin.[29]

Undoubtedly, American leaders did sometimes fail to consult properly, and they also resorted to coercion on occasion. During the Cuban crisis, for example, US officials effectively forced the Norwegian government to recall ships bound for Cuba by threatening the termination of American arms supplies.[30] The smaller and less materially capable members of NATO sometimes complained of a lack of consultation and American disregard of their views.[31] Major European states were not immune either. Denis Healey, British chancellor of the exchequer from 1974 to 1979, recalled in his memoirs an American attempt in 1976 effectively to dictate the terms of a planned loan to the UK by the International Monetary Fund.[32] Helmut Schmidt, West German chancellor between 1974 and 1982, later complained about a general lack of consultation by the US, of its NATO allies, during the Carter and Reagan administrations in the late 1970s and early 1980s.[33]

It would be inaccurate therefore to imagine some kind of golden age of consultation ever having existed between the US and its European NATO allies. It is equally misleading, on the other hand, to suggest, as some have done, that the US simply ran the NATO alliance through a combination of manipulation, bribery and sometimes plain coercion.[34] In reality, American leaders resorted to a variety of approaches in their dealings with allies. The point here is that the consultative approach was *at least* as important a feature of relations during the Cold War years overall as more manipulative or coercive methods, although it is instances of the latter that have tended to be remembered and more often discussed. Furthermore, decision-making amongst NATO allies was not simply – or even mainly – determined by the United States' greater material (military and economic) resources. Skill in social interaction – in this case manifested in complex and continuous networks of intra-alliance consultations – could be just as important.

In this context, the academic work of Thomas Risse-Kappen has been pioneering in its analysis of the complex interactions and 'give and take' of NATO decision-making. The nature of these interactions has often given European member states significantly greater influence over US policy and attitudes than might be expected by a simple consideration of the respective material balance.[35] Non-material sources of influence have sometimes been publicly acknowledged by American leaders. In 1973, for example, then Secretary of State Henry Kissinger accepted that 'military muscle does not guarantee political influence ... countries can exert politi-cal influence even when they have neither military nor economic strength.'[36]

Multilateralism

Most American leaders in practice accepted the view – explicitly or implic-itly – that the most effective and mutually productive way to engage with their NATO allies was through a multilateral approach. John Gerard Ruggie, the leading academic theorist of multilateralism, has defined its essential premises thus:

> [It is] an institutional form that coordinates relations among three or more states on the basis of generalized principles of conduct ... which specify appropriate conduct for a class of actions, without regard to the particularistic interests of the parties or the strategic exigencies that may exist in any specific occurrence.[37]

The consultative structures and processes of NATO, first established in the late 1940s and early 1950s, provided the permanent organizational frame-work within which such 'generalized principles of conduct' amongst member states could be developed and entrenched. In doing so, over time they acted, in the words of political scientist David Calleo, 'as a training ground for life in a pluralistic world [where] even the greatest countries are subject to a balance of power and ... national self-interest has to be defined and pursued in a cooperative framework'.[38]

American leaders were, on occasion, willing to alter their stated views and policies, even on issues judged to be very important to US interests, as a result of political and diplomatic pressure exerted by their allies. For example, allegations of coercive American pressure on certain allies during the Cuban missile crisis, noted above, are balanced by research showing the ways and extent to which *American* policy and attitudes during the crisis was influenced and conditioned by what NATO allies thought (or by what American policy-makers believed that they thought). This degree of European influence was substantially facilitated by the generally held belief amongst American leaders that nothing should be allowed to happen that would risk splits within NATO at such a delicate time.[39]

More recently, European influence over American policy was evident in the context of the divisive debates between 1979 and 1984 over the prospective deployment of new intermediate-range nuclear forces in

Western Europe. During this anxious time, the Reagan administration conducted a concerted diplomatic and political campaign in order to try and ensure that the missiles were deployed on schedule. Consultations were held, presentations were given and intelligence information on the scale of the supposed Soviet nuclear threat was shared (despite opposition to the latter from within some US government agencies). Even so, the US had to accept that neither Belgium nor the Netherlands would agree to take their share of the new missiles according to the originally agreed NATO timetable. The Dutch were further able to negotiate specific *quid pro quos* with the US. These saw them being relieved of some existing NATO nuclear roles in return for agreeing, eventually, to deploy the new missiles.[40]

The contrast with the pre-Gorbachev Soviet approach to alliance management on the same issue was stark. An insight into this was given by a former foreign minister of communist Czechoslovakia, Bohuslav Chňoupek. Chňoupek recalled that, late in 1983, his ministry

> got a note from the Soviet embassy with no more than 50 words on it saying that medium-range missiles would be deployed on the territory of Czechoslovakia and the GDR...I called Berlin and an official answered that the same message had been received [there]...The deployment had not been discussed with us.[41]

The longer-term debilitating effect of this *diktat*-based approach contributed to the eventual collapse of the whole Soviet alliance system in Europe between 1989 and 1991.

The essential differences between the US-led NATO and its Soviet-led counterpart, the Warsaw Treaty Organization (commonly called the 'Warsaw Pact' amongst NATO member states), have been well captured by John Lewis Gaddis:

> NATO...was an *organic* alliance: it proved to be deeply rooted, in tune with its environment...But both the Warsaw Pact and the Sino-Soviet alliance seem today to have been *inorganic*...they were impressive to look at and hard when touched; but under strain they shattered easily. (Emphases in the original)[42]

The arguments developed above point to the conclusion that the relative 'organic' strengths of NATO (to use Gaddis's term) lay in the extent to which its formal organizational structures provided a framework for the development of underpinning *social* networks of virtually continuous discussion, consultation and bargaining amongst representatives of its member states. Often these went unnoticed by contemporary observers, and, as suggested earlier, attention tended to focus on the transatlantic alliance only when something went wrong. In retrospect, however, it is apparent that the existence and evolution of these social processes did in fact form a significant part of the basis of NATO's core relative strengths.

Overall, data collated by Stephen Walt in 1987 showed that the international alliance system led by, and centred on, the United States during the Cold War years was significantly stronger and more extensive than its Soviet-led counterpart when measured by total population size, total economic product, and the aggregate size of the respective military establishments.[43] On the basis of the discussions above, it can be argued that this reflected the extent to which successive American governments since the 1940s had managed to make their alliance system significantly more attractive than had their Soviet counterparts. They had achieved this, as John Ikenberry has suggested, largely by institutionalizing multilateral consultations and negotiations, and thus giving their smaller and less materially powerful allies both an input and a stake in the American alliance system.

After the Cold War: the unipolarity debate

What is unipolarity?

'Unipolarity' has been succinctly defined by the American scholar William Wohlforth as 'a structure in which one state's capabilities are too great to be counterbalanced'.[44] Its existence could, therefore, engender a robust sense of self-confidence and also self-sufficiency on the part of the leaders of the state in pole position (i.e., the US). They might, as a consequence, opt for increased international disengagement (often called an 'isolationist approach'), on the grounds that their state had no pressing need or wish to maintain significant engagement with other states and international organizations. They might, on the other hand, opt to maintain engagement, but to do so increasingly on the basis of a unilateral – rather than multilateral – approach. This could see less effort being devoted to soliciting, engaging with, or incorporating into their own posture and policies the views or sensitivities of other states and their leaders.

With both of these theoretical possibilities, unipolarity could lead to the significant attenuation and degradation of international social interaction on the part of the leading state. Without this, a liberal hegemonic structure of the kind discussed above might be seriously threatened. If power is, in the final analysis, a social process, it is also possible that, were the state in pole position to begin to act in either of the ways outlined above, its own power might degrade from the superior, increasingly to the inferior, kind.

Unipolarity is another voguish concept in the current world politics and international relations debates, and it is widely assumed that, since the early 1990s, the world has, in fact, been unipolar. Rather than simply going along with this assumption, it is sensible to ask at this juncture whether it is, in fact, the case.

At the end of the twentieth century, the well-known American scholar Samuel Huntington argued that, despite the fact that 'there is now only one superpower', the world had not become unambiguously unipolar. His benchmark for unipolarity was a theoretical world order that contained 'one superpower, no significant major powers, and many minor powers'. In reality the contemporary world, in Huntington's view, had not been like that because 'significant major powers' such as Russia and China do in fact exist, although the US does not necessarily consistently engage with them to the degree and in the ways that it arguably should.[45] With this in mind, Huntington came up with the rather inelegant – but arguably more accurate – term 'unimultipolar' to describe the actual configuration of power relations amongst leading states, at least at the outset of the post-Cold War era during the 1990s.[46]

Such qualifications on the existence of unipolarity have been robustly challenged by those who are convinced that a unipolar world does indeed exist, and has done so since the end of Cold War bipolarity. Sometimes, unipolarity's proponents have seemed quite exasperated by the unconverted. William Wohlforth and Stephen Brooks, for example, declared in 2002 that, 'if today's American primacy does not constitute unipolarity, then nothing ever will. The only things left for dispute are how long it will last and what the implications are for American foreign policy.'[47] The journalist and commentator Charles Krauthammer, meanwhile, also accused Huntington of setting the bar too high, asserting that he was 'applying a ridiculous standard: that America be able to achieve all its goals everywhere all by itself. This is a standard not for unipolarity but for divinity.'[48] Krauthammer's views are of particular interest because he is often credited, through a famous article published in *Foreign Affairs* in 1990, with introducing the notion of unipolarity into the international relations debates.[49]

Krauthammer did not invent the term itself. It can be traced back at least as far as the work of Harold Lasswell and Abraham Kaplan, published in 1950. These authors argued then that a unipolar pattern of international power might be formed through essentially coercive domination by an especially strong state in material terms. Alternatively, and perhaps more benignly, it might form as a result of increasing cultural homogenization within a region. This could have the effect of creating a permissive environment in which 'a single state emerged, consolidating itself over an enormous region, thanks to the efficiency of cultural unity and the prestige of a rising civilization'. They further argued that, historically, 'military dominion not preceded and accompanied by cultural homogeneity soon broke up'.[50]

Given the *bipolar* Cold War context in which Lasswell and Kaplan were writing, concepts of unipolarity presumably appeared to many at the time to be of little more than historical interest. Unipolarity did not, therefore, become a commonly used tool for analysing world politics and international relations until after Charles Krauthammer reintroduced it into the debates in the early 1990s, at a time when it was clear to many that the Cold War international structure was ending. Lasswell and Kaplan did perform a useful service in their work, however. They effectively argued that unipolarity – at least of a sustainable kind – does not depend on pre-eminent material capabilities and elements of coercion. A unipolar order would – they thought – be better founded on the basis of increasing perceptions of rising cultural homogeneity. The basis for this, in turn, might well be primarily attraction rather than coercion – what today, therefore, might be called soft power.

The social structure of unipolarity

Overall, for Lasswell and Kaplan, it is apparent that unipolarity could be essentially a *social* structure as much as a material one. As noted earlier, for sociologists and many philosophers, the whole concept of structure is intrinsically social. This has not been the case for many international relations scholars. The prevalent understanding on this issue has been strongly influenced by thinking associated with the American political scientist Kenneth Waltz, and termed 'structural realism'. Structural realist thinking, set out by Waltz in his 1979 book *Theory of International Politics*, suggests that the international structure is the key determinant of relations amongst states, and in particular the 'leading powers' of the day. 'Structure' in this context is, however, *materially* rather than socially determined and based primarily on states' relative military and economic capabilities.[51]

An individual analyst's understanding of structure can have a major impact on their overall view of the nature and distribution of power in the international arena. For many it is axiomatic that the Cold War era was bipolar in terms of the basic structure of international politics, with the United States and the Soviet Union as the two superpowers at the heart of it. Torbjørn Knutsen, however, has put forward the iconoclastic view that the post-1945 world order was really based on a variant of American *uni*polarity. Knutsen justifies his assertion with the liberal hegemonic argument that:

> The key to America's pre-eminence [lay] in the normative dimension of America's power...it enjoyed massive support abroad – notably from the great powers of Western Europe...[Thus] the United States...was a strong power as well as a strong state, the Soviet Union was 'merely' a strong power.[52]

For many, the argument that an international system containing the Soviet Union could in any meaningful sense be described as being based on American unipolarity will likely seem too much of a stretch. Whether one agrees with him or not, however, Knutsen's provocation does serve as a useful caution against neglecting the social and ideationally based dimensions of both power and international structure. This is a key mistake made by structural realists.

In a 2009 article, Martha Finnemore developed a relatively rare analysis – for an international relations scholar – making precisely this case: that 'the structure of world politics...is social as much as it is material'. For Finnemore, the key finding to emerge from a social analysis of unipolarity is that, in order to maximize its ability to operationalize power, a unipole must limit its willingness and hence its ability to do so unilaterally. This is a significant paradox. This is because, for many, the existence of a unipolar world order in material terms means that the predominant state enjoys unprecedented scope to achieve its aims without effective opposition or counterbalancing. Finnemore reminds us of the key importance of legitimacy as a factor of power, however. She writes: 'Using power as more than a sledgehammer requires legitimation, and legitimation makes the unipole dependent, at least to some extent, on others.' This dependence accrues for the obvious reason that 'actors, even unipoles, cannot create legitimacy unilaterally. Legitimacy can only be given by others.'[53]

Despite his own assertion that the post-Cold War international system 'is unambiguously unipolar',[54] William Wohlforth did accept that the US is not entirely in a class of its own. He argued that 'unipolarity should not be confused... with an imperial system containing only one major power'. Frustratingly, Wohlforth failed to quantify clearly what the essential differences between these two systems are supposed to be. Neither did he identify what the US is supposed to be if not the 'one major power' in the current 'unambiguously unipolar' world.[55] Wohlforth's circumlocutions on these points suggest that, in spite of his own apparent certainty, it is not in fact 'unambiguously' clear either what unipolarity is or whether the contemporary world can actually be characterized as being clearly unipolar in character.

Finnemore's arguments provide a means to address the implicit question raised – but not answered – by Wohlforth: i.e., what is the difference between unipolarity and an 'imperial system'? Using the insights offered by Finnemore, the following answer can be suggested: an effective unipole must self-limit the consequences of its material preponderance in order to employ fully the social dimensions of power. Above all, this means limiting the temptation to think and act unilaterally. If this happens, then there is no intrinsic reason why a unipolar international system cannot also incorporate liberal hegemony. An 'imperial' state, on the other hand – in the kind of world suggested by analysts such as Paul Kennedy and John Mearsheimer – would be unlikely to appreciate the benefits of doing this. Its leaders would likely be of the view that they could rely on their material (and especially their military) capabilities in order to achieve desired objectives and ends. Further, this could be done without reference – and indeed in opposition – to the views and wishes of other actors.

If one accepts that the social dimensions of power matter, this latter approach becomes problematic. Finnemore rightly argues that 'preponderant power can only be converted into social control if it is diffused. To exercise power to maximum effect, unipoles must give up some of that power to secure legitimacy for their policies.'[56]

Reflecting on the history of the Cold War, John Lewis Gaddis used the notion of lubrication in an attempt to capture what this could mean in practice. He argued that the elements of consultation and consent which underpinned the American-led alliance system, compared with its Soviet counterpart, made an enormous difference quite unrelated to the military strength each side could bring to bear...influence, to be sustained, requires not just power [in a material sense] but also the absence of resistance...Anyone who has ever operated a vehicle knows the need for lubrication, without which the vehicle will...grind to a halt.[57]

This brings us back, finally, to multilateralism, and specifically to the idea that multilateral structures, norms and processes constitute the essential lubrication that keeps an international system running most effectively. This applies as much from the perspective of a unipole as it does from that of other actors in the system. Measured materially, the other actors may be quantifiably inferior or subordinate to the unipole. They should not be treated with disdain, however, for they have it within their means to withhold cooperation and support and – most importantly – the legitimation that often accompanies these.

With the above points in mind, the discussions will now proceed to examine in detail in the next three chapters the post-Cold War record of the 'unipolar' United States. Special attention will be paid here to the ways and the effectiveness with which American leaders have adapted to and employed this status, with particular reference to the impact of their policies and actions on the ability of the United States to operationalize effective power in the social sense suggested in Finnemore's analysis.

4

The Multipolar Moment? The US and the World in the 1990s

In 1990, even before the final collapse of the Soviet Union, Charles Krauthammer proclaimed, as noted in the previous chapter, the dawning of a 'unipolar moment' in international affairs – a 'moment' that he envisaged lasting for a generation or more.[1] Others have seen the first post-Cold War decade as witnessing the – albeit somewhat uneven – emergence of a more *multi*polar world, a development that was, they believe, subsequently disavowed and undermined by the policies adopted by the administration of George W. Bush from 2001 to 2008.

The approach of this particular administration will be the focus of the analysis in the next two chapters. Here, attention will be concentrated, firstly, on elaborating a definition and a usable model of multipolarity. This is something that has rarely been done in the academic literature to date. It will provide a framework for analysis of the foreign policy approaches followed by the administrations of George H. W. Bush and Bill Clinton in response to key international security challenges during the 1990s. These discussions, in turn, will facilitate the drawing of conclusions about the extent to which the 'new world order', proclaimed by the former in 1990, did in fact display any significant and recognizable multipolar characteristics.

Multipolarity

As discussed in the previous chapter, there has been a lively debate – at least amongst American scholars – concerning the nature and meaning of unipolarity. There has not, thus far, been a similarly systematic debate about multipolarity. Rather, the term is often used loosely, frequently in juxtaposition to unipolarity, where it is widely and simply assumed to be its more positive and desirable opposite.

There were the beginnings of a debate about multipolarity in the early 1990s. The ending of the Cold War order was accompanied by some speculation that the collapse of bipolarity would (or should) produce a new international arrangement based on something akin to the nineteenth-century 'Concert of Europe'. Although the term 'multipolarity' itself was used relatively rarely at this time by international relations and world politics scholars, it is apparent that many of those who wrote about concert systems had in mind something similar.[2] It is, therefore, worth identifying the main elements of their thinking in order, in turn, to begin to tease out a working understanding of multipolarity in the post-Cold War world.

The first thing to become apparent from a study of the literature that made up these early debates is that the concert system envisaged in a post-Cold War international system would be made up of three or more 'significant powers'. This is a basic definition of a multipolar system. It is distinguishable from both unipolarity, which is based, as we know, on the presence of a single pre-eminent centre of international power, and bipolarity, which is based on two such centres.

Analysts who were favourably disposed to a concert-type international arrangement generally premised their view on the idea that it would likely be more cooperative, and therefore a better underpinning structure for international stability and security, than potential unipolar or bipolar alternatives. In a widely cited 1985 article, Robert Jervis had identified the main distinguishing feature of the nineteenth-century Concert of Europe, at least during its strongest years, as being 'an unusually high and self-conscious level of cooperation among the major European powers. The states did not play the game as hard as they could; they did not take advantage of others' short-run vulnerabilities.'[3]

Not everybody has been persuaded that a multipolar system is best for international security and stability. Kenneth Waltz famously argued during the Cold War that a *bipolar* system is likely to be more stable than a multipolar one.[4] In Waltz's view, multipolarity negatively complicates the calculations of political leaders in terms of who their potential friends and enemies are. In this way, it can increase the dangers of mistrust or miscalculation, heightening tensions and possibly provoking conflict. Waltz's more recent work shows that he has maintained these concerns.[5] They are a useful corrective to simplistic assumptions that a multipolar world will *automatically* tend to produce more cooperation amongst the leading states, and thereby produce a more stable international system.

It is also useful in this context to suggest that the concept of multipolarity be treated in a similar way to unipolarity in Martha Finnemore's work – i.e., that its social dimensions be considered, as well as its material and structural features. With this in mind, it can be argued that an important advantage of a multipolar arrangement of international power distribution could be to make relatively more likely a cooperative multilateral approach to international policy and action than would be the case in a unipolar one. This is not because multilateralism and unipolarity are in some sense inherently incompatible. It can, however, be argued that, in a multipolar order, leaders are more likely to choose to act multilaterally rather than unilaterally. In other words, perhaps multipolarity promotes what might be termed social conditioning amongst leaders in favour of multilateral approaches.

In the first instance, this could be the case because the 'temptations of a superpower' (to use Ronald Steel's phrase)[6] may not be as great in a multipolar world, on account of greater structural equilibrium between and amongst the leading states. Multipolarity does not necessarily presuppose the existence of three or more states of basically *equal* power capabilities. It does, however, suggest a widespread acceptance and inculcation of the belief that there is essential *equivalence* amongst several states. This means that leaders of each of the states involved accept that the others contribute vital assets or public goods that could be withdrawn or made unavailable as a consequence of unilateral action, to the detriment of all. These assets could be material capabilities, such as military forces. They might also be less easily quantifiable, but just as important in context. Examples of the latter could include support for the maintenance of core international institutions from which all leading actors derive essential benefits. They could also include supporting, diplomatically and politically – and hence helping to confer legitimacy on – particular actions in the international arena, even if others choose not to participate actively themselves.

Over time, multilateral processes amongst a group of 'equivalent' states in the sense outlined here may increasingly become self-reinforcing. This was apparent in the NATO example used as the case study in chapter 3. It was suggested in the discussions in this chapter that participation by the United States in a standing multilateral framework with its European allies served – as David Calleo put it – 'as a training ground for life in a pluralistic world'.[7]

Having thus, in these brief discussions, established a working understanding of multipolarity, the analysis that follows in this chapter will assess, within this framework, the approaches adopted by the George H. W. Bush and Bill Clinton administrations during the 1990s, focusing on key international security challenges during that decade.

The George H. W. Bush administration and the Persian Gulf crisis, 1990–1

As is well known, in responding to the invasion of Kuwait by Iraq in August 1990, and the subsequent refusal of Saddam Hussein's regime to withdraw voluntarily, George H. W. Bush made the construction of a multinational diplomatic – and subsequently military – coalition the centrepiece of his approach. This was, indeed, maintained following the eviction of Iraqi forces from Kuwait in Operation Desert Storm in January–March 1991. International pressure on Saddam was kept in place subsequently through the maintenance and periodic bolstering of a substantial series of UN-mandated economic and commercial sanctions, originally imposed in response to the invasion of Kuwait.

It may also be recalled from the discussions in chapter 3 that, for some analysts at least, the essence of unipolarity exists when the material resources of a single state are too great to be realistically counterbalanced, even by any likely combination of other states' resources. The proposition put forward by Charles Krauthammer, in his 'unipolar moment' thesis, presupposed that the US was becoming structurally dominant in material terms as the Soviet Union was weakening. Yet, in the Persian Gulf crisis, the American administration did not appear to act in a manner that such a position of predominance might have suggested was well within its capabilities.

Some at the time argued that in part this was because, whilst the US may have been structurally dominant, this did not mean that it was *self-reliant* in either military or economic terms. At the conclusion of Desert Storm in March 1991, *The Economist* observed that 'to defeat a country with the national product of Portugal took 75% of America's tactical aircraft and 40% of its tanks'. The journal also noted that, given its substantial budget deficit at the time, the American government had set great store by its ability to persuade rich allies such as Japan, Germany and Saudi Arabia to defray a substantial part of the financial costs of fighting the war against Iraq.[8]

This jarred with the opinions of those who argued that the US could, in fact, have fought and won the Gulf War on its own, without the need for practical operational and financial support from allies. Krauthammer evidently subscribed to this view. He referred to the military coalition assembled under US leadership in the Gulf as being an example of 'pseudo-multilateralism'. By this he meant that it had been put together essentially for presentational reasons, rather than from any kind of necessity.[9] In reaching this conclusion, however, Krauthammer overlooked the fact that, whilst it might have been true that the American armed forces could have defeated Iraq without assistance *if* they were able to devote all their resources to this mission, they were not in fact able to do so.

Although the Cold War bipolar structure was clearly changing – and the forces that had opposed and restrained the US during the Cold War were substantially weakened by 1990–1 – bipolarity was still, in significant measure, intact. The Warsaw Pact was not formally dissolved until July 1991, and the Soviet Union survived until the end of that year. The US required approval from its NATO partners in Europe to remove forces from their existing NATO taskings in order for them to be sent to the Gulf. Because the bipolar 'East–West' stand-off had not yet been fully overcome, NATO members such as Germany, which did not itself contribute militarily to operations in the Gulf, did agree that their forces could 'backfill' NATO roles in place of the American troops that had been redeployed. These arrangements were not made simply for political convenience. The US, as a NATO member, had legal obligations to undertake significant military roles in Europe's defence, requiring the basing of substantial military resources there on an ongoing peacetime basis. It would have been politically costly to have been seen to be abrogating these obligations without the agreement and compensatory support from its allies in NATO.

A second source of motivation encouraging the American government to act multilaterally – and specifically within the legal and political framework of the United Nations – during this time was a concern to ensure that the Gulf operations were viewed to the greatest possible extent internationally as being legitimate. Even critics such as Charles Krauthammer acknowledged the significance of this factor, although Krauthammer professed himself frankly bemused as to why it should matter. It clearly did, however, as he acknowledged.[10] The degree to which legitimization through the UN was sought and conferred on the US-led Gulf effort in 1990 and 1991 was to prove to have durable long-term effects.

Whatever one thinks of the policy of keeping – and, indeed, further strengthening – the sanctions on Iraq *after* its forces were evicted from Kuwait, it is difficult to deny that this approach enjoyed significant and enduring international support through the 1990s. This in itself offers evidence of its legitimacy. During the twelve years that this sanctions regime lasted, the UN Security Council passed no fewer than seventeen authorizing resolutions to adjust or add to it. The last of these – Resolution 1441, passed in November 2002 – drew particular attention at that time. This was, firstly, because it was passed unanimously by the Council, notwith-standing increasing international divisions over the George W. Bush admin-istration's apparent determination to invade Iraq and remove Saddam Hussein from power. Secondly, the resolution was strongly worded by UN standards. It declared that Saddam's government had 'a final opportunity to comply with its disarmament obligations' under previous resolutions, and further asserted that the Iraqi government would 'face serious conse-quences' if it failed to do so.[11]

In 1990, Charles Krauthammer had argued that the United Nations was essentially irrelevant to the US in dealing with the Gulf crisis. He grandilo-quently asserted then that 'the United Nations is guarantor of nothing. Except in a formal sense, it can hardly be said to exist.'[12] The extent to which the George W. Bush administration would have to deal with some 'serious consequences' of its own when it opted to invade Iraq without specific UN authorization in 2003 casts doubt on this judgement. It suggests that the UN's role as a legitimizer of international sanctions and – in the last resort – military action can be a key enabler and facilitator of state power. Conversely, the absence of the UN from the picture can make power – at least of the superior kind – more difficult to operationalize.

It is of course true that the United Nations could not impose *structural* constraints on the US in order to prevent it from invading Iraq in March 2003. Its refusal to sanction and therefore legitimize that act, however, was instrumental in helping to condition and shape the attitudes and approaches of other states towards the US – in Iraq and elsewhere. This arguably made it appreciably more difficult for the American government to secure pre-ferred outcomes on a variety of issues.

The approach followed by the George H. W. Bush administration in 1990 and 1991 was also substantially more multilateral in the sense that the non-American members of the political and military coalitions assembled to deal with the Gulf crisis were not there simply to make up the numbers. Having said this, the coalitions were clearly not partnerships of equals either. The administration's approach was predicated on the idea that the US could and should be able and willing to act as an – if not always *the* – international leader, but that it should do so, where possible, within a clear multilateral framework.

In his memoirs, co-authored with his former national security adviser Brent Scowcroft, the first President Bush argued that his basic foreign policy premise, evident in his handling of the Gulf crisis, was that, with the Cold War coming to an end: 'The United States henceforth would be obligated to lead the world community to an unprecedented degree...and...we should attempt to pursue our national interests, wherever possible, within a framework of concert with our friends and the international community.'[13] As is usual with memoirs, a certain degree of caution should be exercised here. Bush might, of course, have been seeking to put the best possible *post facto* spin on his administration's record in office. Such recollections do not therefore necessarily fully reflect actual thinking and motivations at the time. Having said that, the record discussed above does suggest that notions of the desirability of multilateral leadership did underpin the Bush administration's basic approach to managing the Persian Gulf crisis in 1990–1.

The prevailing international structure during most of Bush's presidency did not encourage a more assertive and unilateral American approach. As noted earlier, and *pace* Krauthammer, it was not really unipolar during 1990 and 1991. It was still, essentially, *bi*polar. American policy was, therefore, constrained to a significant extent by this still prevalent (though undoubtedly weakened) international structure. Because it was nonetheless clear by then that profound structural changes were under way, it was also apparent that the US would almost certainly need to base its international leadership in future on new foundations. The prospect of the US ceasing to play an international leadership role was evidently not seriously considered within the administration.

During the Cold War, in the context of the perceived threats emanating from the Soviet-led communist bloc, the United States' international leadership claims had been founded to a significant extent on a (self-)ascribed role as 'leader of the free world'. With the Eastern bloc now significantly diminished, the Bush approach shifted to a broader and somewhat more nebulous idea of the US leading the 'international community' generally in the construction of a more peaceful and stable 'new world order'. Bush was often criticized for being vague when he tried to articulate these ideas publicly during his presidency. In fairness, however, it is hard to see how he could – and, indeed, should – have been more specific and precise, given the great uncertainties of the time.

Evidence of ongoing debates within the Bush administration became public in the spring of 1992, when a draft of the Defense Department's military planning guidance was leaked to the *New York Times*. It reportedly stated that the main goal of post-Cold War American security policy should be to 'prevent the re-emergence of a new rival' anywhere in the world. On the face of it, therefore, the planners seemed to be suggesting that the US should adopt an assertive approach, designed to try and accelerate the creation of a unipolar world, based substantially on American military capabilities. As such, the draft guidance probably reflected dissatisfaction amongst some mid-ranking officials in the Defense Department at the direction in which policy appeared to be heading.

Having said that, the original guidance recommended that American leaders pursue the task of preventing the emergence of new rivals by developing a strategy of accommodation, rather than coercion. It reportedly stated: 'The US must show the leadership necessary to establish and protect a new order that holds the promise of convincing potential competitors that they need not aspire to a greater role or pursue a more aggressive posture to protect their legitimate interests.' Further, it was argued that, in pursuit of this objective, the US 'must account sufficiently for the interests of the advanced industrial nations to discourage them from challenging our leadership or seeking to overturn the established political and economic order.'[14]

These elements sounded more multilateral and designed to help bolster and maintain American international leadership in an essentially cooperative way. The reference to seeking to preserve 'the established political and economic order' was significant in this context. Based on security institutions such as the UN and NATO, together with the Bretton Woods economic, financial and commercial institutions, this order was inherently a multilateral and 'liberal hegemonic' one, as noted in chapter 3.

Notwithstanding this, the public controversy generated by the press leak in 1992 led to the planning guidance being redrafted and toned down. The revised version was also leaked (quite possibly with official connivance). It differed from its forerunner most notably in one important respect. The original draft had stated that the US would 'retain the preeminent responsibility for addressing selectively those wrongs which threaten not only our interests but those of our allies or friends'. The new version reportedly amended this so that the key passage now read: 'Where our allies' interests are directly affected, we must expect them to take an appropriate share of the responsibility, *and in some cases play the leading role*; but we maintain the capabilities for addressing selectively those security problems that threaten our own interests' (emphasis added).[15]

By the time that Bill Clinton took over the presidency in January 1993, therefore, it was becoming apparent that American policy was moving in a direction suggesting that, whilst it should retain broad leadership capabilities, the US should not in practice always expect – or indeed want – actually to *be* the international leader in responding to a particular challenge. This should not be interpreted as some kind of abrogation of responsibility or an indication of American weakness. To a significant extent, leadership is about choice. Choosing *not* to play the central role on occasion, either because sufficiently important national interests are not judged to be at stake or in the reasonable expectation that others will play that role, is in itself an important element of effective leadership. From the end of 1991, the collapse of Cold War bipolarity provided a newly permissive international environment. This allowed American governments a greater degree of leeway in choosing which international security issues they wished to become actively engaged in dealing with.

Bush, Clinton and the Balkans, 1991–9

These factors were relevant with regard to the emerging conflicts that accompanied the break-up of the Socialist Federal Republic of Yugoslavia from mid-1991. In the early 1990s, American political and public opinion was unconvinced that, with the Cold War clearly ending, the US had sufficient interests at stake in South-East Europe to warrant a military commitment there. Epitomizing this attitude, James Baker, Bush's then secretary of state, was supposed to have said: 'We don't have a dog in that fight'. Whether he actually did so is open to question, and this author has found no actual source for the quote. It is certainly the case, however, that the sentiments allegedly expressed by Baker did fairly reflect the position taken by the Bush administration in 1991–2 and maintained by its successor during its first two years in office in 1993–4.

The role of economic constraints should not be overlooked as an influencing factor here. The Bush administration had faced a significant recession at the beginning of the 1990s, and the president's perceived inattention to the US's economic problems was the major factor that prevented his re-election in 1992. His successful opponent – Bill Clinton – had, during the election campaign, made his own intention to focus 'like a laser' on reviving the American economy very clear. This was to provide fresh impetus to the approach already sketched out by his predecessor during his last months in office. Partners and allies would be expected, and indeed encouraged, to take the lead in dealing with international security challenges when the US government did not itself judge vital national interests to be at stake.

The EC, NATO and Bosnia

It also appeared, in the Balkan context, as if there might be other actors able and willing to step up to the plate. Members of the then European

Community (EC) were in the process of deliberating whether to extend the latter's remit to include a formalized security and defence dimension. Predictably, there were varying shades of opinion amongst its member states about the possibility or desirability of doing so. Those who favoured this development, however, evidently saw the unfolding Yugoslav crisis as an opportunity both to demonstrate and to develop the EC's relevance as a post-Cold War European security actor. They attempted to seize the moment with alacrity and also, it seemed, a perceptible degree of hubris. Jacques Poos, the then foreign minister of Luxembourg (which held the EC's rotating presidency in the second half of 1991), grandly declared, as he departed on an early diplomatic mission to Yugoslavia: 'This is the hour of Europe, not the hour of the Americans.' In similar vein, Jacques Delors, then president of the European Commission, stated: 'We do not interfere in American affairs [and] we trust that America will not interfere in European affairs.'[16]

Public statements such as these were gratuitously unnecessary, because it was already clear that the American government had no wish to take the lead in dealing with the Yugoslav crises. They later also became embarrassing, in view of the failure of successive EC peace missions and peace plans to stem the advancing tide of war – most especially in Bosnia from the spring of 1992. In addition to evident hubris, it is possible that such statements reflected evidence of a nascent interest, in some quarters amongst EC members and officials, in promoting the idea of the emergence of a new multipolar international order. In such an order, regional Great Powers might define 'spheres of interest', in which they expected to deal with security issues and challenges themselves. Such was the extent to which the EC quickly became overwhelmed by the problems in Yugoslavia, however, that this essentially conceptual debate did not gain further traction in Western Europe during the early 1990s. The EC's failure to broker peace in Bosnia, despite its various efforts, ensured that no prospective multipolar architecture emerged along the lines that some in Europe may have been hoping to see.

The discrediting of any such notion is evident in the extent to which, increasingly, Western European leaders began to call for greater *American* involvement in responding to the worsening civil war in Bosnia. It should be noted that, notwithstanding the widespread view domestically that the US had 'no dog in the fight' in the Balkan region, it *had* been involved from the beginning in several ways in the international response to the Yugoslav break-up. Diplomatically, the US had supported the imposition by the UN Security Council of economic sanctions against the central Yugoslav government, and also an embargo on arms sales to any of the warring parties in the various conflicts in the Balkan region. From 1992, American warships participated in an ongoing maritime operation designed to enforce the embargo, in particular against the warring parties in Bosnia.

This and other American operational contributions in the region were facilitated to a significant extent through the use of military assets – such as planning and command and control – provided by NATO. Bosnia thus became NATO's first ever actual military operation. It is significant that both the Bush and the Clinton administration insisted on NATO providing the institutional framework for managing American involvement in the Balkans, rather than opting for a more informal US-led coalition effort, as Bush had done during the Persian Gulf crisis. NATO was an established European security institution with developed procedures for ensuring at least some measure of 'burden-sharing', in terms of contributions to its activities, from a cross-section of its member states. In this respect, using NATO's multilateral structures and processes was viewed as working in important ways in the American interest.

The other side of the coin was that, as noted in chapter 3, in this established and fairly robust multilateral arrangement, the US could not expect simply to dictate terms. In the context of the Bosnian civil war, this was somewhat mitigated in practice by the failure of EC efforts to tackle it effectively. This helped to ensure that American proposals tended to be accepted by NATO allies without significant dissent. This was especially evident in 1995, when the US effectively inspired, organized and commanded a major coercive air campaign against Bosnian Serb military forces. Additionally, having thus helped secure a ceasefire in Bosnia, the Clinton administration followed this up with an imposed peace agreement in talks which it hosted at Dayton, Ohio. The US's European NATO allies were barely represented in the Dayton deliberations, and they raised no serious objections to the terms of the agreement set out there.

Such unilateralism, however, proved to be the exception rather than the rule in the American response to the Balkan crises during the 1990s. A principal lesson, taken from the events of 1995 by the Clinton administration, was that maintaining NATO as a viable and important international security institution was a core American security interest. This was made very clear by the president and senior officials in his administration as they strove – successfully – to persuade Congress to support the deployment of American troops as part of the NATO-led force in Bosnia with responsibility for helping to police the implementation of the Dayton agreement. Thus, for example, then Secretary of State Warren Christopher publicly warned of 'the end of NATO' if the US was not prepared to help by deploying troops on the ground. Defense Secretary William Perry, meanwhile, told a congressional committee that the successful implementation of the agreement would 'demonstrate the credibility of NATO'. Finally the president himself, in a televised address to the American people, said: 'If we're not there, NATO will not be there; the peace will collapse... and erode our partnership with our European allies.'[17] These persuasive efforts were ultimately effective. There had been a widespread expectation that Congress would be reluctant to support a US troop presence in Bosnia. Not only did it in fact do so in the autumn of 1995, but it subsequently consented to several extensions of the NATO forces' mission there. This mission, indeed, was not effectively terminated until the end of 2004, when NATO formally transferred command and control of the remaining stabilization forces in Bosnia to the European Union.

The discussions here illustrate the key point that multilateralism and burden-sharing cuts both ways. In order to secure the perceived benefits of formalized burden-sharing and participation in stabilizing Bosnia by its allies, the US was expected by them in turn to take the leading role – and it did so. Clinton had said, as noted above, that, 'if we're not there, NATO will not be there'. Possibly the most telling illustration of the extent to which US policy was influenced and shaped by this consideration is that the United States went from a seemingly firm determination to put no 'boots on the ground' in Bosnia, when civil war erupted there in spring 1992, to contributing 30,000 troops – one half of the total – when a NATO peace implementation force went in, to face a still uncertain and unstable situation, in January 1996.

The Kosovo crisis

The influencing effects of multilateralism were also evident in the response to the second significant Balkan crisis of the 1990s. This was in Kosovo, where the early stages of a programme of Serb 'ethnic cleansing' of the indigenous Albanian population seemed to many to be under way by late 1998. In response, NATO members eventually decided to launch an extensive air operation – Operation Allied Force – to coerce the Serb government, led by Slobodan Milošević, into ceasing this campaign and effectively handing Kosovo over to international administration.

By this time, there was little question that NATO would be the central instrument of choice for this effort, or that the US would be in the lead in terms of making the single largest operational contribution to the air campaign. Equally important, however, was the fact that, as before, the Clinton administration wanted the overall effort to be a multilateral one. This was not only for reasons of military and financial burden-sharing, but also in order to try to bolster the operation's legitimacy. Operation Allied Force took place *without* an authorizing resolution from the UN Security Council, owing to Russian opposition. Much was made, therefore, of the extent to which NATO, as an alliance of nineteen democratic states, could help legitimize the operation itself. For this argument to be convincing, neither the US nor the other militarily significant member states felt that they could afford to be seen simply to be running the operation on their own, with NATO merely providing 'top cover'.

This resulted in a series of uneasy compromises between perceived political requirements to maintain legitimacy, on the one hand, and operational efficiency and effectiveness, on the other. During the first phase of the operation, decisions even over individual targets for bombing missions required the approval of all nineteen NATO member states. After about ten days, it was recognized that this was too cumbersome and was in danger of impairing operational effectiveness. Thereafter, there emerged an arrangement that came to be known as the 'Quints' group, comprising the US, the UK, France, Germany and Italy.[18] The other NATO members informally agreed that political decisions affecting the day-to-day running of the operation would be discussed and agreed amongst these five, although overall strategic direction of the campaign would remain with the full NATO Council. In return for this, the other member states agreed to maintain NATO-wide political consensus and solidarity behind the core objectives of the Kosovo campaign.[19] Membership of the Quints group was capabilities and contributions based. The five participating states between them provided over 80 per cent of the almost 1,000 aircraft which were involved in the latter stages of Operation Allied Force. The US, the UK and France reportedly functioned as a kind of subgroup within the Quints framework, again based on their operational contributions.[20]

With the creation of the Quints group, the US was no longer obliged to seek the agreement of eighteen other states for day-to-day operational decisions. On the other hand, its four Quints partners could and did significantly influence operational decision-making, sometimes against American wishes. This was particularly the case with regard to targeting decisions. The US possessed greater intelligence-gathering and processing resources than any other NATO state, and so most decisions regarding target selection were made by American national authorities alone. Target *approval*, on the other hand, was done multilaterally amongst the Quints group collectively. This reportedly created delays, to the chagrin of many American political and military leaders,[21] and there is evidence of both the British and French governments sometimes blocking approval of particular targets suggested by the US.[22]

During the course of Operation Allied Force – which lasted from late March to early June 1999 – prominent Americans expressed disquiet, sometimes vigorously so, about the extent to which the US was constrained by the Clinton administration's sense of the need to keep its NATO allies on board. In April 1999, for example, Congressman Steven Kuykendall asserted: 'We are actually the hammer in NATO, the rest of them just come along for the ride . . . we are the leader and we need to act like the leader. We are not doing that in NATO right now.'[23] This showed striking ignorance on the part of an American lawmaker of the whole basis of a multilateral process. It should have been apparent that NATO's European members were not simply 'along for the ride', and that the US was relying significantly not only on operational burden-sharing contributions from its Quints partners but even more so on the important political and diplomatic contributions to the legitimization of the effort from NATO members as a whole.

By the time of Operation Allied Force in 1999, the two conditioning factors noted above – i.e., burden-sharing and legitimacy – had been supplemented by a third. This was the increasingly held belief that NATO's 'credibility' was on the line in its Balkan operations. This concern had been apparent as early as 1995 in relation to Bosnia, when Defense Secretary Perry asserted that the US and its allies had to ensure the success of the post-Dayton peace implementation mission in part in order to 'demonstrate the credibility of NATO'. Judging by the increasing number of public statements made about credibility during the Kosovo campaign four years later, by the end of the 1990s it had clearly become firmly entrenched as an important political consideration for both American and European decision-makers.

Soon after the start of Operation Allied Force, for example, then British Foreign Secretary Robin Cook was quoted as saying: 'The whole credibility of NATO is at stake – not just loss of face after earlier commitments, but confidence in our own security. It is in the national British interest to maintain NATO's credibility.' In the US, meanwhile, Senator John McCain, who was to challenge for the Republican presidential nomination the following year, stated: 'Credibility is our most precious asset. We have purchased our credibility with American blood.'[24] Perhaps most significantly, the US

Defense Department released an *After-Action Report* on the Kosovo campaign in 2000. This identified 'ensuring NATO's credibility' as being one of the 'primary interests' of the US and its allies in conducting the operation.[25] It could be said, therefore, without much in the way of exaggeration, that Operation Allied Force was fought, to a significant extent, for the credibility of NATO.

During the 2000 presidential election campaign, candidate George W. Bush had suggested that, as president, he would end the US contribution to the NATO-led stabilization operations in both Bosnia and Kosovo (the latter having been deployed as part of the agreement with the Milošević government that ended Operation Allied Force in June 1999) and expect European NATO member states to fill the resulting gaps. In fact, American troops were maintained in both theatres until the agreed handover of command from NATO to the EU in Bosnia in December 2004. US troops continued to be deployed in Kosovo well beyond that date, albeit in progressively diminishing numbers.[26]

As early as February 2001, the new Bush administration demonstrated that, whatever might have been said during the previous year's election campaign, in office it was committed to maintaining NATO as a key international security institution, and this entailed the US undertaking continuing commitments in the Balkans. Then Secretary of State Colin Powell told his European colleagues that a unilateral American withdrawal from the Balkans was effectively ruled out, stating that 'we went into the Balkans together, and we will leave together'.[27] This stance was subsequently modified when the US did withdraw from the Bosnian stabilization mission in 2004, although this was carried out as part of an agreed transition from a NATO- to an EU-led operation, as noted.

Several pertinent observations can be made on the basis of the case studies under consideration here. Firstly, to reiterate: it was not self-evident in the 1990s that the United States was a unipolar power, even in military terms. The earlier discussion of the Persian Gulf crisis suggested that the US had to devote very significant military resources to the campaign to force Iraq out of Kuwait in 1991. It is, therefore, questionable whether it could have achieved this on its own, even if its president had been minded to do so. As noted, the US was not able to devote *all* its military resources to the task at hand because of its ongoing alliance commitments in Europe (through NATO) and also Asia (through bilateral security treaties with Japan and South Korea).

At the time, these commitments might have appeared to some to be residual holdovers from the era of Cold War bipolarity, and therefore likely to wither or be subject to substantial modification. Since the early 1990s, these alliance arrangements have indeed been somewhat modified. However, the US has remained substantially committed to them. As of 2011, it retained over 50,000 troops assigned to NATO roles in Germany, 35,000 in Japan and 25,000 in South Korea.[28] These are not occupation forces. The deployments are maintained by agreement with the host countries and, in the case of NATO, as part of a well-established multinational planning, training and command regime dating back to the early 1950s.

These overseas military deployments can be seen as an important component part of what might be called the international networks of American power. Through its unparalleled overseas military presence, the US has been, and remains, engaged in a frequent and sometimes virtually continuous process of mutual influence and bargaining with individual host states and, in the European case, within the multilateral NATO framework too. On occasion, American attitudes and policies have been significantly influenced and changed, in part at least, as a result of this. This was particularly apparent in the Balkan case study discussed here. The US went from a stance of studied detachment in the early 1990s, to playing the leading role in the Bosnian peace implementation force in 1996 (contributing 50 per cent of the troop numbers) and in Operation Allied Force in 1999 (where the US contributed 75 per cent of the aircraft involved and flew 80 per cent of the strike sorties).

The puzzling 'hyperpower' critique

With these points in mind, it is interesting to observe that the US was criticized at the end of the 1990s for allegedly displaying 'hyperpower' characteristics. This critique was especially pertinent as it came from one of its established NATO allies. The actual term 'hyperpower' was coined by then French Foreign Minister Hubert Védrine in 1999, during the Kosovo crisis. Védrine defined a hyperpower as 'a country that is dominant or predominant in all categories', meaning one that had gone beyond predominance in traditional military and economic capabilities to encompass also 'domination of attitudes, concepts, language and modes of life'.[29] This notion posited a type of unipolar world order where the predominant state would have little need – and presumably little inclination, therefore – to act multilaterally or cooperatively. Given the argument that has been developed here – that the US had *not* been acting in this manner during the 1990s – the French critique at first sight appears somewhat puzzling.

In the event, public use of the term had a short shelf life, and the evidence suggests that it was developed as a tactical political expedient in the context of French domestic politics, rather than as a significant and considered perspective on the contemporary United States. It is noteworthy that the foreign minister began using the term, in the immediate aftermath of a bilateral agreement between France and the UK in October 1998, to support the development of a military capability for the European Union. Officially, this was being presented as compatible with NATO and the established American role in European security affairs. However, there has long been a distinct constituency of political and popular opinion in France which has been sceptical of alleged American dominance over Europe's security affairs. It is, therefore, possible that, by reinforcing the public image of an overweening US, Védrine was signalling to this group that the French government continued to recognize and respect their concerns, despite the new EU initiative having been formally presented in pro-NATO and pro-American terms.

Additionally, the French government, under then President Jacques Chirac, had begun a process of reintegrating France with NATO command and planning structures, from which President Charles de Gaulle had withdrawn during the 1960s. Again, the increase in rhetoric about American hyperpower provided a degree of political cover for these moves. Rhetorical assurances were offered, suggesting that the ongoing *rapprochement* with NATO did not represent a fundamental softening in traditional French concerns about the dangers of an overly dominant United States.

In part also, the phrase may have been brought into use in response to hubristic language that had increasingly begun to permeate the Clinton administration's own official pronouncements about the American role in the world. The president and some of his senior advisers had begun to refer publicly to the US as 'the indispensable nation'.[30] On occasion, this rhetoric seemed designed almost deliberately to be gratuitously grating to non-American ears, as when then Secretary of State Madeleine Albright declared: 'We are America. We are the indispensable nation. We stand tall. We see further into the future.'[31] Hubert Védrine's criticism of the American 'hyperpower' can, therefore, be seen as one piece of hyperbolic rhetoric simply feeding off another.

The perceived need to strike a balance between appealing to certain domestic constituencies of opinion, on the one hand, and avoiding antagonizing American leaders, on the other, was reflected in Védrine's careful articulation of his hyperpower concept. It was couched as a warning against the undesirable consequences which he suggested might follow *if* American leaders were to act in future without due consultation with, and regard for, the concerns of their allies.

With this in mind, it may be considered to be no small irony that – presumably because the French government felt that airing the notion had served its purpose and its continued use might become counterproductive – the term 'hyperpower' was allowed to drop from official rhetoric during the course of 2000. This occurred just as George W. Bush was beginning his ascent to the presidency, and when American behaviour in the international arena would soon begin to resemble, in many people's eyes, precisely that of the overweening hyperpower that Hubert Védrine had earlier cautioned against.

American power in the 1990s

An important conclusion emerging from the case studies examined here suggests that there was little evidence during the 1990s that a multipolar world was coming into being. In both the Persian Gulf and the Balkans, the US was clearly the pivotal actor around which the overall international responses to the respective security challenges coalesced. Its central position at the time may be further adduced from the absence of any effective wider international responses to challenges from which the US withdrew, such as Somalia in 1993–4, or with which it decided not to become involved in the first place, as with the Rwandan genocide during 1994.

States or groups (such as the EC/EU) that might conceivably have aspired to balance the US – either individually or in concert – during this decade were either too weak (Russia and the EC) or too preoccupied with their own internal development (China and India). Any interest that there may have been amongst European Community member states and officials in using the collapse of Yugoslavia as a platform to seek some kind of multipolar order, based on privileged spheres of interest, was quickly sublimated by the EC's failure to operationalize effective power in the Balkans. It is probably no coincidence that academic interest in the possibility of the formation of a new Concert of Europe (or similar arrangement on a global scale) virtually disappeared at about the same time.

Notwithstanding this, a key common denominator in the case studies examined here was the willingness of American governments during the 1990s to act extensively with and through established multilateral institutions and processes. This in itself does not prove the absence of a unipolar world order. Multilateralism is essentially a social process and is not, in the final analysis, structurally determined. The leaders of unipoles can always *choose* to operationalize power through multilateral institutions and processes, in order to achieve more efficiently and effectively their preferred outcomes in the international arena.

5

A New Era? The George W. Bush Administration's 'War on Terror'

Whilst it is sometimes asserted rather grandiloquently that the events of September 11, 2001 (9/11) 'changed everything', it is not of course possible to know with any real certainty what the George W. Bush administration, which by then had been in office for only eight months, might have done if the events of that date had never happened. Nevertheless, some of its most controversial international initiatives were taken, or at least set in train, during the immediate *antebellum* period.

Chief amongst these was the immediate declaration by the president that the al-Qaeda attacks on the World Trade Center and the Pentagon on 9/11 meant that the US was 'at war' with militant Islamist terrorists and the states that were deemed to be harbouring or supporting them.[1] This proclaimed 'war on terror' led directly to the American military intervention in Afghanistan from October 2001 in operations that were designed to overthrow the Taliban regime, degrade al-Qaeda's operational facilities and – subsequently – support the creation and development of new structures and processes of governance. Later, in 2003, the Bush administration launched an invasion of Iraq to remove the regime of Saddam Hussein from power, partly because of alleged links between it and al-Qaeda operatives.

These actions, and the ways in which the administration carried them through, proved to be highly controversial, with some suggesting that the Bush approach amounted to a 'revolution' in the conduct of American foreign policy[2] and an 'assault' on the established world order.[3] Those who argued in such dramatic terms were typically concerned not just about the administration's policies themselves, but also about its approaches to pursuing them. 'Arrogantly unilateralist' was a common description used by such critics.

The policies and approaches of the George W. Bush administration are of pivotal importance to the discussions in this book. Hence analysis of them will be spread over two chapters here. It is, firstly, relevant to ask whether and to what extent the Bush approach really did represent a significant – or even radical – departure from past practice, and, if so, in what ways and with what consequences. These issues will be the focus of the analysis in the current chapter. A key underlying question will be what impact the Bush approach had on the effectiveness of American power with regard to important security challenges during the 2000s.

The US, NATO and Afghanistan

It may be recalled from earlier discussions that NATO had remained an institution of prime importance in US (and European) security policy during the 1990s. It is true that its developing roles and functions at that time were regionally limited to Europe itself. On the other hand, the *de facto* decision on the part of its member states to utilize NATO in order to address security challenges in the Balkans, which had not involved responding to a direct attack on one of them, was itself a radical departure from the institution's core Cold War purposes. By 2001, NATO members had demonstrated a clear willingness to adapt it to the changing international security environment.

On 12 September 2001, member states agreed to invoke Article 5 of the 1949 NATO Treaty for the first time in the institution's history. This is the well-known article stipulating that an attack on any one member state shall be considered an attack on them all, and it was the basis of NATO's Cold War role. The unprecedented nature of its invocation, in response to the terrorist attacks on Washington and New York the previous day, was always likely to ensure that what happened next would be widely interpreted as having the most profound consequences for the whole future of NATO, and for the transatlantic security alliance that it had come to embody.

Security analyst Anne Deighton summed up a common – indeed, perhaps the prevalent – view at the time, both in describing the decision of 12 September as 'a crucial moment' for NATO and in proceeding to note that 'Article 5 failed to trigger a NATO-led military response' to the terrorist attacks. This alleged inaction, she asserted, 'exposed the conditional nature of Article 5' and therefore, by implication, called into question the whole basis of NATO's continued existence.[4] Former NATO Secretary-General Javier Solana was more luridly alarmist in his choice of words. He was quoted as saying: 'NATO invoked its most sacred covenant, that no one had dared touch in the past, and it was useless! Absolutely useless!'[5] In similar vein, the then Secretary-General, Lord Robertson, 'and the whole Nato establishment' were reported to have been 'flabbergasted' by the Bush administration's lack of 'appropriate' response to the invocation of Article 5.[6]

At first sight, these responses seem rather exaggerated. Regardless of practical follow-up (or lack thereof), the very decision to invoke Article 5 was itself important. As Philip Gordon noted shortly thereafter: 'With very little public or official debate, NATO had now interpreted Article 5 to include a terrorist attack on a member state.'[7] This was a contingency that was not remotely in the minds of those who had drafted the NATO Treaty back in the 1940s. Perhaps more significantly, NATO member states *did* make a practical collective response to the 9/11 attacks, and thus did effectively follow up their declaratory invocation of the article. A package of no fewer than eight measures was agreed under NATO auspices. The two most prominent elements were the deployment of a multinational naval task force to undertake counter-terrorism patrols in the Mediterranean, and thereby relieve pressure on the American ships already there, and the dispatch of NATO early warning aircraft to help patrol US airspace.[8]

There was certainly scope for differences of opinion over how important this package really was. Some analysts, such as David Brown, downplayed it.[9] Others emphasized its significance. Philip Gordon, for example, called it 'a good demonstration of the value of political commitment and integrated and interoperable military forces' [within the NATO framework].[10] There was clearly a debate to be had. Simply to assert, however, that the invocation of Article 5 produced 'no NATO action' was neither accurate nor, therefore, entirely fair.

The precise terms in which Article 5 is couched can usefully be recalled at this point:

> The Parties agree that an armed attack against one or more of them in Europe or North America shall be considered an attack against them all and consequently they agree that, if such an armed attack occurs, each of them, in exercise of the right of individual or collective self-defence recognised by Article 51 of the Charter of the United Nations, will assist the Party or Parties so attacked by taking forthwith, individually and in concert with the other Parties, such action as it deems necessary, including the use of armed force, to restore and maintain the security of the North Atlantic area.[11]

The basis of Article 5, as drafted, was the preservation of the decision-making rights of individual signatory states. This is evident in the inclusion of the phrases: 'each of them...', 'taking forthwith, individually and in concert with...', and 'such action as [each] deems necessary, including the use of armed force...'. In a strict legal sense, therefore, it would be possible for each signatory to decide to take no – or limited – military action in response to an armed attack on an ally. Although not stated explicitly in the treaty itself, it is reasonable to suppose that a correlation of this is that those attacked are also not formally obliged to avail themselves of what-ever assistance may be offered.

All of this may be true in a strict legal sense, as suggested. Politically and psychologically, however, the prevalent attitudes amongst NATO member states – particularly in Europe – had evolved significantly since the treaty was originally signed. During the Cold War, the relative legal looseness of the security guarantee offered by Article 5 was purposely but-tressed by member states with what was sometimes called a 'presumption of automaticity'. From the early 1950s, members had deliberately created a dense and demanding network of integrated and collaborative military structures and arrangements. These were viewed as effectively guarantee-ing that states would be so tightly bound together in defence terms that their leaders would have little choice about becoming involved in repelling a Soviet attack collectively if one of them were attacked. This conscious effort to create and lock in the presumption that a collective response to aggression would, in actuality, be automatic directly inspired the most controversial elements of NATO's Cold War military strategy and doc-trine. Such elements included forward defence of the inner German border, the related notion of a 'tripwire' force and, not least, a consistent refusal to rule out the possibility of the first use of nuclear weapons.

Thus, when, in the aftermath of 9/11, the Bush administration was widely deemed to have failed to utilize NATO structures and processes fully in the first thrusts of its war on terror, the impact of this was more profound than might have been expected from a simple reading of the formal legal terms of the Article 5 commitment. Fifty years of history and the evolution of normative practices and procedures within NATO's formal structures ensured that many European leaders and NATO officials did indeed view Article 5, in Solana's words, as being their institution's 'most sacred covenant'. The Bush administration's perceived failure to 'honour' this covenant in the way many European governments seemed to expect, by involving NATO directly in Afghanistan, was widely viewed as being an affront to – if not an assault on – the very credibility of the institution itself. This was important. It had, indeed, been a prime concern for the Clinton administration at the time of the Kosovo crisis just two years previously, as noted in chapter 4. Over time, it was also increasingly seen as another indicator of the still relatively new administration's generally hostile attitude to formal multilateral processes, institutions and agreements such as the Kyoto environmental protocol, the Anti-Ballistic Missile Treaty with Russia, and the International Criminal Court.

This was compounded by what seemed to be a brusquely dismissive attitude on the part of senior administration officials. The president himself had presumptuously asserted shortly after the terrorist attacks that 'every nation, in every region, now has a decision to make. Either you are with us, or you are with the terrorists.'[12] Being 'with us' appeared to be a one-way street, however. It did not seem to extend to an American willingness to operate as a component part of a multilateral consultative coalition of the kinds that had prosecuted the campaigns in the Persian Gulf and, especially, Bosnia and Kosovo during the 1990s. In late 2001, then Deputy Defense Secretary Paul Wolfowitz was clear enough about the new administration's attitude: 'If we need collective action we will ask for it; we do not anticipate that at the moment.'[13]

'Informal' multilateralism?

Perhaps most (in)famously in this context, Wolfowitz's boss, Defense Secretary Donald Rumsfeld, asserted, with regard to the post-9/11 military operations in Afghanistan and subsequently Iraq: 'The mission determines the coalition; the coalition must not determine the mission.' With this formulation, Rumsfeld was not simply asserting that the US could and should go it alone. As the Defense Secretary explained:

> We need a lot of help to do this. And nations will help in some ways and some other nations will help in other ways, and that's fine. Countries ought to participate in a way that they can contribute and feel comfortable with. It's important because if it were a single coalition, and a coalition member decided not to participate in one way or another, it would be charged that the coalition was falling apart. On that basis the weakest link in the chain would end the mission, which is why we don't have a single coalition, we have flexible coalitions for different aspects of the task. In this way, the mission determines the coalition; the coalition must not determine the mission.[14]

This approach has been described as one of 'informal multilateralism', as opposed to straightforward unilateralism.[15] Proponents of this view have argued that, contrary to popular stereotyping, the administration was not straightforwardly unilateralist and simply dismissive of the benefits of working together with allies and partners. Rather, its approach was to avoid potentially cumbersome, frustrating and inconclusive negotiations and bargaining within established formal institutional and organizational frameworks, preferring instead the 'flexibility' afforded by more informal arrangements. The latter were often termed in academic and popular discussion as 'coalitions of the willing', and they were put together in practice on the basis of bilateral arrangements with selected governments and states.

Multilateralism is essentially a social rather than a structural construct, based on 'generalized principles of conduct' amongst participants, as noted earlier. Thus it could be argued *prima facie* that there is no intrinsic reason to privilege formal and more institutionalized and structurally based approaches over more informal kinds. In practice, however, 'informal multilateralism', at least as practised by the Bush administration, has appeared to some to be no kind of 'real' multilateralism at all. The well-known American analyst Francis Fukuyama articulated this view when he wrote, in describing his own increasing disagreements with the administration's approach, that 'being willing to work within a multilateral framework does not mean accepting support only on your terms; that is just another form of unilateralism'.[16]

Although it is not structural in essence, multilateralism does, nonetheless, essentially depend on tried, tested, established and, above all, accepted structures and institutions. By working within established and formalized multilateral structures and processes, therefore, the US – in John Ikenberry's phrase – 'makes its power safe for the world'. It does this by purposely creating and enhancing opportunities for materially less capable states to have an input into collective decision-making and policy formulation. Further, as in the case of consultations within the NATO framework during the Cold War or over Balkan issues in the 1990s, the US has allowed itself to be influenced in its own decision-making by the arguments and attitudes of its partners and allies.

This, to be sure, had not always happened. In institutions such as NATO, however, it had occurred with sufficient regularity so as to persuade both American and other participants that the consultative process was useful, meaningful and in their own interests. The *quid pro quo* for the US of maintaining such processes had been the frequent (though not inevitable) willingness by its fellow participants in multilateralism to accept American leadership on issues which American governments considered to be in their national interests.

This helps to explain the concerns that existed in Europe in the wake of 9/11 about the extent to which the Bush administration wanted to build 'flexible coalitions', in the sense in which Rumsfeld had used that term. Its approach did seem to many European governments to be a significant departure from tried and tested multilateralism. As Fukuyama's critique quoted above suggested, multilateralism is not simply a numbers game, with several actors gathering together to discuss an issue of common concern. A coalition or alliance is essentially a social arrangement, resting as it must do on some kind of understanding between two or more actors in the pursuit of *shared* objectives. To some European NATO governments in 2001–2, however, it appeared as if the administration's preference for flexible coalitions was based on little more than an attempt effectively to dictate the terms of their participation, with scant attention being paid to securing their 'buy in' through consultations on what the shared goals, and means of achieving them, should be.

Such an approach arguably, therefore, did not constitute effective international leadership on the part of the United States. The essential requirements for such leadership (or 'social control', as she calls it) have been summed up by Martha Finnemore:

> Effective and long-lasting social control requires some amount of recognition, deference, and, preferably, acceptance on the part of those over whom power is exercised. Paradoxically ... preponderant power can only be converted into social control if it is diffused ... unipoles must give up some of that power to secure legitimacy for their policies.[17]

With this in mind, perceptions by potential partners of an unwillingness to seek agreement from them is likely to result in a would-be leader finding that its ability to operationalize its own power effectively is diminished. Power, as noted earlier in this book, is not simply about making things happen. In its most effective form – called 'superior' power here – it is premised on achieving intended or preferred outcomes. This, in turn, suggests a significant degree of control of outcomes on the part of the initiating actor. Producing effects which are less controllable, or which turn out to be unintended, can in turn be described as an 'inferior' form of power. During the presidency of George W. Bush, the practical consequences of this kind of degradation of American power were most clearly evident with regard to the war in Iraq and its aftermath in the months and years following the invasion of spring 2003.

The Iraq War

Far from seeking to consult in order to try and develop consensus approaches with important allies and partners on dealing with the Iraq issue, if anything the Bush administration seemed intent on wilfully pursuing a contrary course during 2002–3. In January 2003, for example, Defense Secretary Rumsfeld had attempted publicly to divide France and Germany – whose governments were the two foremost opponents in Europe of an early drive to war with Iraq – from the rest of the NATO membership. This was at an (in)famous press conference when, in response to a question about the mood in Europe – and France and Germany in particular – *vis-à-vis* a possible war, Rumsfeld had said:

> Now, you're thinking of Europe as Germany and France. I don't. I think that's old Europe. If you look at the entire NATO Europe today, the center of gravity is shifting to the east. And there are a lot of new members. And if you just take the list of all the members of NATO and all of those who have been invited in recently – what is it? Twenty-six, something like that?...Germany has been a problem, and France has been a problem.[18]

The main 'problem' from the perspective of American allies and partners was not simply unilateralism, in the sense of the US acting, or seeking to act, alone. Rather, it was the extent to which the Bush administration seemingly expected other states to join its war on terror more or less automatically – on pain of ostracism, stigmatization and possible sanction if they did not ('either you are with us, or you are with the terrorists'). Moreover, it appeared that, having joined the US-led coalition(s), they could expect little if any substantive consultation by the self-appointed leader, even over the fundamentals of what they were supposed to be fighting together for. The crucial social dimensions of American power, in other words, were substantially – and it seemed quite deliberately – being attenuated by the administration's basic approach.

In a major speech at the West Point Military Academy in June 2002, President Bush had stated: 'The 20th century ended with *a single surviving model* of human progress, based on *non-negotiable demands* of human dignity, the rule of law, limits on the power of the state, respect for women and private property and free speech and equal justice and religious toler-ance' (emphasis added). All of these values might well seem highly desir-able in the abstract. However, 'respect for women', for example, means different things in different societies with different histories and traditions. Yet Bush's choice of words in describing the values explicitly as 'non-negotiable' (and implicitly, therefore, as the only valid universal choices) seemed to make no allowance for this, or for the possibility and desirability of discourse and dialogue amongst different cultural traditions about how core values could and should be interpreted and developed in their own social contexts.

At West Point, Bush did acknowledge that 'America cannot impose this vision' by force. He nevertheless suggested that it might be promoted by using American material assets and resources to 'support and reward gov-ernments that make the right choices for their own people'. This implicitly raised the possibility of those making the 'wrong' choices – in the judge-ment of the United States government – being subject to some kind of sanction or punishment.[19]

In September 2002, the administration released a new core *National Security Strategy* document. This reiterated themes that the president had previewed in his West Point address, repeating, and indeed amplifying, the notion of 'non-negotiable' universal values. It did acknowledge the exis-tence of 'different histories and cultures', but at the same time it still asserted that these could and should 'successfully incorporate these core principles into their own systems of governance'.[20] In similar vein, market economics were identified as being 'relevant for *all* economies – industrial-ized countries, emerging markets, and the developing world' (emphasis added).[21] One contemporary analyst aptly concluded from all of this that, under Bush: 'Washington's main message to the world seems to be, Take dictation'.[22] Little or no space was seemingly allowed for consultation, negotiation or, indeed, any kind of meaningful multilateral engagement.

'Hubris'

This impression was reinforced by the military campaign in Iraq from March to April 2003. In searching for the 'real' underlying reasons for the administration's decision to launch this war, some critical analysts and commentators concluded that a key facilitator was sheer American 'hubris', ultimately unconstrained by any significant sense of what others might think or how they might respond. This was not, to be sure, the first time that perceptions of hubris had entered the picture – an example involving the European Community and Yugoslavia in 1991 was noted in chapter 4. In that case, however, the EC and its member states had realized fairly quickly that they did not possess the means necessary to achieve their declared objectives of securing a peaceful resolution to the emerging conflicts there, and attention had progressively shifted to finding alternative means of doing so. Eventually, as noted, NATO was the main institutional vehicle through which the conflicts in both Bosnia and Kosovo were addressed during the later 1990s. In the case of the US and Iraq in 2003, however, it seemed evident to the Bush administration that the US *did* have the means – military, economic and political – to achieve its declared goals of regime change, followed by the creation of a new, stable and democratic state. No significant modification in its essential approach to this issue was therefore evident.

An evocative attempt to capture the attendant sense of hubris, evident to some at the time, was made by the British journalist Robert Fisk. He argued that the Bush administration's drive to war had been driven by the:

> visceral need to project power on a massive scale, based on neo-conservative fantasies no doubt, but unstoppable, inexorable. Our army can go to Baghdad. So it *will* go to Baghdad. It will pour over Sumeria and Babylon and all the caliphates and across the land where civilisation supposedly began. (Emphasis in the original)[23]

Fisk was a well-known critic of American policy, and his evaluation of the administration's motivations was, therefore, hardly surprising. Many others, however – not all of them essentially sceptics about the US role in the world – argued along similar lines.[24] These criticisms were often conceptualized in terms of the alleged presence of hubris in the administration's thinking and approaches. An important specific premise, which often underpinned the criticisms, was that the Bush administration oversimplistically reduced 'power' primarily to military capability, and that it had little or no understanding or appreciation of the nature and importance of its social dimensions.

Perceptions of arrogance and hubris on the part of the administration were reinforced by candid suggestions from some of its senior officials that the main *stated* rationale for going to war – Saddam Hussein's alleged development of weapons of mass destruction – had not really been believed, even within the administration's own higher echelons. It had thus effectively been an excuse for a conflict which would likely have been sought in any event.[25] One 'senior adviser to Bush' was quoted by the American journalist Ron Suskind in October 2004. If reported accurately (and they were not officially repudiated), his comments would hardly have seemed out of place if spoken by a member of the Inner Party in George Orwell's *1984.* According to Suskind:

> The aide said that guys like me were 'in what we call the reality-based community,' which he defined as people who 'believe that solutions emerge from your judicious study of discernible reality.' I nodded and murmured something about enlightenment principles and empiricism. He cut me off. 'That's not the way the world really works anymore,' he continued. 'We're an empire now, and when we act, we create our own reality. And while you're studying that reality – judiciously, as you will – we'll act again, creating other new realities, which you can study too, and that's how things will sort out. We're history's actors ... and you, all of you, will be left to just study what we do.'[26]

The term 'hubris' is often used generically and loosely to describe actions and attitudes which those employing it do not approve of. As such, its use is frequently subjective, and often pejorative, and it might therefore appear to have little role in scholarly analysis. The frequency with which it was used – including by reputable analysts – during George W. Bush's presidency, however, argues in favour of some effort being made to quantify it, and also to determine whether it might be used as a more objective analytical tool.

In terms of its original conception and understanding in ancient Greece, it did appear to have a more objective resonance compared with much modern usage. Displaying hubris (or 'hybris', as the word is often translated by classicists) in the ancient Greek context was primarily a social offence, as well as, on occasion, a legal one. In the view of Douglas MacDowell, in Greek thought hubris sprang from 'having energy or power [deriving from material sources] and misusing it self-indulgently'.[27] Douglas Cairns, another classicist, has defined it in similar terms, arguing that hubris 'involves over-valuing one's own qualities to the extent that one under-values the claims of others and neglects one's social role'.[28]

As discussed earlier, in ancient Greek thought, *hegemonia* was a concept of legitimate consensual leadership, as opposed to hierarchical control (*arkhe*). In international affairs, the main danger posed by perceptions of hubristic behaviour, on the part of a dominant actor, is that this is likely to make it more difficult to develop and maintain essential alliances and similar forms of support from others. Earlier in this book, it was suggested that this is one of the main themes apparent from a reading of Thucydides' *History of the Peloponnesian War*.[29] It is also a view which has endured down the ages. In the 1940s, for example, the prominent realist scholar Hans Morgenthau wrote: 'A nation that . . . finds itself at the peak of its power is particularly exposed to the temptation to forget that all power is relative. It is likely to believe that the superiority it has achieved is an absolute quality to be lost only through stupidity or neglect of duty.'[30]

This brief discussion suggests that hubris can be an analytically respectable tool for identifying and formulating criticisms of the damaging effects – not least to the actor(s) who display it – of an arrogant and excessively self-centred view of one's own power. This, indeed, is the context in which the term was used by most of the critics of the Bush approach.

Causes and consequences of the Bush approach

In the post-9/11 era, analysts such as Christian Reus-Smit, David Calleo and Barry Buzan argued that American policies and approaches influenced by a hubris inspired, in turn, by material preponderance was likely to weaken rather than strengthen US power in overall terms.[31] Evidence that this was indeed the case, during the early years of the George W. Bush era, is most clearly apparent when looking at the aftermath of the 2003 Iraq invasion and the fate of efforts to replace Saddam Hussein's regime with a friendly, stable and recognizably democratic state.

Hubristic assumptions

From the second half of 2003, two evidently unexpected challenges became apparent in Iraq. The first was the extent to which postwar developments failed to follow the trajectory expected by the administration. Iraq progressively descended into a widespread and increasingly vicious series of insurgencies. A debate has since developed as to the nature of the Bush administration's principal failings in this regard. The prevalent view has been that it naively went into Iraq without realistic, tested and developed plans for post-conflict stabilization and reconstruction, simply assuming that, once Saddam had been deposed, the Iraqi people would themselves lead the way to a better and more stable and democratic future.[32] Others have argued that the US had gone into Iraq with a plan, but that this made too many poorly founded assumptions about what the Iraqi population, and the various religious and tribal groups within it, wanted, or at least were prepared to tolerate. As a result, attempts to implement it proved impractical and, indeed, counterproductive.[33] Some critics of the invasion, finally, argued that whether the US had plans or not was largely irrelevant. This was because local perceptions that any kind of new political order was being imposed by outside forces of occupation was almost certainly bound to generate resistance.[34]

It is not necessary to enter into debate about the respective merits of these arguments here. What is of relevance in the context of these discussions is to note that *all* of these distinct strands of opinion attribute the failure of the US to achieve its intended effects, of creating a stable and democratic Iraq from spring 2003, at least in part to what might properly be called hubris. This manifested itself as arrogance and naivety in the assumptions that were made about the likely course of developments in the aftermath of regime change. It was also apparent in the evidently unanticipated attitude of ordinary Iraqis to the presence of foreign military forces and civilian administrators in their country. This suggested that the assumptions evident in the president's 2002 West Point speech, and subsequent *National Security Strategy*, about apparent, singular and non-negotiable principles and values of human behaviour were indeed essentially flawed.

Limited legitimacy

Compounding the administration's mounting difficulties after the invasion was the marked absence of practical international support when the going started to get tough in Iraq from late 2003. As Ivo Daalder and James Lindsay have documented, when the Bush administration began to request international military assistance to help counter the growing insurgency, few states responded – and very few made more than token contributions.

This imposed obvious financial and military costs on the United States, especially as the original post-invasion plan, overseen by Donald Rumsfeld, had envisaged rapid American military drawdowns following the overthrow of Saddam Hussein.[35] More pertinently for the discussions here, there was also a price to pay in terms of lost legitimacy. This was both cause and consequence of the limited support internationally for the Iraq invasion. The substantial absence of meaningful multilateralism in the administration's approach to post-9/11 challenges in both Afghanistan and Iraq had helped progressively to undermine the perceived legitimacy of what it claimed it was trying to do, most especially in the latter case.

As discussed in chapter 2 of this book, legitimacy is an important power resource in its own right. Its value rests on the extent to which it helps to confer authority on an actor. This, in turn, can be instrumental in persuading other actors to acquiesce in, and indeed cooperate with, what it is seeking to achieve. If legitimacy is limited, or absent altogether, any utility accruing to material resources can in turn be limited or even rendered ineffective in sustaining the production of intended power effects.

Legitimacy theorist David Beetham illustrated this point with reference to the Iranian revolution of 1978–9. He argued: 'The chasm between the enormous [material] power of the Shah and the justifiability of that power was what ultimately rendered that power itself impotent.'[36] The various popular uprisings which together made up the 2011 Arab spring offered further evidence to support this proposition. These occurred in states such as Egypt, Libya and Syria, notwithstanding the fact that the material power resources – including those available for internal repression – of the governments of these states had not markedly declined or weakened. What *had* changed, rather, were popular perceptions of the continuing legitimacy – or lack thereof – of the regimes in question. This engendered an increasing willingness on the part of many sectors of society to challenge openly their right to remain in government. The effects were perhaps most dramatically seen during August 2011 in the rapid collapse of the Gaddafi regime in Libya, despite its apparent continued command of significant military and financial resources.

The point was also stressed earlier, in chapter 2, that legitimate power is, by definition, (self-)limited. This should not be seen as a negative. As Ian Clark has argued: 'Legitimacy enhances power by making its maintenance less costly. Legitimacy does not simply constrain power: it makes it more effective through "consensual empowerment".'[37]

The Bush administration did not neglect legitimacy altogether. Rather, the difficulties encountered by the US arose in large part because of its emphasis on *domestic* sources of legitimacy providing sufficient justification for American action in the *international* arena. This was both coupled with, and derived from, the scepticism of many senior officials about the whole idea of the US being bound or limited by international institutions, processes or agreements in pursuit of what they considered to be vital national interests.

Domestic legitimacy is not in itself an invalid concept, and some Bush critics have erred in dismissing it as simply a 'truncated notion of legitimacy'.[38] Issues of legitimacy are inextricably bound up with sovereign statehood. As former Secretary of State Henry Kissinger has noted: 'A state is by definition the expression of some concept of justice that legitimizes its internal arrangements and of a projection of power that determines its ability to fulfil its minimum functions – that is, to protect its population from foreign dangers and domestic upheaval.'[39]

Some analysts have argued that latent tensions between domestic and international sources of legitimacy are particularly evident in the American context. They suggest that the reason for this is the particular respect – indeed, reverence – with which the domestic system of law, based on the founding constitution, is treated by the American body politic. As a report produced for one Washington think tank argued in 2007: 'Most Americans would like to conform to international norms, but do not wish to have domestic laws that have been written and passed by elected representatives superseded by international institutions over which Americans feel they have little input or control.'[40]

Thus, any American government will likely be faced with the challenging task of attempting to reconcile domestic and international legitimacy interests and concerns. Further, some have argued that the demise of Cold War bipolarity only increased the magnitude of this challenge. During the Cold War, according to this line of reasoning, the existence of the Soviet Union and its allies effectively counterbalanced the US. This had the effect of making the latter appear less potentially threatening to smaller states than would have been the case had it been less evidently constrained. It also provided the US with a potent claim to international legitimacy, at least amongst non-communist states, as the leader of the free world.[41]

As Max Weber suggested, legitimacy is at least partly subjective, residing as it does in perceptions of the justifiability of one's actions on the part of others. Thus legitimacy – and the closely correlated concept of authority – cannot reliably be established simply by being asserted by an actor, particularly in the international arena. However, some Bush administration officials appeared determinedly oblivious to this, and indeed disdainful of the whole concept of international legitimacy. For them, domestic legitimacy seemed to be the only kind that really counted. In November 2003, then Under Secretary of State John Bolton articulated this view clearly:

> Our actions, taken consistently with Constitutional principles, require no separate, external validation to make them legitimate. Whether it is removing a rogue Iraqi regime and replacing it, preventing WMD proliferation, or protecting Americans against an unaccountable [International Criminal] Court, the United States will utilize its institutions of representative government, adhere to its Constitutional strictures, and follow its values when measuring the legitimacy of its actions. This is as it should be, in the continuing international struggle to protect our national interests and preserve our liberties.[42]

The lessons arising from the American difficulties over Iraq strongly suggest that international legitimacy *is* an important asset, however. This is especially so in helping to shape and condition the international environment in ways likely to increase the chances of other states and institutions helping out when even the materially strongest cannot effectively do the job alone, or with only limited support.[43] Overall, the Bush administration's principal shortcoming in this area was not that it stressed domestic legitimacy *per se*. It was, rather, the failure to balance this with an appreciation of the importance of *international* legitimacy.

Mishandled soft power

Related to the above, some critics of the Bush approach have focused on the alleged indifference, if not actual hostility, to the value and use of soft power within the administration. Francis Fukuyama has nuanced this somewhat by arguing that the Bush administration did not simply dismiss the value of soft power *per se*: 'No one was opposed in principle to the use of soft power; they simply hadn't thought about it very much.'[44] Illustrating this, Joseph Nye – the principal exponent of the concept – recorded an occasion during 2003 when Defense Secretary Rumsfeld, asked about his attitude to soft power, claimed that he did not know what the term meant.[45] It is not, perhaps, surprising that the instinctive response of senior members of the administration to the events of 9/11 and its aftermath was to reach for 'harder' instruments and options, but this approach did of course have consequences. As Fukuyama has laconically noted: 'When your only tool is a hammer, all problems look like nails.'[46]

During the second Bush term, from January 2005, greater rhetorical interest at least was given to the soft power concept. In November 2006, for example, Paula Dobriansky, under secretary of state for democracy and global affairs, provided an insight into the administration's emerging understanding of it:

> The values Nye singles out are indeed seductive, but they are more than that. They are universal. Democracy and human rights are enshrined in the [UN] Universal Declaration of Human Rights. They are the cornerstones and the promise of the United States, virtually every European nation, and the European Union. We agree that human rights and freedoms, including the right of the governed to have a say in the direction of their country, are both inalienable and imperative, applying not just to us but to all – regardless of race, sex, religion, or nationality.[47]

It was apparent from this, and similar statements by senior officials, that soft power was seen primarily in the context of the administration's universalist worldview developed during 2002. As noted earlier in this chapter, this was essentially premised on the belief that prevailing American understandings of norms and values were essentially valid for all states and societies throughout the world.

The potential for cultural imperialism is, in the view of some, latent in the soft power concept in any event. The Bush administration's particular approach, however – manifested most clearly in its declared pursuit of 'democratization' in the wider Middle East – compounded this potential problem. In part this was because of the tone of much of its rhetoric, which, as noted, explicitly presented American conceptions as 'non-negotiable'. The president and his senior advisers sometimes adopted a messianic tone in their public statements. In a major speech in November 2003, for example, Bush grandiloquently announced that 'the United States has adopted a new policy, a forward strategy of freedom in the Middle East'. He then proceeded to declare:

> We believe that liberty is the design of nature; we believe that liberty is the direction of history. We believe that human fulfillment and excellence come in the responsible exercise of liberty. And we believe that freedom – the freedom we prize – is not for us alone, it is the right and the capacity of all mankind. Working for the spread of freedom can be hard. Yet, America

has accomplished hard tasks before. Our nation is strong; we're strong of heart. And we're not alone. Freedom is finding allies in every country; freedom finds allies in every culture. And as we meet the terror and violence of the world, we can be certain the author of freedom is not indifferent to the fate of freedom.[48]

These kinds of statement amounted for some to what one critic called the 'self-sacralization' of the American role in the world.[49] By thus appearing to claim 'God on our side', they arguably also helped fuel perceptions of a covert anti-Islamic agenda on the part of the American government.

Joseph Nye noted, during the early 2000s, that the US under Bush was showing itself to be no longer as capable of producing effective soft power as had previously been the case.[50] The administration was, perhaps, attempting to do so to some extent, on its own terms, but the effort was counterproductive and ultimately self-defeating. The overt universalism upon which its messages were based did not prove to be inherently attractive to many non-Americans, in spite of wishful thinking on the part of the president and many of his senior advisers. This suggests that the administration had *over*estimated the extent to which attractiveness can be intentionally generated by an actor, and *under*estimated the extent to which soft power is inherently an ascribed – rather than an assertive – power factor. The military campaigns in Afghanistan and Iraq also made it easy for critics to suggest that the US was seeking to impose its values at the point of a bayonet. The Bush administration could thus be seen as being guilty of pursuing the contradictory objective of seeking soft power ends by hard power means. Overall, in this context, the analyst Edward Rhodes has rightly surmised that 'power's ability to change behaviour is well documented. No tyrant, terrorist, or torturer doubts it. Power's ability to change *beliefs*, though, is far more limited, more indirect and more slowly operating' (emphasis added).[51]

Could it nonetheless be argued that the events of the 2011 Arab spring – characterized by popular protests and uprisings calling for greater freedom and 'dignity' – originated in part in impulses first stimulated by Bush's 'forward strategy of freedom' in the Middle East during the preceding decade? This proposition is difficult to prove either way, especially as the events in question are ongoing at the time of writing, and it is not yet clear what the long-term prospects for democratization and liberalization in the affected states will be.

Having said that, a striking feature of the 2011 protest movements was their essentially home-grown nature and responsiveness to domestic drivers and developments. The US, as with most other outside states, was evidently taken by surprise by the sudden and dramatic upsurge in protest at the beginning of that year. The Obama administration did not automatically support the aspirations of the protesters in states such as Egypt and Yemen, where the US had established ties to the incumbent regimes based on shared interests in, for example, countering militant Islamist terrorism.

Barack Obama's approach reflected the traditional one followed by the US in the Middle East since the mid-twentieth century. It placed regional stability and the protection of established American interests in the region above the unpredictable and potentially destabilizing consequences of democratization and liberalization. Some have suggested that the Bush administration itself had earlier effectively reverted to this approach and, indeed, was never really serious about departing from it in the first place, despite its rhetoric to the contrary. In this context, Francis Fukuyama has noted that Bush himself began speaking publicly about democratization in the Middle East only immediately prior to the attack on Iraq in spring 2003.[52] This suggests that his approach may have reflected a political tactic to try and boost the legitimacy of the invasion, rather than a sincere and committed belief in democracy promotion in the region as a whole.

Evidence to bolster this view can be found in a comparison of two major speeches – both given in Cairo – by then Secretary of State Condoleezza Rice. In the first, delivered in 2005, Rice proclaimed what seemed to be a significant break from the traditional American approach. She signalled that the Bush administration's priority in the Middle East would, from henceforth, be aiding and promoting democratization rather than automatically supporting the *status quo* for reasons of stability.[53] Less than two years later, however, Rice took almost exactly the opposite position, concentrating instead on the primary importance of regional stability and hardly mentioning democracy and freedom at all.[54]

It was not hard to see what might have changed minds in the meantime – particularly if the American commitment was already fragile and tactical in nature. A much heralded series of elections in Iraq from January 2005, whilst notably free and fair by the prevailing standards amongst Arab states at the time, had had little impact in stabilizing the country and damping down the various insurgencies within it. In the Palestinian Territories, meanwhile, relatively free and fair elections had brought to power a new government led by Hamas – regarded by successive American administrations as being an anti-Israeli terrorist organization.

Overall, it can be argued that, although the Bush administration was not ignorant of – or intrinsically hostile to – notions of soft power, its efforts to operationalize it were critically misapplied. This was mainly because its worldview, based on universally applicable non-negotiable norms and values, took insufficient account of the extent to which attraction is inherently a two-way process. At the least, its effectiveness relies as much on the 'target' actors being attracted as it does on the initiator seeking to attract. Indeed, in a relationship based on attraction, the *main* determinants of success reside ultimately with the former rather than the latter. The George W. Bush administration made few allowances for this in practice, however. As a result, its attempts to operationalize soft power were largely ineffectual.

The degradation of American power under George W. Bush

The overall lesson for American power of the various issues and problems, discussed here, has been clearly and effectively summarized by Ivo Daalder and James Lindsay. Simply put, they argue: 'The more others questioned America's power, purpose, and priorities, the less influence America would have.' If the 'others' were sufficiently alienated and dissatisfied, they could refuse to support the US. If this happened, 'Washington would need to exert more effort to reach the same desired end.' This, in turn, could threaten 'not only what the United States could achieve abroad but also domestic support for its engagement in the world'.[55] Daalder and Lindsay's assessment here neatly encapsulates what has been called in this book 'inferior' power.

Following its 2003 invasion, the US was hardly 'powerless' in Iraq *per se*, despite the mounting problems that it faced there. It was a key player in determining the course of events on the ground. On the other hand, it is apparent that its ability to achieve *intended* effects in post-invasion Iraq became markedly diminished, at least until the impact of the 'surge' of extra troops, ordered by Bush into the country, began to be felt during 2007.[56]

To write of the simple 'loss' of American power, as a result of the Bush approach to prosecuting its 'war on terror', would therefore be too crude. Rather, it can be argued that it resulted in a noticeable *degrading* of American power, so that, on key security challenges such as Iraq and Afghanistan, the US became increasingly unable to generate intended effects. The United States remained a principal player – indeed for many *the* principal player – in the international arena. On these key issues, however, what was increasingly apparent, both to outside observers and to growing numbers of Americans,[57] was the ineffectiveness of the Bush administration's attempts to secure its declared objectives. Consequences still followed as a result of American decisions and actions, but they were not what the Bush administration had intended. American power was, therefore, effectively degraded.

6

Return to Multilateralism?

In the previous chapter it was argued that the approach adopted by the George W. Bush administration in pursuing its proclaimed 'war on terror' in Afghanistan, and especially in Iraq, counterproductively led to a noticeable degradation in American power in the international arena. In this chapter, attention will focus on the questions of whether, why and to what extent the administration effectively learned from this – without necessarily admitting so publicly – and moved towards more cooperative approaches, in particular during the course of its second term in office, from the beginning of 2005.

Two case studies will be employed in order to facilitate consideration of these questions. Attention will focus, firstly, on the administration's changing attitude and approach towards the emerging International Criminal Court (ICC). The second case study will concentrate on American attempts to foster a process that would eventually lead to the denuclearization of North Korea – an ongoing effort that Bush had inherited from his predecessor.

The International Criminal Court

The initial Bush approach

The ICC has been selected as a case study in this chapter, both because it proved to be especially controversial during the 2000s and because it is particularly revealing of the consequences of the Bush administration's early approaches for the production of effective American power. This is partly because the administration's early decision to 'unsign' a major international agreement, announced during 2002, rather than just leaving the ICC statute unratified by Congress, as is the case with plenty of other treaties and agreements in American history, was virtually unprecedented. This move seemed to many outside the US, including – indeed, perhaps especially – amongst its major international allies, as being deliberately provoca-tive and gratuitous. This impression was heightened when the administration refused to engage in any sort of international consultation or negotiation over its decision – not even formally explaining it to its co-signatories. The decision not to become a party to the treaty was simply announced in a bald three-line letter to the UN Secretary-General, sent under the signature of then Under Secretary of State for Arms Control and International Security John Bolton in May 2002.[1] Even the choice of signatory was seen by some as deliberately inflammatory, given Bolton's reputation as one of the Bush administration's most sceptical senior officials when it came to the value of international multilateral agreements *per se*.

Overall, the unilateral manner in which the administration made and announced its decision on the ICC mattered almost as much internation-ally as the substance of it. This, in itself, contributed to the degrading of American power. Evidence of this can be seen most obviously in the fact that the administration's May 2002 decision failed to stop the ICC's statute from going into effect, with many US friends and allies signing up. Indeed, by refusing to engage in significant negotiation or consultation with any of the sixty states which had ratified the statute by that time, the adminis-tration not only failed to prevent the Court from being established, it also failed to effect any significant changes to its scope or terms of reference.[2]

At the time of the May 2002 announcement, senior Bush administration officials had virtually pledged that the US government would not only oppose but would actively work to undermine the ICC. Pierre-Richard Prosper, ambassador-at-large for war crimes issues, declared that Bolton's letter to the UN 'frees us from some of the obligations that are incurred by signature. When you sign you have an obligation not to take actions that would defeat the object or purpose of the treaty.'[3] These words carried a clear – if implicit – threat: that the administration might seek to obstruct the ICC in future. This was followed through in two related ways. From 2002, Bush administration officials sought to pressure other UN member states not to adhere to the ICC statute, or at least to support special exemp-tions from its jurisdiction for US military personnel serving on overseas operations. At the same time, and *apropos* of the latter, the administration threatened to veto the renewal of mandates for UN peace operations unless American personnel were given *de facto* immunity from possible ICC investigation or prosecution.

In fairness to the administration, the attempted spoiling tactics were not confined to the executive branch of the American government. The admin-istration could have claimed, with some justification, that its hand was being forced in part by congressional sentiment and action, although it did not in fact do so and gave little impression of being unenthusiastic about obstructing the ICC. In August 2002, Congress had passed a measure called the American Service-Members' Protection Act (ASPA). The terms of this Act were suggestive of a defensive and, indeed, somewhat vulnerable mentality on the part of the American body politic, as well perhaps as a desire not to see constraints imposed on US freedom of action in pursuing its war on terror. Whilst this was understandable in the immediate post-9/11 context, some of this sentiment at least was misplaced, and it also reflected apparent ignorance about how the ICC was designed to work.

It was – and is – an accepted premise of the international law of armed conflict that international courts and tribunals will only operate when national legal processes are absent or seriously deficient, a situation that hardly pertained in the United States. Yet the terms of the ASPA asserted that US military personnel might still find themselves being prosecuted by the ICC. It was also claimed that 'the President and other senior elected and appointed officials of the United States Government' might be similarly liable. The main thrust of the legislation was to prohibit US government agencies from cooperating with or assisting the ICC in any way. However, the clause that generated most comment and controversy, and some measure of ridicule, was the one that stated: 'The President is authorized to use all means necessary and appropriate to bring about the release of any [American citizen] who is being detained or imprisoned by, on behalf of, or at the request of the International Criminal Court.'[4]

Critics suggested that this clause theoretically opened the door to possible US military action against the Netherlands, a NATO ally, on the grounds that the ICC was based at The Hague. They mockingly dubbed the legislation 'the Hague Invasion Act'. The ASPA thus exposed the United States to a measure of ridicule, as noted above. This, in itself, was not an irrelevant factor in terms of its negative impact on US international legitimacy, prestige and soft power. Furthermore, passage of the Act demonstrated not so much strength as weakness. Successive administrations had expressed concerns about the terms of the ICC statute, both during and since its original negotiation in 1998.[5] Yet neither the Clinton nor the Bush administration engaged multilaterally with other signatories in the four years that elapsed between the completion of the original negotiation and the decision to unsign. Thus, American leaders in 2002 were faced with an agreement which they had signally failed to influence or change since it was originally negotiated. In the meantime too, as noted in the text of the ASPA itself, by spring 2002, 138 other states had signed the statute and thirty had successfully ratified it. By then the United States was, therefore, very much on the defensive with regard to the ICC. Indeed, the proximate source of the Bush administration's decision to unsign, and Congress's passing of the ASPA, was the fact that sufficient other signatories had ratified the ICC statute by mid-2002 so as to ensure that it could now come into legal effect.

Subsequently, the American government did win an apparent victory. This came in July 2002, when the UN Security Council agreed to Resolution 1422, effectively exempting American personnel from the ICC's jurisdiction in exchange for the US dropping its threats to veto the renewal of mandates for UN operations.[6] Given that, as noted above, the chances of American civilian or military personnel actually finding themselves before the ICC were slight, this was not in fact a substantial practical achievement. Indeed, it could be argued that the main function of Resolution 1422 was to provide face-saving cover to facilitate an American climb-down from a position that was becoming politically untenable in terms of damage to the country's prestige generally, as well as its ability to influence international legal debates. To that end, the American government had compromised on its original demand for *permanent* exemptions for US citizens. Instead, the exemptions contained in Resolution 1422 were subject to annual renewal by the Security Council.[7] In an additional retreat, the US subsequently abandoned efforts to secure further annual renewals of the exemption from 2004. This followed criticism of the adverse impact that this process was having on the stature of the Security Council, which had arguably acted with questionable legal authority in granting consent to such exemptions in the first place.[8]

Evidence of a revised approach

Overall, the period 2004–5 saw a significant change in the Bush administration's approach. In March 2005, the Security Council passed Resolution 1593, authorizing the ICC to begin investigations into possible war crimes committed in the course of the conflict in the Darfur region of Sudan. The US government had chosen to abstain rather than veto this resolution, and had thus consented *de facto* to its being passed. As a result, and for the first time, the ICC was given a UN mandate to pursue investigations into a specific conflict, and all UN members were 'urged' to 'cooperate fully' in facilitating this.[9] The passing of Resolution 1593 and the US stance on it were important. The latter represented the effective abandonment of American attempts actively to undermine the ICC.

Why was the American approach changing? One important reason, naturally, was that its former approach had evidently failed in its principal objective of stopping the ICC from becoming operational. It also risked engendering negative spillover effects in other important policy areas. Not only had the American government been unable to prevent the ICC from being established, it had also failed to persuade signatories to follow its own example and unsign the statute. Thus it found itself caught on the horns of a dilemma. On the one hand, much had been made by the Bush administration of the importance of apprehending and prosecuting alleged international war criminals more effectively in places such as the Balkans and – latterly – Sudan. On the other hand, the American government had simultaneously opposed and sought to obstruct the main internationally agreed means of doing just this.

Hitherto, as noted, the administration had not bothered to discuss with other states the possibility of addressing its concerns about the existing ICC arrangements. In a social context this mattered. Conversations and negotiations are a basic, but vital, lubricant of any social system. In order to produce positive and beneficial results for *all* involved parties, these basic kinds of social interaction must – by definition – involve *two-way* processes of influence and give and take. This was precisely what had been absent in the early Bush approach to the ICC, however. The administration's representatives had hardly been reticent in talking about their hostility to the Court *per se*. What had been missing, however, was any real suggestion of a willingness to enter into multilateral conversations – as opposed to delivering unilateral monologues and diplomatic *démarches* – about addressing what may have been valid concerns. This approach had helped effectively to degrade American power on ICC matters, as the failure to impede the activation of the Court's structures and mechanisms had clearly demonstrated.

Whilst there was no public acknowledgement of a change of attitude and approach to the ICC, it was evident towards the end of the first Bush term in 2004 that one was emerging. Then Secretary of State Colin Powell declared in September 2004 that events in Darfur amounted in some instances to acts of genocide.[10] This brought the Bush administration's self-induced dilemma to a head. Under Article I of the 1948 Genocide Convention, states 'undertake to prevent and to punish' acts of genocide. Further, it is stipulated in Article VI of this international convention that 'Persons charged with genocide...shall be tried by a competent tribunal of the State in the territory of which the act was committed, or by such international penal tribunal as may have jurisdiction with respect to those Contracting Parties which shall have accepted its jurisdiction.'[11]

It seemed hardly likely that the Sudanese government itself would rigorously and fairly investigate, try and punish the alleged perpetrators of genocide in Darfur. The perpetrators were widely assumed to be either acting at the behest of that government or working directly for it. That effectively left a choice between a competent 'international penal tribunal' and nothing. The only such tribunal available was the ICC. Secretary of State Powell was – perhaps intentionally, in view of his relatively internationalist ideological position within the Bush administration – instrumental in paving the way for the negotiation and adoption of UN Security Council Resolution 1593 and, concurrently, the effective end of active American attempts to undermine the ICC.

This did not signal a complete *volte face*, and the administration's stated position remained that there were no conceivable circumstances in which the US itself would actually join the ICC. Nevertheless, the change was significant, and officials let it be known that the US was now willing to offer practical assistance to ICC officials in, for example, gathering evidence and preparing indictments and cases against alleged war criminals in places like Sudan.

The evolving course of Bush administration policies and attitudes towards the ICC, from 2002 to 2005, had not come about because the administration was faced down on the issue by any state or coalition of states opposed to its stance. Rather, it began to alter its own course as it became clear that its previous approach was in danger of undermining its ability to pursue its wider interests effectively in the international arena. This *de facto* policy shift was not advertised in public, and indeed may not have been conceived in these terms by administration officials at the time. The practical cooperation that began to take place with the ICC (often behind the scenes) and the discontinuation of previous bellicose rhetoric about actively seeking to undermine the Court were in themselves sufficient substantially to reduce the salience of the issue as a power liability for the United States as the 2000s progressed.

Increasing socialization

From 2009, senior officials in the administration of Barack Obama were evidently keen to build on the more positive American approach evident in the later Bush years, whilst, as one might expect for political reasons, sometimes claiming actually to have adopted a *new* approach. In some respects, claims to newness were in fact justified, as when Secretary of State Hillary Clinton publicly raised the possibility of the US actually (re)signing the ICC statute at some point in the future.

Most relevantly, in the context of the discussions here, Obama officials evidently accepted the evidence which suggested that the Bush administration's original obstructive approach had attenuated, rather than strengthened, American power on this issue. In August 2009, on a visit to Kenya, Hillary Clinton was asked whether the US not being a signatory to the ICC had hindered its efforts to ensure that alleged human rights violations were properly investigated and, if necessary, prosecutions brought. She replied: 'That is a great regret, but it is a fact that we are not yet a signatory. But we have supported the work of the court and will continue to do so under the Obama administration.' Clinton also suggested that earlier multilateral engagement and dialogue on the part of the US might have yielded a better result for her country: 'I think we could have worked out some of the challenges that are raised concerning our membership by our own government, but that has not yet come to pass.'[12]

In June 2010, two senior Obama administration legal officers addressed the question of the US relationship with the ICC in a similar way. At a press briefing in Washington, Ambassador-at-Large for War Crimes Issues Stephen Rapp, and State Department Legal Advisor Harold Koh, developed the theme that the Obama administration was pursuing an approach of 'principled engagement' with the ICC. Referring to a recent ICC review conference, Koh asserted:

> After 12 years, I think we have reset the default on the US relationship with the court from hostility to positive engagement. In this case, principled engagement worked to protect our interest, to improve the outcome, and to bring us renewed international goodwill. As one delegate put it to me, the US was once again seen, with respect to the ICC, as part of the solution and not the problem. The outcome...demonstrates again principled engagement can protect and advance our interests, it can help the states parties find better solutions, and make for a better court, better protection of our interests, and a better relationship going forward between the US and the ICC.[13]

Doubtless, simple partisanship helped, to an extent, to inform such statements. More interestingly, in the context of these discussions, it can also be argued that they suggested a process of progressive 'socialization' was taking hold, in terms of evolving American attitudes to the ICC. Socialization in this context means that, over time, an actor's attitudes and behaviour become increasingly conditioned by unwritten principles and norms of behaviour which evolve within a social system – in this case the international system. Such norms help to define what constitutes 'acceptable' behaviour within the system, and hence that which is most likely to work in an actor's own interests, as well as that of others.

Academic interest in this kind of socialization has thus far tended to focus on its impact on 'secondary states' in the system, rather than the more powerful.[14] The example under consideration here, however, suggests that it can be just as influential in helping progressively to shape the attitudes and approaches of a hegemonic state. The Bush administration, over the course of its two terms in office, clearly altered its approach to the ICC and adopted a markedly more constructive attitude to working with it, whilst remaining outside formal membership. The Obama administration maintained the more cooperative approach. Furthermore, it strengthened it as the accepted basis of American policy-making by publicly declaring its virtues – something that its predecessor had not really done.

Overall, in the ten years between 2001 and 2011, American policy towards the ICC had changed to a remarkable degree. This happened as a consequence, firstly, of what might be called pragmatic corrective learning by the Bush administration. Under his successor, Barack Obama, this was increasingly being bolstered and entrenched by an emerging socialization process. Officials serving under both presidents doubtless believed that they were helping to develop and articulate policies and stances designed to serve the national interests of the United States. The onset of a socialization process helped progressively to shift their calculus about how those interests might best be served and advanced in relation to the ICC.

North Korea's nuclear weapons programmes

North Korea's alleged nuclear weapons development programmes had first been an important issue on the Clinton administration's agenda during the 1990s. In 1994, this administration had signed an agreement with the North Korean government, whereby the latter's development of a plutonium programme was frozen and placed under international safeguards in exchange for pledges of various kinds of economic and technological aid and assistance, primarily from the US. The implicit threat of possible American air strikes against North Korean nuclear installations was also, apparently, a background factor in the negotiations that took place.[15]

The initial Bush approach

In his 2004 memoirs, Bill Clinton stated – perhaps with an element of *post facto* mischievousness – in deciding not to go to North Korea personally in late 2000 to secure an agreement on long-range missiles: 'I was confident the next administration would consummate the deal based on the good work that had been done [by his own team].'[16] This view, of the desirability of continuity, does appear to have been shared initially by some of George W. Bush's own principal advisers. In 2000, prospective National Security Adviser Condoleezza Rice had written that the Clinton administration's agreements with North Korea 'cannot easily be set aside'.[17] Even more clearly, Secretary of State Colin Powell announced at the outset of the new administration, in March 2001: 'We do plan to engage with North Korea to pick up where President Clinton and his administration left off. Some promising elements were left on the table and we will be examining those elements.'[18]

Powell's remarks were made the day before a visit to Washington by then South Korean President Kim Dae-Jung. This visit provided the first opportunity for Bush personally to declare his intentions with regard to North Korea. The president appeared to go out of his way to disavow Powell's suggestion that his policy would be characterized by continuity with the Clinton administration's approach. In a press conference with Kim, Bush was highly sceptical about the possibility of maintaining any agreement with North Korea.[19] Most strikingly, Powell was required at the same time to 'clarify' (that is, effectively, repudiate) his stance of the previous day. He now said: 'The President forcefully made the point that we are undertaking a full review of our relationship with North Korea . . . coming up with policies unique to the administration . . . And in due course, when our review is finished, we'll determine at what pace and when we will engage with the North Koreans.'[20]

It was perfectly reasonable for a new administration to want to conduct a review of its options before agreeing on a policy approach. Yet, the immediate backdrop to the Powell statement quoted above suggested that the Bush administration's emerging policy towards North Korea was being shaped less by careful consideration of the complex issues involved, and more by a reflexive determination not to adopt or follow the Clinton approach. This desire was such that the president was prepared to embarrass his own secretary of state in public and, in doing so, demonstrate disunity and significant division at the top of his own administration.

The Bush approach can also be faulted for gratuitously and unnecessarily offending both the North Korean government (which had proved itself to be prickly and difficult to deal with at the best of times) and the US's South Korean ally. The latter had not been consulted or even briefed in advance about a possible departure from the established American approach to negotiating with the North. As in the case of the ICC, discussed earlier, the dominant strand of thinking within the new administration at the time seemed quite prepared deliberately and gratuitously to ignore, or even denigrate, established and often laboriously constructed international agreements and processes. President Kim Dae-Jung had invested considerable political capital in developing the so-called sunshine policy of greater political contacts with the North. This policy had been actively supported by the Clinton administration, which in June 2000 had sent Secretary of State Madeleine Albright on the highest ranking official US visit to North Korea since the Korean war of 1950–3.

The new Bush approach saw strong – some would say inflammatory – rhetoric in the president's 2002 State of the Union address, placing North Korea, together with Iraq and Iran, in an 'Axis of Evil', coupled with his reported personal denigration of North Korean leader Kim Jong Il.[21] This was accompanied, in the autumn of 2002, by the unexpected announcement from the administration that it was in possession of evidence that the North Korean government had been cheating on its 1994 agreement with the US, by proceeding with additional covert nuclear programmes. The unheralded nature of this revelation provoked some suspicion that the administration had at least partly manufactured a political crisis so as to give itself a pretext for finally dispensing with the Clinton-era approach and agreements.[22] When, in 2003, the North Korean government responded by announcing its withdrawal from the Nuclear Non-Proliferation Treaty (NPT), the situation was literally back to square one – it had been an earlier threat to withdraw from the NPT that had persuaded the Clinton administration to establish the diplomatic process which had produced the 1994 agreement. The overall balance sheet subsequently turned even more negative when the North Korean government tested atomic devices in 2006 and again in 2009.

The Bush administration's approach in 2001–2 had effectively undercut American efforts in advancing the stated core goal of ensuring that North Korea did not develop a nuclear weapons capability. The deliberate and, frankly, gratuitous renunciation of the established international framework for dealing with the issue, coupled with public demonization of the North Korean regime and its leader, made it virtually inevitable that the 1994 agreement, which was already showing signs of stress, would fall apart. Moreover, during its early years, the administration had evinced little interest in negotiating with North Korea in *any* format.

Evidence of a revised approach

During the Bush administration's first term, no progress was made in advancing the denuclearization of the Korean peninsula. During its second, however, there were clear indications of a process of pragmatic corrective learning getting under way on this issue. Indeed, from late in its first term, administration officials, in response to North Korea's NPT withdrawal, had begun to explore the possibility of establishing a new international negotiating framework, and indeed one that was more explicitly *multilateral* than that adopted by its predecessor. The Clinton approach had been essentially bilateral between the US and North Korea, with informal consultations taking place on the side with Japan and South Korea, the two principal American allies in the region. The new approach was formally multilateral, with the process being channelled through a so-called six-party framework. This involved the US and North Korea, together with China, Japan, South Korea and Russia, all operating within a single negotiating forum.

Considering its earlier approach – eighteen months of non-contact with the North Koreans, followed by an abrupt accusation of cheating and the effective termination of the 1994 agreement – it had been a dramatic moment when the Bush administration announced a new outline denuclearization agreement with North Korea in September 2005. The virtues of the multilateral framework within which this was negotiated were positively trumpeted by an administration spokesman: 'The format this time has led North Korea to understand this is more than a bilateral conversation. It's not one voice speaking to the North Koreans. It's a coalition of five all saying the same thing.'[23] After a delay caused mainly by a dispute over the unfreezing of North Korean financial assets held in foreign banks and the 2006 nuclear test explosion (which may have represented an extreme form of pressure from the North Koreans for a resolution of this issue), implementation of the agreement began in early 2007, although it has thus far remained incomplete.

In his memoirs, Bush was evidently concerned to allay any suggestion that the decision to move from bilateralism to a formal multilateral approach was in some way a product of American weakness. He claimed that he pursued this course because he had decided that the US 'was done' with putting up with what he characterized as infantile behaviour by Kim Jong Il. He also suggested that he had successfully pressured the Chinese government to join the prospective six-party forum by effectively threatening, if North Korea's own programmes were not controlled, to turn a blind eye to the possible acquisition of a nuclear weapons capability by Japan. At the same time, Bush conceded that American influence over the North Korean government was 'mostly negative' when compared with that of China.[24] The Bush administration could, in fact, be fairly sure that the US would remain the single most important interlocutor with the North Koreans, even within the six-party framework. American influence, therefore, was unlikely to be significantly diluted by participation within it, and may, indeed, have been enhanced by participation in a formal multilateral effort alongside China.[25]

From the North Korean perspective, the importance of the American role rested on two bases. Firstly, there were the material assets which it could bring to the table. For all its truculence in the successive nuclear negotiations, North Korea is materially in many ways an extremely impoverished state. This is the case not only in economic and financial respects, but also because its political system and totalitarian nature ensure that its government is effectively unable – and arguably even unwilling – to provide basic services to its population at large. Of the other five state participants in the negotiations, the US was best able, by virtue of its own relative material resources, to offer shipments of oil and the prospect of eventually providing the North Korean government with technologies for the peaceful production of nuclear energy, in exchange for a verifiable renunciation of its weapons-making capability.

In addition, the leaders of the other states in the negotiations accepted that the US would be the pivotal player in brokering any successful outcome. This is not to say that the part played by the others was irrelevant or merely decorative. This was not the case with the Chinese government, in particular, as Bush acknowledged in his memoirs, as noted above.[26] It remains fair to say, however, that the US was expected to play the central and leading role in consummating the deal, most importantly by the North Korean government itself. This had been made quite clear in a statement that North Korea put out to mark the outline agreement of September 2005.[27] It had earlier also been apparent in an initial North Korean reluctance to engage in multilateral – as opposed to bilateral – negotiations at all. The North Korean government had earlier stated a clear preference for negotiating directly with the US alone.[28]

Adopting a formal multilateral approach was advantageous to the US in other respects. It allowed fence-mending to take place with its South Korean ally following the bruised relations engendered by Bush's initially dismissive approach to the negotiating process he had inherited from his predecessor. It also provided a practical opportunity to engage China in a multilateral process. This in itself could help practically to advance the notion, then being promoted by senior administration officials, of encouraging the Chinese government to become a more 'responsible stakeholder' in the established international system (discussed further in chapter 9).

This is interesting because it suggests that some within the administration believed that it might be possible to harness the benefits of a putative multilateral socialization process, on the North Korean issue, in order to draw China into a more supportive and less potentially threatening international role more generally. To have a reasonable prospect of success, such an effort would require the provision of clear evidence of an *American* willingness, in turn, to participate constructively and effectively in a multilateral process itself. The revised approach to North Korea, evident during the second Bush term, can be viewed in this light.

At the time of writing, the various approaches tried by successive American administrations to dealing with the North Korean nuclear programmes had failed to achieve definitive and final success. The Obama administration, whilst maintaining the six-party framework, had thus far added little new impetus to the process embodied within it. Whatever its other relative virtues, this is a reminder that adopting a multilateral approach in itself offers no guarantee of success in achieving stated objectives. Having said that, if the argument, suggested above, about the progressive socialization of official Chinese attitudes and approaches is accepted, then there is some evidence available to support the view that these have indeed started to shift in a more favourable direction from the American point of view.[29] Thus, in a 'bigger picture' perspective, it can be said that the six-party effort has had discernible and positive effects beyond those relating specifically to North Korea.

From unipolar assumptions to multilateral accommodation?

Were the shifts noted and discussed in the two case studies here engendered purely or mainly by drivers specific to the issues and circumstances involved? Or is there evidence of more general underlying and deliberative change in the Bush administration's thinking and approaches to international affairs over the course of its two terms in office? If the latter is indeed the case, where did the main impetus for this come from? The discussions in this section will attempt to answer these questions.

In the autumn of 2002, when debates about a possible US-led invasion of Iraq were moving into high gear, John Ikenberry contended that, historically: 'The secret of the United States' long brilliant run as the world's leading state was its ability and willingness to exercise power within alliance and multinational frameworks, which made its power and agenda more acceptable to allies and other key states around the world.' Ikenberry added that, in his view, 'This achievement has now been put at risk by the [Bush] administration's new thinking.'[30]

Subsequent events, especially in Iraq, lent substance to Ikenberry's forebodings. The consequences of the administration's downgrading – if not indeed denigration – of multilateralism in its early years became apparent in the run up to the Iraq War. As noted in chapter 5, two of the major NATO allies – France and Germany – consistently opposed the use of military force, at least within the timeframe that the Bush administration was suggesting in late 2002 and early 2003. Far from attempting to conciliate the governments of these states, Defense Secretary Rumsfeld chose instead to stigmatize them publicly as 'old Europe'. By the spring of 2003, there was a virtually complete breakdown in effective consultation and multilateral interaction amongst the four states which had formed the heart of NATO since the 1950s (the fourth being the UK, which, under Tony Blair, was solidly on the US side).

This marked the Iraq crisis out from previous instances of strained relations amongst NATO allies, such as during controversies over the deployment of intermediate-range nuclear missiles in Western Europe during the early 1980s. In these cases, although strained, multilateralism had not broken down to the same extent as in the early 2000s. The discipline imposed by the bilateral Cold War international structure, and the consequent shared perceptions that alliance solidarity was a paramount requirement for Western defence and security, was no doubt important before the 1990s. By definition, this same discipline did not hold good in the era of the post-Cold War 'unipolar moment'. Comparisons should not simply be based on structural changes, however. Just because earlier structural constraints no longer existed, the US government did not *have* to choose a markedly less consultative and more unilateral approach to the conduct of its international relations. This was not pre-determined.

As discussed in chapter 5, a prime consideration characterizing the Bush administration's approach to fighting its post-9/11 war on terror was not to have the military effort impeded by 'inflexible' coalitions. By placing the main emphasis on military effectiveness, however, the administration risked losing more than it gained: by undermining its ability to produce power effects beyond the relatively narrow parameters of what could realistically be attained by the use of armed force.

The negative consequences of this approach were apparent to some, even before the occupation of Iraq began to face serious insurgencies from 2004. Thus, Christopher Layne had noted in 2003:

> Despite widespread predictions that they would fold diplomatically and acquiesce in a second UN resolution authorizing the United States and Great Britain to forcibly disarm Iraq, Paris and Berlin (and Moscow) held firm. Rather than being shocked and awed by America's power and strong-arm diplomacy, they stuck to their guns.[31]

The Iraq War and its aftermath suggested significant limitations on the utility of military force in the contemporary international arena. There was no real doubt as to what the initial outcome would be of a US-led military invasion. Saddam Hussein was quickly toppled, forced into hiding and finally apprehended at the end of 2003. In this narrow sense, the US had clearly used its military capability to produce power of a superior kind during the course of 'major combat operations' in spring 2003. Subsequently, however, the unfolding insurgency and enduring failure, of either the American occupation authorities or local Iraqi politicians, to create a stable and effective system of governance in the country demonstrated that American power in post-conflict Iraq was progressively degrading and becoming inferior.

This was substantially due to the lack of genuine international support for both the invasion and the subsequent occupation. Only three states – the UK, Australia and Spain – had made significant supporting military contributions on the ground, and Spain withdrew in mid-2004 following the Madrid train bombings and a change of government. Unlike in the cases of Bosnia and Kosovo during the 1990s, NATO was conspicuous by its absence from Iraq. The United Nations never really had more than a half-hearted presence and commitment. France, Russia and China had the means, on the Security Council, to veto any more significant effort.

The US-led occupation was, therefore, critically short-staffed and under-resourced from the beginning.

Soft balancing?

In the mid-2000s, some analysts began to refer to an emerging process of international 'soft balancing', allegedly acting increasingly to constrain the United States. By this they meant that, rather than formally aligning against the US in order to counterbalance it in material terms – a difficult and potentially costly option in a structurally unipolar world – the leaders of other states chose to withhold support from, and participation in, the Bush administration's chosen courses of action. Such an approach might not prevent a unipole from pursuing its own course initially. It may, however, have the effect of limiting and restricting its ability to achieve its intended goals and objectives, at least easily and at an acceptable cost. It might also significantly degrade any claims of legitimacy, of the international kind, for the chosen course of action.[32]

The existence of such soft balancing has been questioned, on the grounds that the term describes actions that are indistinguishable from normal foreign policy activity.[33] The concept could also be said to be rather mis-leading, in that it perhaps encourages those sceptical about the Iraq War to over-interpret the significance of certain developments. Thus, for example, David Calleo claimed to detect in early 2003 a 'nascent Great Eurasian coalition' forming between France, Germany and Russia in oppo-sition to the Iraq War.[34] In reality, this 'coalition' turned out to be a short-lived, tactical and essentially symbolic diplomatic expedient, with no significant or lasting impact.

Perhaps the strongest criticism of soft balancing is that it is not really a form of balancing at all. Traditionally, the term 'balancing' has been used in international history to describe concerted action by one or more states designed to deter behaviour considered undesirable or unacceptable on the part of others. Clearly, whatever soft balancing might have taken place during 2002 and 2003, it failed to prevent the Bush administration from orchestrating and leading its invasion of Iraq. Nor is there much evidence to suggest that sceptical governments at that time seriously believed that it would have been possible to do so.

By withholding cooperation at the time and subsequently, however, other states could certainly impose increased costs – political, financial and in terms of degraded legitimacy – on the United States. James Steinberg, who was later to serve as deputy secretary of state in the Obama administration, rightly noted in this context that:

> By appearing to defy important allies' advice and by short-circuiting the UN process that the United States itself had helped put in place, Washington complicated its ability to gain the support of other countries on actions that were far more central to US interests [than Iraq], including constraining Iran and tackling terrorist cells globally.[35]

This kind of 'blowback', which the Bush administration encountered following its invasion of Iraq, offers another important illustration of the point that unipolarity is a social as much as a material construct. To be sure, the US had the material capabilities to override international objections and proceed with its military action, and it did so. The rapid defeat of Saddam Hussein's armies also showed plainly that the American armed forces could quickly and effectively fight and win against a weakened, but not wholly inconsiderable, foe. The limitations of unipolarity became increasingly evident in the aftermath of this victory, however. The administration's failure effectively to solicit and engage the support and commitment of other important states significantly increased the United States' political, financial and reputational costs in Iraq.

To its credit, the Bush administration learned from its shortcomings in Iraq, and subsequently began to modify its approach to the conduct of its international relations, as suggested in the two case studies discussed earlier. The US benefited little from these shifts in Iraq itself, however, where the antipathy generated during 2002 and 2003 helped to ensure that little substantial international assistance was forthcoming in the difficult years from 2004. In Afghanistan, however – the other main front in the war on terror – the picture was somewhat different. Initially, as discussed in chapter 5, the US had sidelined NATO from any substantial involvement in the military operations which followed 9/11. Having subsequently made a decision to remain in Afghanistan and lead a process of post-conflict stabilization and reconstruction, however, the Bush administration began to seek international military and financial contributions for this ongoing effort.

Sensibly, it chose to make NATO a major institutional means for facilitating this. In August 2003, the latter's member states agreed that NATO would assume command of the international stabilization force supporting reconstruction efforts in Kabul, and progressively thereafter extending into most Afghan provinces. By 2009, all twenty-eight NATO member states were contributing to the international operations in Afghanistan in some way, with some providing troops, others contributing military or police trainers to programmes designed to train up indigenous Afghan security forces, and others helping to defray the costs of major troop contributors such as the United States. Tellingly, significant contributions of troops and trainers were made by both France and Germany, the two 'old European' states which had been conspicuous by their absence from supporting, still less participating in, the operations in Iraq.

This was important, firstly, from a financial and military burden-sharing perspective. Such concerns became increasingly significant in the wake of the 2007–8 financial crisis and economic downturn in many parts of the developed world. In Washington, the Congressional Research Service estimated that, by fiscal year 2011, the cost to the US of sustaining its ongoing operations in Iraq had been nearly twice as much ($800 billion) as its contribution to the multinational operations in Afghanistan ($440 billion).[36] Multinational participation and burden-sharing was equally important from a legitimacy perspective, and indeed the two are related. Greater and more widespread perceptions that operations in Afghanistan were legitimate helped to persuade more states to contribute and participate. This, in turn, further bolstered the operations' international legitimacy. At the same time, it helped to share the economic and financial burdens that might otherwise have been borne largely by the US, as in Iraq.

Pragmatic corrective learning

The case studies discussed in this chapter, coupled with the discussions in chapter 5, have offered evidence to support the view that the administration of George W. Bush altered course appreciably following its invasion of Iraq and adopted a markedly more cooperative stance on important international issues. This process – called here pragmatic corrective learning – involved modifying apparently entrenched opposition to the very existence of the International Criminal Court; moving from what might be described as bilateral hectoring of North Korea to being a leading participant in a formal multilateral engagement with it; and, finally, pushing successfully for a NATO-centred approach to ongoing stabilization and reconstruction operations in Afghanistan.

The Afghanistan case is especially significant. Not only were the ongoing operations there of central importance to the administration's war on

terror, its approach also offers perhaps the most direct evidence of deliberative learning. In less than two years, the US went from opposing – indeed,
sometimes actively denigrating – the prospect of any significant NATO
involvement in Afghan operations to being the main sponsor of a drive to
have the overall effort conducted within a NATO command, planning and
political consultative framework. This shift was particularly evident from
2003. By then, it was beginning to become apparent that the Bush administration's initial expectations about the course of events in post-invasion
Iraq were far from being fulfilled. Evidently, the administration had no
wish to see a repeat of these negative trends in the second major theatre
of its war on terror.

7

Russia as a 'Continuing' or 'Reviving' Great Power

Since the end of the Cold War, Russia has been in a distinctive position in the international arena. Although contemporary Russia is a new state – one of fifteen to emerge from the wreckage of the former Soviet Union in December 1991 – its leaders have generally not claimed that it is a new power. The core idea that underpinned the Russian government's view of its rightful place in the world during the 1990s was that Russia was, and should be treated as, a *continuing* Great Power. When this approach was widely seen, by the end of that decade, to have failed, a revised one was adopted. This has been focused on the idea that Russia is a *reviving* Great Power. The discussions in this chapter focus on how these core notions were developed and played out in practice in the policies and approaches adopted by the governments led, firstly, by Boris Yeltsin from 1991 to 1999 and, latterly, in which Vladimir Putin has been the dominant political figure since 2000.[1]

Apropos of these domestic political debates, the Russian debates and discussions about multipolarity in the international arena have become comparatively sophisticated and developed. Because these relate directly to the core themes of this book, and are therefore interesting and important in their own right, they will be considered separately in chapter 8.

The Yeltsin approach, 1991–9

Russia as the Soviet successor state

From the beginning of Russia's current existence as an independent state, in December 1991, the governments led by Boris Yeltsin demonstrated a clear sense that they both wanted and, indeed, expected it to be treated as a Great Power by other leading states – and most especially by the US. To that end, President Yeltsin and his first foreign minister, Andrei Kozyrev, set great store by ensuring that Russia was recognized by other states – especially the permanent members of the UN Security Council – as being legally the 'successor state' to the Soviet Union.[2] This formal status was viewed as validating Russia's position as a Great Power. Once it had become clear that the Soviet state was unsustainable, Yeltsin and Kozyrev believed that the new Russia could and should assume its international status and rights more or less automatically. The most important international assets in this regard were being a legally recognized nuclear weapons state and the permanent membership seat on the Security Council. Soviet-era responsibilities and obligations – for the Soviet Union's international debts, for example – were also taken on, as a burdensome but necessary correlation of taking over the assets.

Yeltsin and Kozyrev evidently worked assiduously to assure legal successor status. In April 1992, Kozyrev publicly hinted at the diplomatic effort that had been expended when he stated: 'It seems to many people that Russia became the legal successor automatically, but this was by no means the case.'[3] This does not necessarily mean that their efforts met serious resistance from other leading states. On the contrary: in January 1992, the UN Security Council met for the first time ever at the level of heads of government. Ostensibly, the purpose of this meeting was to initiate a review of the UN's roles in the emerging post-Cold War world. It can be argued, however, that the real purpose was formally to confirm Russia's accession to the permanent seat previously held by the Soviet Union. To that end, Russia was simply inducted as a permanent member without there having been any debate or discussion about the issue – at least publicly.

This was a significant *de facto* legal and political coup for the Russian government. The five permanent members – including the Soviet Union – are specifically named in Article 23 of the UN Charter, and there is no formal legal basis or mechanism provided within that document for simply transferring a seat to a new state.[4] Russia's status as a recognized nuclear weapons state was related to this, although – contrary to popular opinion – there is no formal requirement for a permanent member of the Security Council also to be a nuclear weapons state.

Perhaps most important, in this respect, was the supportive role played by the United States. Again, with little public discussion or debate, the administrations of George H. W. Bush and Bill Clinton simply recognized Russia, as the Soviet Union's declared legal successor, as a party to the various bilateral nuclear arms control and disarmament agreements, such as the Anti-Ballistic Missile Treaty and the Strategic Arms Reduction Treaty, that had been concluded by the two Cold War superpowers.

Russian power under Yeltsin

The inheritance issue

Several distinct elements underpinned official Russian views about the nature of international power in the early 1990s. Firstly, as should be evident from the discussions above, it was seen as being in part a *legal* construct, or at least one that was underpinned by important legal entitlements, such as the UN permanent seat and nuclear weapons status. It was also evidently viewed as an *inheritance* from the Soviet Union. This was a somewhat delicate issue politically. The Yeltsin government, on the other hand, certainly did not want Russia to be seen as the Soviet Union 'mark two'. This would hardly have been conducive to establishing a positive status and reputation for Russia in many parts of the world, and particularly with the US and its NATO allies in Europe.

These concerns were reflected at the time in the extent to which mainstream Russian leaders often deliberately eschewed using the Cold War term 'superpower' in describing their state. Andrei Kozyrev, for example, generally preferred to use 'normal Great Power'.[5] This did not carry specific Soviet-era connotations. Instead, it harked back to pre-Soviet historical epochs. 'Superpower' never disappeared completely from the official lexicon and was still used from time to time even by relative liberals such as Kozyrev. In an article published in *Izvestia* in March 1994, for example, he wrote: 'Russia . . . will remain a superpower not only insofar as nuclear-missile and military might as a whole are concerned but also in space exploration and the creation of the latest technologies, not to mention in terms of natural resources and geostrategic position.' It was significant that Russian leaders and commentators tended to use the 'superpower' descriptor when discussing Russia's relations with the US in particular. Kozyrev did so in the article quoted above, for example. He argued there that, in terms of its relationship with the US, 'superpower' Russia could 'only be an equal partner, not a junior one'.[6]

There was a further dimension of the Soviet legacy in evidence here. Statements such as Kozyrev's echoed the consistent desire of Soviet-era leaders to be accorded formal equality in their Cold War bilateral relationship with the United States. Russian officials, nearly all of whom had spent their earlier careers working for the Soviet state, appeared almost instinctively to use the term 'superpower' when they were speaking specifically of their country's relations with the US – and most often in response to perceived slights from it.

Relative weakness and the 'spoiler' approach

The idea that an inherited 'reputation for power' can constitute part of a state's overall portfolio of power resources is not new. At the beginning of the 1960s, for example, the international relations scholar A. F. K. Organski had argued that states 'that have been great powers in the past may continue to trade upon their reputations for some time'.[7] A key asset in complementing, reinforcing and underpinning such a reputation is international prestige. As with legitimacy, 'prestige' is essentially socially constructed because it is, primarily, 'a function of other actors' perceptions'.[8] Such perceptions may be based, in part, on material holdings. At least as important, however, is the skill with which a state's leaders succeed in positioning it positively in the key networks of international life.

Russia during the 1990s was, by most accounts, materially relatively weak – and getting progressively weaker. The declining effectiveness of its military capabilities was widely remarked upon by analysts at the time. The overall impression of many observers was effectively summed up in 1999 by Coral Bell, who defined Russia as being, increasingly, a 'Potemkin power' in the military sphere.[9] In other words, whilst Russia might maintain the façade of pre-eminent military capability, its armed forces had actually degraded substantially due to persistent underfunding, and were increasingly seen by the leaders of other states as incapable of mounting sustained and significant military operations.

Economically and financially, the situation was even more debilitating, most especially in the aftermath of a spectacular financial crash and debt default in the summer of 1998. All told, by the late 1990s Russia's very survival as a viable state was occasionally being called into question. Thomas Graham, a former US diplomat who had served in Moscow, wrote in 1999: 'Arguably we are witnessing a geo-political and geo-economic shift of historic proportions, one in which Russia will become less and less an actor in world affairs, while running the risk of becoming an object of competition among more advanced and dynamic powers.'[10] Condoleezza Rice, who acted as security adviser to candidate George W. Bush during the 2000 presidential election campaign, argued in similar vein at the time that 'American security is threatened less by Russia's strength than by its weakness and incoherence'.[11]

Such pessimistic assessments were by no means confined to American observers. Russian political scientist Vyacheslav Nikonov argued that, by the time Yeltsin announced his retirement at the end of 1999:

> Big business...was running the country, appointing ministers, adopting laws in its own interest, choosing governors in its 'domains,' and availing itself of broad access to the state's resources, but had yet to acquire the habit of paying taxes. For all practical purposes, Russia was not being governed.[12]

Russian leaders during the 1990s were well aware of their state's weak resource base. Robert Legvold, a noted American analyst of Russian affairs, remarked that they nevertheless maintained their belief in Russia's innate Great Power status, at least in public. Legvold argued that this was reflected in the relative frequency with which Russian leaders publicly declared their state to be a significant international power. He also suggested, however, that this need for public declaration (and, preferably, affirmation from others) reflected their persisting uncertainties about its actual status.[13]

Their regular public declarations about Russia's leading international status may, however, arguably have helped induce in Russian leaders a false sense of self-confidence. This, in turn, may have inclined them to adopt increasingly hostile rhetoric and obstructive positions when other states – and most especially the US – proposed taking action that did not accord with their perceptions of their state's national interests. These instances could be described as being counterproductive, when it was clear that Russia was not strong enough actually to block developments which its leaders had stridently and publicly opposed. A good example of this was evident in March 1999 in the build-up to the NATO decision to commence the bombing of Serbia over its government's actions in Kosovo.

During 1998 and 1999, the Russian government had been determinedly hostile to any suggestion of NATO military action over Kosovo – to the point where, for months before the actual bombing began, it had consistently threatened to block any discussion of such action in the UN Security Council. In October 1998, for example, then Foreign Minister Igor Ivanov had stated publicly that, if NATO sought a UN mandate for military action, then Russia would 'undoubtedly exercise its veto'.[14] This position was rigidly adhered to thereafter.[15]

The problem was not with the Russian stance *per se*. Rather, it arose from the inflexible and unimaginative way in which Russian diplomats and officials went about seeking to pursue and advance it. Basically, Russian representatives were very clear about what they did *not* want. They were, however, much less forthcoming in pursuing or suggesting any potential *alternative* course of action, which might have rendered a military option unnecessary or at least delayed its initiation. In essence here, the Russian government was attempting to play what critical analysts would later call the role of 'spoiler' in the international arena. This somewhat patronizing, but not entirely inaccurate, description has been used to describe Russian efforts to block what its leaders have perceived to be undesirable actions (most often by the US and its allies) but without suggesting any other, better, alternatives.[16]

By any measure, Russian efforts to play the spoiler role effectively, with regard to the Kosovo issue in 1998–9, ended in spectacular failure. Most obviously, NATO members ignored its attempts to block discussion of military action in the Security Council and simply decided to go ahead with their air campaign anyway, without specific UN authorization. Moreover, Russia was widely blamed for effectively making this course of action inevitable. In a 2000 report, an independent international commission studying the lessons of the Kosovo crisis concluded that Russia's 'rigid commitment to veto any enforcement action' against Serbia had been 'the major factor forcing NATO into an unmandated action'.[17] The then UN secretary-general, Kofi Annan, had also criticized Russia implicitly when he declared, with reference to the Kosovo crisis, that: 'the choice...must not be between...Council division, and regional action...the Member States of the United Nations should have been able to find common ground in upholding the principles of the Charter, and acting in defence of our common humanity.'[18] Even some of its own officials joined in the criticism, with one publicly agreeing with the view that Russia's policy on Kosovo had been inflexible and unimaginative throughout.[19]

Pragmatic corrective learning

This mini case study offers a good example of the production of substantially inferior power. The Russian approach had produced a limited power effect, in that it had prevented NATO members who favoured seeking UN authorization for military action against Serbia from actually securing it. Clearly, however, this was not the main intended effect, which had been to prevent military action by the US and its European allies *at all*. NATO went ahead with its bombing campaign anyway, and Russia was blamed as much, if not indeed more so, than its member states for the fact that they did not enjoy UN authorization for their action.

More positively for Russian power over the longer term, the Kosovo case and its aftermath suggest that Russian leaders did both recognize and subsequently learn from their mistakes. This apparent learning process has had both short- and long-term implications. In the short term, the Yeltsin government decided to try and play a more positive and proactive role on the Kosovo issue once the NATO bombing was actually under way in spring 1999. This eventually took the form of a leading Russian role in diplomatic efforts to bring about a Serb security force withdrawal from Kosovo, and the concomitant end of NATO bombing. These efforts bore fruit in June 1999. Russia's role in brokering the Kosovo settlement – widely and rightly seen as being key – helped to restore a measure of international prestige in the aftermath of its 1998 financial crisis, as well as enabling its leaders to achieve specific political and diplomatic objectives in Kosovo itself. The latter included both ensuring that the UN Security Council would have the final say over Kosovo's eventual status and demilitarizing the armed anti-Serb Kosovo Liberation Army. Neither of these elements had been present in NATO's own initial terms for ending the conflict. The Russian government also secured for itself a significant military presence on the ground in Kosovo, as part of a NATO-led international peacekeeping and stabilization force. This was conceded in spite of initial resistance from some NATO members, including the United States.[20]

Over the longer term, since 1999 successive Russian governments have generally avoided temptations to play spoiler over major international questions in which the US has identified its own vital or important national interests as being involved. This was the case with the response to the 9/11 attacks and the subsequent US-led military intervention in Afghanistan. It was also substantially the case with regard to the Iraq crisis and eventual war in 2002–3. In this instance, it is true that the Russian government, under President Putin, did publicly align itself with those opposing a potential war. It did so, however, in a careful and calibrated way, as will be discussed further below and in chapter 8. This stood in marked contrast to the intemperate spoiling tactics used over Kosovo in 1998–9 and suggested that Putin had learned from the earlier experience.

Also significant, in this context, was the Medvedev–Putin government's decision, in March 2011, to abstain on – rather than veto – a UN resolution authorizing NATO-led military action, in the context of the popular uprising in Libya, to forestall further depredations by the Gaddafi regime against civilians. This operation – centred on an air campaign – bore significant comparison with that which had taken place in Kosovo twelve years previously.[21] The markedly different position adopted by the Russian government can, therefore, be seen as further evidence in support of the view that deliberate and long-term efforts have been, and are being, made to avoid repeating the counterproductive, and ultimately debilitating, approach pursued during the Kosovo crisis.

The Putin approach, 2000–

By the time he took over from Yeltsin as acting president of Russia on the eve of the new millennium, Vladimir Putin was already convinced that his predecessor's basic approach – resting as it did on the presumption that Russia was a 'continuing' Great Power – had failed. Instead, he believed that Russia's international power status would effectively have to be rebuilt and thus 'revived'.

Putin had already set out his views on Russia's problems, and his priorities in tackling them, in a public document called *Russia at the Turn of the Millennium*.[22] The basic claim to Great Power status was evidently not in question here. The document argued that:

> Russia was and will remain a great power. It is preconditioned by the inseparable characteristics of its geopolitical, economic and cultural existence. They determined the mentality of Russians and the policy of the government throughout the history of Russia and they cannot but do so now.

Putin further argued: 'It will not happen soon, if ever, that Russia will become the second edition of, say, the US or Britain in which liberal values have deep historic roots.' He claimed that, nevertheless, 'our future depends on combining the universal principles of the market economy and democracy with Russian realities'.

Overall, there was little evidence here of any view that Great Power status depended upon positioning Russia within a 'European' or 'Western' cultural and political mainstream. Russia's reviving power credentials would essentially be home-grown. This opinion rested on the belief that evident domestic strength leads, in turn, to greater international prestige, respect and willingness on the part of other states to cooperate with Russia on the basis of a partnership of equals. Putin rejected, in *Russia at the Turn of the Millennium*, Soviet-era 'nationalist conceit and imperial ambitions'. He envisaged, instead, Russia's contemporary power credentials being based primarily on the promise of economic modernization and governmental consolidation at home. Together, these would form the basis for Russia's 'own path of renewal'.

Essentially, Putin was signalling that his forthcoming presidency would mark the end of attempts to base Russia's international power primarily on its legal role as the successor state to the Soviet Union. Instead, Russian power would, from henceforth, be based on 'a strong state' at home, which Putin claimed could be compatible with a healthy democracy:

> Our state and its institutions and structures have always played an exceptionally important role in the life of the country and its people. For Russians a strong state is not an anomaly to be discarded. Quite the contrary, they see it as the source and guarantee of order, and the initiator and the main driving force of change. Contemporary Russian society does not identify a strong and effective state with a totalitarian state. We have come to value the benefits of democracy, a law-based state, and personal and political freedom. At the same time, people are concerned by the obvious weakening of state power. The public wishes to see the appropriate restoration of the guiding and regulating role of the state, proceeding from the traditions and present state of the country.

It became clear during the early 2000s that the thinking laid out in *Russia at the Turn of the Millennium* did subsequently form the basis of a discernible political and economic strategy, with both domestic and international implications. In practice, this was manifested in three distinct, but related, policy elements. The first involved abandoning certain high-profile elements of the Soviet Union's Cold War international 'infrastructure'. The second focused on state-based domestic consolidation. The third entailed renewed interest in promoting the evolution of a multipolar world order. The first two will be considered in the remainder of this chapter and the third, as noted earlier, will be examined in detail in chapter 8.

Abandoning old Soviet infrastructure

The first of these was evidently an early priority for Putin, and it was reflected in particular in two key decisions that he made, not without domestic opposition, during 2001. These were to close the Soviet-era naval base at Cam Ranh Bay in Vietnam and an intelligence-gathering facility at Lourdes in Cuba.[23] Both of these had been major facilities during the Cold War, and they had been retained by the Russian armed forces in the Yeltsin era. Given Yeltsin's overall approach to Russian power, the retention of these facilities was probably due less to their continuing military value than to their political and symbolic importance in underpinning 'continuing' Russian claims to global influence and military presence. In this context, it was surely not coincidental that the facilities in question were situated in two states of particular sensitivity as far as the United States was concerned.

From the early 1960s, close relations with the Castro government in Cuba in particular had formed a major part of the Soviet Union's global interests. Given its core 'successor state' strategy, it is not surprising that the Yeltsin government evidently had this in mind in formulating its own Cuban policy after 1991.[24] Notwithstanding Russia's straitened finances, the army had signed a new leasing agreement for the Lourdes facility in 1994 for the equivalent of $200 million per annum. To many in Russia (and elsewhere), this and other initiatives to maintain or boost its presence in Cuba were undoubtedly seen as being 'mainly a political demarche to spite the United States'. One Russian newspaper, in 1995, went so far as to evoke the Cold War's greatest crisis, hubristically asserting that, 'if NATO starts preparing in earnest to deploy nuclear weapons in Poland [as part of its impending membership enlargement], our missiles may turn up on the approaches to Cuba again'.[25]

In the early 2000s, Putin was evidently prepared to run the risk of provoking accusations of making Russia look (temporarily) weaker internationally, in order to begin moving away from the Yeltsin approach. The allegations of weakness were predictably forthcoming.[26] This raises the question as to why Putin chose to go down this particular path. Several contributory factors suggest themselves. In the context of Russia's parlous economic condition since the late 1990s, and Putin's political focus on domestic economic consolidation and restructuring, the financial costs of maintaining facilities in places like Cuba and Vietnam were not negligible. There may also be evidence of the 'anti-spoiler' social learning process, discussed earlier, with Putin seeking to begin his term of office by eliminating aspects of Russia's international posture that had hitherto been maintained solely or mainly to 'spite' the United States.

The implicit paradox in this was identified by some Russian commentators and analysts at the time. In October 2001, for example, Dmitry Shusharin had argued: 'Russia is...destined to be a superpower in the world taking shape before our eyes. And in casting off the legacy of the old world – such as our bases in Cuba and Vietnam...Russia is only strengthening its position.'[27] Others went further, and argued that Putin was seeking a basic realignment in Russia's international relations. This view became increasingly prominent in the aftermath of the events of 9/11. In a typical example, Dmitry Furman, of the Russian Academy of Sciences' Institute of Europe, claimed that:

> A radical shift has occurred...from attempts to continue the great-power policy of the Soviet Union in a somewhat 'parodic' form (because our grand claims were inconsistent with our limited capabilities) to a policy aimed at building an alliance with the West and integrating our country into Western structures.[28]

Russia and the US in the wake of 9/11

Was Putin really aiming, after 9/11, at 'building an alliance with the West and integrating our country into Western structures', as Furman and others were suggesting? In his May 2003 State of the Nation address to the Russian Parliament, the president made the case that it was necessary to look forward, rather than back to the Soviet era, in order to ensure that Russia was treated as a Great Power in the new post-9/11 world. Putin asserted:

> All our decisions and actions must be dedicated to ensuring that, in the foreseeable future, Russia will firmly take its place among the truly strong, economically advanced and influential states of the world. This is a qualitatively new task, a qualitatively new step for the country. A step which we were unable to take earlier because of a number, a multitude of pressing problems. We have this opportunity and we must take it.[29]

As he suggested here, Putin's approach was premised primarily on consolidating and developing Russia's perceived status as a reviving Great Power. Russia's domestic condition and international status were closely linked in his mind, as noted earlier. Putin's early post-9/11 posture, of cooperation with the United States, was intended to reflect the alleged benefits of his approach to domestic consolidation in terms of increased prestige, status and power in the international arena.

To some critics, this approach met with only limited success. In Russia, by the beginning of 2002, there was an emerging sense that, as the dust settled after 9/11, it was becoming clear that little had really changed in terms either of overall relations with the US or of attitudes towards Russia on the part of its leaders. In January 2002, for example, an editorial in

Izvestia asserted that 'everything [is] just like it was before... Sept. 11 changed nothing. The Americans are the same as they were before. Russia and its president need not expect a special approach, leniency or solidarity on the part of the sole superpower.'[30] *Vremya MN*, meanwhile, commented acidly that 'the latest illusory honeymoon in relations with the US lasted less than five months'.[31]

To a substantial extent, such criticisms missed the point. Putin was evidently taking a longer view, in two respects. Firstly, he was seeking at least tacit American acceptance of key Russian policy objectives. Most obviously and importantly, this was the case with respect to ongoing 'counter-insurgency' operations in the war-torn southern republic of Chechnya. This was a totemic issue for Putin, as he had risen to power during 1999 largely on the back of his pledge to suppress the Chechen insurgency once and for all. After 9/11, he was successful in effectively gaining American acquiescence in his approach there, which might well otherwise have been even more extensively condemned internationally for its brutality.

More widely, Russia did seem to be in general good standing with the George W. Bush administration during the early 2000s. Whilst the Putin government opposed the growing indications of American interest in military-led regime change in Iraq during 2002 and early 2003, Russia was not ostracized and censured by the American government to the extent that had been the case with other prominent dissenters – chiefly France and Germany. An announcement in August 2002 of plans for enhanced long-term economic cooperation between the Putin government and the regime of Saddam Hussein, for example, was reportedly greeted with 'surprising calm' by the administration. According to one Russian commentator, this demonstrated 'a high level of trust in relations between Russia and the US', and it was speculated that, in order to damp down any potentially negative political impact, the Russian government might even have given the Americans advance notice of its plans.[32] More likely, an evident tacit understanding reflected the interest of both parties in maintaining the other's support for fundamental international objectives: the continuing 'war on terror' in Afghanistan on the part of the US and, for Russia, advancing its self-ascribed status as a reviving Great Power.

In November 2002, Russia voted in favour of UN Security Council Resolution 1441. It was also reported at the time that the Russian government had claimed credit for promoting a compromise between those seeking immediate war and those arguing in favour of fresh arms inspections in Iraq. It was further suggested that the Putin government viewed the outcome of the UN negotiations as attesting to 'the mature and partnerlike nature' of Russia's relations with the US.[33] The ability to be seen to be taking and maintaining a position mid-way between those of the Bush administration and the more entrenched opponents of US policies was a key element of the whole Putin approach on this issue. To facilitate it, Russian political leaders had been careful not to close off any options completely in late 2002 and early 2003, and thus risk seriously or permanently antagonizing the Bush administration by adopting an upfront spoiler posture on an issue that the latter clearly regarded as being very important.

With this in mind, in February 2003 Putin indicated publicly that, if Saddam did not improve the nature and extent of his compliance with Resolution 1441, Russia might even eventually support military action in Iraq.[34] Foreign Minister Ivanov, meanwhile, declared that his government would use 'all available political and diplomatic means to avoid a situation in which it would be necessary to exercise our veto power' in the Security Council.[35] This stood in marked – and no doubt deliberate – contrast to Russian policy during the Kosovo crisis, when Ivanov had also been the foreign minister. As noted earlier, the approach then had been consistently and publicly to threaten veto action against any proposal to authorize a NATO-led military operation.

In the Iraq case, the Russian government successfully avoided most of the blame for the failure in the Security Council of American and British attempts to obtain a follow-up resolution to 1441 explicitly authorizing the use of force. Condoleezza Rice, then Bush's national security adviser, allegedly described post-invasion American policy as being to 'punish France, ignore Germany, and forgive Russia'. Rice, in fact, never publicly acknowledged using those words. Nevertheless, the sentiments behind them did reflect the view of many at the time, that enough of the post-9/11 US–Russia *rapprochement* had endured to mitigate appreciably the impact of their differences over Iraq.

Neither Putin nor anybody else was, of course, able to prevent the United States from using military force against Iraq in order to overthrow Saddam Hussein. This should not necessarily be seen as a power failure on the part of the Putin government, however. The discussions above have suggested that preventing invasion may not have ranked that highly on its list of priorities. More important priorities, arguably, were to avoid antagonizing the US to the extent that it became hostile to – and even potentially sought to obstruct – the domestic economic and political consolidation that formed the basis of Putin's whole approach to reviving Russia. In addition, Putin had successfully ensured that Russia had been a constructive actor of sorts, and not simply an impotent spoiler, in the international dramas which had accompanied the build-up to the Iraq War.

Domestic state consolidation and 'sovereign democracy'

Once he had been elected as post-Soviet Russia's second president in spring 2000, Putin had moved quickly to implement his pledges in *Russia at the Turn of the Millennium* to create a 'strong state'. It was soon apparent from policy decisions that, in practice, this would be based on a revamping of the federal presidency's executive authority and reinforced by what Putin referred to as 'an effective vertical chain of authority in the country' (often known to Western observers simply as the 'power vertical').[36] This, in turn, would be based on the creation by the president of seven 'federal districts', each under the authority of a federal representative to be personally appointed by him.[37]

Any Western criticisms of the apparently undemocratic nature of these reforms, which were limited in the first place, were muted further by the fact that Putin and his overall reform package proved to be enduringly popular inside Russia itself. In explaining this, the legacy of the 1990s should be recalled. As noted earlier, there had been many suggestions that Russia had become seriously enfeebled – or even effectively ungovernable – by the end of that decade. With this in mind, it can be argued that Putin's reforms were less an attempt at personal or statist aggrandisement and more a necessary *defensive* set of measures, taken against the backdrop of grave concerns about Russia's very future as a viable unitary state.

A major presidential address in May 2000, outlining the initial reforms, was replete with references to Russia's internal weaknesses. In justifying his reform programme, Putin asserted:

> It's a scandalous thing when – just think about this figure – a fifth of the legal acts adopted in the regions contradict the country's Basic Law, when republic constitutions and province charters are at odds with the Russian Constitution, and when trade barriers or, even worse, border demarcation posts are set up between Russia's territories and provinces. These things are happening. Experience has shown that the consequences of such violations are catastrophic. It is seemingly isolated instances

> like these that, drop by drop, give rise to separatism, which
> sometimes becomes the springboard for an even more danger-
> ous evil – international terrorism... once again I want to stress
> that the time of forced compromises that lead to instability is
> over.[38]

A second major round of state consolidation was announced in the wake
of the Beslan hostage crisis in September 2004. Again, Russia's alleged
inherited domestic weakness was the key justifying *leitmotif*. Putin famously
declared at the time that the Beslan incident had occurred because 'we
showed ourselves to be weak and the weak get beaten'.[39] Beslan in itself did
not usher in a new round of state consolidation. Rather, it confirmed – and
perhaps accelerated – plans that were already in gestation, chiefly to ensure
a role for the federal president in the selection of regional leaders.[40] Having
said that, there is little doubt that Beslan did crystallize domestic concerns
about Russia's possible 'dismemberment', and it thus helped to create a
permissive environment for the Putin government to take its next steps.

In this context, presidential aide Vladislav Surkov came to prominence
as the public face of efforts to use Beslan in justifying new measures to
strengthen the 'effective vertical chain of authority'. Making a direct link
between the domestic and the international contexts, Surkov argued that
Beslan demonstrated that the goal of 'interventionists' was to 'destroy
Russia as a viable state'. Therefore, 'faced with such a threat, the president
has no choice but to fully realize the constitutional principle of unified
executive authority',[41] with the objective of 'slightly [*sic*] increasing the
political system's margin of safety'.[42]

The view that Putin's state consolidation was designed to have both
domestic *and* international ramifications had been evident to some from an
early stage. In March 2002, for example, Sergei Karaganov, one of the best-
known Russian analysts of international affairs, had written of the 'hopes
for successful domestic development' as representing 'the prime condition
for our recovering the title of real great power, as opposed to virtual one'.[43]
However, it was only after the Beslan tragedy that the connection became
more generally apparent. In large measure, this was because Putin himself
evidently chose to make it so. Concurrently with the president's own efforts
in this regard, his aide, Surkov, articulated it as a core feature of what he
began to call the concept of 'sovereign democracy'.

Putin's first post-Beslan State of the Nation address was delivered in
April 2005. Three key – and interrelated – themes underpinned it. One was

the importance of further strengthening Russia – domestically and internationally – in order to reduce the risk that it would 'get beaten' by malevolent outsiders again. The second, closely related, was a stress on sovereignty. The third was a reassertion that the Russian government would ultimately pursue its own course and not be dictated to by outsiders.

Outside Russia, this particular speech became well known for Putin's declaration that 'the collapse of the Soviet Union was a major geopolitical catastrophe of the [twentieth] century'.[44] On the basis of this statement, Putin's critics were quick to denounce him for allegedly harbouring ambitions to re-create some kind of Soviet-type internationally expansionist state. In the context of the speech as a whole, however, he used the statement as a lead in to a familiar itemization of the security, economic and social problems which had characterized the Yeltsin era. It is also apparent that he was using it to draw a comparison between the Soviet Union, as a fully sovereign actor in the international arena, and contemporary Russia. The latter, by implication, had *not* been fully sovereign during the Yeltsin years – but was on the way to becoming so under Putin's presidency. This was the crux of the link between the domestic and the international, which lay at the heart of the whole sovereign democracy concept.

Putin equated the growth in Russia's sovereignty with an increasing ability and willingness to chart its own course, both domestically and in the international arena. He asserted: 'It is precisely our values that determine our striving to enhance Russia's independence as a state and to strengthen its sovereignty. We are a free nation, and our place in the modern world – I wish to stress this particularly – will be determined only by how strong and successful we are.' Later in the same address, Putin developed this point further and more explicitly:

> Russia is a country that has chosen democracy for itself, by the will of its own people. It embarked on that path on its own and, while observing all the generally accepted democratic norms, will decide for itself – with a view to its own specific historical, geopolitical and other features – how to ensure that the principles of freedom and democracy are realized. As a sovereign country, Russia is capable of determining, and will determine independently, its own timetable and conditions for moving forward on that path.

The core message of this address – that Russia was progressively acquiring 'real' sovereignty, based on a new determination to pursue its own developmental path – constituted the essence of sovereign democracy. It was designed, as Surkov put it, to 'give our country back its status as a formidable power that isn't independent on paper only'.[45] Attaining and maintaining this status would depend, to a significant extent, on Russia becoming self-sufficient in key resources, both material and non-material (hence Putin's stress on 'our values'). In this context, the Putin government's progressive paying down of Russia's foreign debts (many inherited from the Soviet Union) during the 2000s was regularly cited inside Russia as being an important factor in enabling the country increasingly to assert 'real' sovereignty.[46]

Russia as an 'energy superpower'?

The notion of Russia as an 'energy superpower', which became popular amongst Western analysts and commentators during the 2000s, was *not* popular in Russia itself. Vladimir Putin publicly eschewed use of the term,[47] and virtually all Russian analysts criticized it. This provides something of a puzzle for analysts. One might intuitively have expected the Russian government to have positively embraced a term that seemed to stress its pre-eminent power credentials in at least one vital area – the export of oil and gas. Why was this, evidently, not the case?

The very fact that the descriptor 'energy superpower' was popular in the West in itself probably served to tarnish it in the eyes of some Russian observers. There were concerns in some quarters that a Russia which became over-reliant on exporting non-renewable energy supplies might find itself locked, over time, into an increasingly *subordinate* relationship with its customers. Some, indeed, speculated that this was precisely what the US and its allies wanted to encourage. In this context, Alexei Arbatov, a well-known Russian analyst, argued in 2006: 'There are no energy superpowers; there are suppliers of energy and raw materials to superpowers…either we are a supplier of energy and raw materials to other countries, or we are an advanced, high-tech economic power.'[48] In similar vein, Vladislav Surkov was quoted as saying that an over-reliance on the energy sector might eventually result in Russia's international role being reduced to that of 'pipeline security guards'.[49]

These views also hint at an implicit feeling that, in material terms, Russia may still not be strong enough to hold its own as an international power, even in an area where many outsiders regard it as being a leading player. Increasing international interdependence may further have blunted the extent to which energy resources could realistically be used as a tool, or even a weapon, to advance Russia's national interests in the international arena. In this regard, the experience of a dispute in 2005–6 with Ukraine over gas prices, during which the Russian state gas corporation had briefly shut off supplies to its neighbour, had the sobering effect of bringing home to Russian leaders that any potential 'energy weapon' was in reality a double-edged sword. It demonstrated that international relationships between energy suppliers and energy consumers are essentially symbiotic. Shutting off supplies not only risked hurting Russia financially, it also undermined Russia's reputation as a reliable supplier. Calling this into question could potentially be extremely costly, not only financially but also in terms of Russia's international status, reputation and prestige more generally.[50]

There is additionally some evidence to suggest that wariness has existed in official circles about Russia becoming overly dependent on any one material sector – especially one which relies upon the export of ultimately finite commodities, such as oil and gas.[51] Negative memories of the ultimately ruinous consequences of the 'monodimensional' basis of Soviet material power may have played a role in reinforcing this view.[52] This might, indeed, have made post-Soviet Russian leaders uneasy about basing their state's power on material capabilities to too great an extent *per se*, even had Russia been stronger in its material assets. In this context, Vladislav Surkov suggested, somewhat grandiloquently, in 2006 that 'a carbonated economy appears to have an invigorating and refreshing effect. But if and when it fizzles out, we will see the real worth of its derivatives – bubbly ambitions, sparkling rhetoric and artificially inflated prosperity.'[53]

Other Russian observers have also expressed concerns about the dangers of material monodimensionalism. They have sometimes made comparisons with oil-producing states such as Nigeria and Venezuela. These examples, they argue, show that being a major producer and exporter of fossil fuels is, in itself, not a sufficient basis for developing significant international power.[54] Indeed, for some analysts this can actually *undermine* a state's overall power resources, in view of the economic and social problems – such as increased potential for political corruption – that have been associated with over-dependence on the extraction and exporting of key natural resources.[55]

The irrelevance of soft power

Successive Russian governments have shown little interest in soft power. Like 'energy superpower', it is often seen as a 'Western' concept and thus inherently suspect. Joseph Nye has argued that the Medvedev–Putin government has been inept at operationalizing soft power at important junctures, such as at the time of the Russo-Georgian crisis in the summer of 2008.[56] However, he does not appear to have accounted for the possibility that it might not, in fact, have been interested in doing so. Those who have argued that Russia *has* developed soft power have often found themselves stretching their definitions significantly beyond Nye's notion of attraction in order to accommodate the Russian experience. In some cases, 'soft power' has indeed been used in the Russian context as a catch-all term, embracing virtually every approach and technique barring the application of coercive military force.[57] This, in itself, raises doubts about soft power's analytical applicability and utility in the contemporary Russian context.

The role of ideas

An important characteristic of Putin's approach to government has been a deliberate reluctance to define and articulate a core ideology, at least in the Soviet-era sense. Although he did not reject all aspects of the Soviet legacy, as noted earlier, Putin was clear that Russia under his leadership would not develop a Soviet-style ideology, with inherent 'export potential'. The thrust of the 'big idea' of sovereign democracy has thus been towards suggesting that Russia possesses values *distinctive to itself*, which both qualify and strengthen it in pursuing its own mode of domestic development, without external interference. This is the antithesis of the expansionist worldview which underpinned the Soviet Union's core Marxist ideology. With this in mind, Dmitri Trenin rightly argued in 2007 that, 'in stark contrast to its Soviet past, postimperial Russia stands among the least ideological countries around the world. Ideas hardly matter, whereas interests reign supreme.'[58] Putin himself has repeatedly stressed the importance of 'pragmatism' rather than ideology in Russia's foreign and security policies.

Since the collapse of the Soviet Union, official Russia has not, therefore, seriously attempted to develop and promote its own 'model' of international development. This has not prevented prominent Russian analysts, including Vladimir Baranovsky and Sergei Karaganov, from suggesting that some such model, representing a viable and attractive alternative to the US, might in fact be emerging.[59] Yet, there is little evidence to support their contention, or to suggest that the approach to governance developed in Russia since 2000 has held much international appeal – except perhaps in the case of a few maverick or authoritarian leaders, such as Hugo Chavez in Venezuela or the president of Kyrgyzstan, Kurmanbek Bakiyev (who was overthrown in a popular revolution in April 2010).[60]

The limitations on Russian power since 1991

Despite its sheer geographical size, nuclear arsenal, and other aspects of its Soviet inheritance, Russia has not become a pre-eminent international power in the period since the Cold War ended. The Yeltsin governments of the 1990s evidently believed that it could and should be treated as such, on the basis of its legal status as the successor state to the Soviet Union. Their claims manifestly failed, however, owing to economic, military and political weaknesses, coupled with self-inflicted wounds caused by the failure of attempts to play the role of international spoiler *vis-à-vis* the United States and its allies.

Under the succeeding governments, dominated by Vladimir Putin, there has been evidence of pragmatic corrective learning in terms of Russia's international postures and policies. In Putin's case, this trend manifested itself most clearly in a reluctance to continue to attempt to play spoiler on issues of major concern to the US. Russian governments have also been reluctant, for reasons discussed above, to attempt to assert power on the basis of material assets and capabilities – even in the energy sector, where many would agree that Russia does possess key global assets and resources.

Overall, it can therefore be argued that Russian power has become significantly *self*-limited, as evidenced by the pragmatic corrective learning identified and discussed earlier. The origins of this conscious self-limitation can be ascribed, in part, to negative memories of the Soviet Union's failure, reinforced by the governmental debilitations and counterproductive international policies of the 1990s. In part also, it can be put down to Russia's relative material weaknesses in the military and economic arenas in comparison with the United States (and, increasingly, China). Finally, Russia has become much more inward looking during the Putin era, with little effort being made to develop and promote attractive ideas to the rest of the world. The core notion of sovereign democracy – perhaps the closest Russia has come to a state ideology in the post-Soviet era – has both reflected and further reinforced this trend.

8

The Russian Multipolarity Debates

Following on from chapter 7, the discussions in this chapter examine the debates surrounding the concept of multipolarity that have taken place amongst government leaders, officials and other interested parties inside Russia. These debates are of interest not just for the light that they shed on Russian thinking specifically. Concepts of multipolarity have been debated in Russia to a more significant extent than in either the United States or China (or any other major state). Unlike in the case of unipolarity, which has generated significant debate and an academic literature (discussed in chapter 3 of this book), there has, so far, been little systematic analysis of multipolarity *per se*. It has often simply been asserted as an alternative (and more desirable) configuration of international power relations than unipolarity. Analysis of the relatively sophisticated Russian debates might, therefore, help us achieve a better understanding of the overall concept itself.

'Neo-Gorchakovism' and the concert system

It is instructive to begin an examination of contemporary Russian views of multipolarity by grounding the discussions in what may be called a 'neo-Gorchakovian' framework. This is named after Prince Alexander Gorchakov, who served as Russian foreign minister for a quarter of a century following the Crimean War in the 1850s.[1] In response to Russian military setbacks, and perceptions of societal and technological weakness highlighted during that conflict, Gorchakov developed and articulated the view that the Russian state should avoid over-extensive foreign entanglements, whilst focusing its energies on domestic modernization, at least for a time. This was not an isolationist prescription. Gorchakov did advocate continued Russian involvement overseas, but selectively, and on the basis of advancing core national interests. The likely focus would, therefore, be on Russia's own geopolitical neighbourhoods in Europe and Asia. Famously responding to contemporary criticisms that his approach was premised on either pique or acceptance of long-term Russian weakness following set-backs in the Crimea, Gorchakov wrote: 'They say Russia is being angry. Russia is not being angry, Russia is concentrating.'[2]

As the discussions in chapter 7 have indicated, this approach has found a fresh resonance in the contemporary context, particularly in the stance adopted by Vladimir Putin towards promoting domestic consolidation in Russia as the basis for reviving its international power. This has been noted by contemporary Russian analysts. In 2006, for example, Sergei Karaganov argued that Russia under Putin was 'passing through a natural period of conservative consolidation after the chaos of the 1990s' – i.e., a period akin to that which had confronted Gorchakov in the aftermath of the Crimean War. Another prominent Russian observer, Andrei Tsygankov, noted that Putin's priorities during the 2000s were 'not unlike [Gorchakov's] concentration after Russia's defeat in the Crimean War in 1856'.[3] Perhaps more significantly, two of the four post-Cold War Russian foreign ministers who had served at the time of writing – Yevgeny Primakov and Igor Ivanov – publicly eulogized Gorchakov and stressed the contemporary relevance of his approach during their time in office.[4]

Contemporary neo-Gorchakovians often emphasize the importance of Russia pursuing what, in official statements, is generally called a 'multi-vector' foreign policy. This was, for example, prominently stressed by Primakov in the late 1990s, in response to the alleged distortions brought about by the relative priority given to relations with the US and Europe under his predecessor as foreign minister, Andrei Kozyrev. According to Primakov at that time, Gorchakov had 'realized that without diversification of foreign contacts Russia would not be able to either surmount its difficulties or stay on as a great power'. He added that, in his view, 'this conclusion is likely to be even more relevant in today's interdependent and closely interconnected world'.[5]

To some this formulation may seem rather un-Gorchakovian in the extent to which Primakov appeared to suggest an extensive – rather than a selective – Russian international engagement and presence. A more nuanced view was articulated by his successor, in keeping with President Putin's new emphasis on foreign policy 'pragmatism'. In 2001, Igor Ivanov asserted that:

> Contemporary Russia has given up the global messianic ideology that was practiced by the USSR and that prompted a demonstration of the Soviet presence in the remotest parts of the

planet…What we need is greater efficiency in the promotion
of national interests through Russia's international activities.[6]

Gorchakov's own approach in the second half of the nineteenth century
had been closely influenced by the context in which Russia operated at that
time. This was premised on a form of semi-institutionalized multipolarity,
although the term itself was not used at the time. Russia was an integral
part of the so-called Concert of Europe – a diplomatic grouping of a half-
dozen (self-styled) Great Powers located, or deemed to have key interests,
in Europe (and, to a lesser extent, Asia). The concert system was designed
to provide a mechanism for agreed mutual regulation of relations amongst
participating states in order to avoid major conflicts, which might adversely
affect most or all of them.

It can be argued that the breakdown of cooperative relations, which had
led to the Crimean War, influenced Gorchakov to place decreasing emphasis on the concert system, although without abandoning it altogether. The
thrust behind his thinking and approach from the 1850s was to try and
position Russia to be a self-sufficient state that could cooperate as and when
it chose, whilst also developing the means to pursue, protect and defend
its interests essentially unilaterally if its government deemed it necessary.

With these observations in mind, attention will now turn to a consideration of contemporary Russian debates about what is today called multipolarity. A number of distinct strands are evident in these debates, and the
main ones will now be considered in turn.

Confrontationalist multipolarity

A new bipolarity?

The notion of confrontationalist multipolarity is premised on the view that
a multipolar world order would – indeed, should – be based on a reviving
Russia, or a group of states led by Russia, acting to prevent the US from
establishing and consolidating a unipolar international system. In some
early post-Cold War Russian formulations, this approach actually evinced
only a limited resemblance to any recognizable form of multipolarity.
Rather, a revised version of international *bipolarity* appeared to be what
was envisaged.[7] This was evident in the statements of Russian leaders
even at a time when, it was widely supposed, the Yeltsin–Kozyrev team
was pursuing a significantly – perhaps even slavishly – pro-American and

pro-Western orientation in Russian foreign policy. Thus, for example, an article published in Kozyrev's name in the US academic journal *Foreign Affairs* in mid-1994 was replete with assertions of Russia's supposedly innate Great Power credentials, and its consequent right to be accorded an equal status with the US in the international arena. Kozyrev made little mention of other states, or any potential international concert-type arrangement, in this piece, and it was apparent that he was really arguing for a revived form of an essentially bipolar US–Russia relationship.[8]

'Confrontationalist', in the sense in which the term is used here, did not mean a revival of the tensions and potential for conflict that characterized US–Soviet relations during the Cold War. As Daniel Deudney and John Ikenberry have noted, the ending of that phase of bipolarity was essentially managed through a number of arms-control treaties between the US and the Soviet Union/Russia in the late 1980s and early 1990s. Maintaining and developing this 'settlement order' thus rested to a significant extent on continuing, but essentially *cooperative*, bipolar foundations.[9] Deudney and Ikenberry's analysis further suggests that it could, therefore, have been possible to establish an essentially cooperative bipolar arrangement between Russia and the US in the early 1990s.

Even in this optimistic scenario, however, the *potential* for tension and disagreement – if not conflict – would most likely be a continuing element in the relationship. This was because of Russia's core and enduring interest in blocking any American drive towards the creation and consolidation of a unipolar world order. Russia's relative material weaknesses, in comparison with the old Soviet Union, meant that it could not effectively check this possibility simply by existing, as the latter had done. Blocking unipolarity, therefore, would have to become an *active* goal of Russia's foreign and security policies. For this reason, although the Cold War variant of bipolarity might have possessed an inherent stability, as Kenneth Waltz argued,[10] this new kind was significantly more likely to be essentially fragile and unstable.

Preserving the trappings of bipolarity had evidently been a priority for the Yeltsin government from the start. Indeed, it was an essential underpinning of its core interest in having Russia recognized as the legal successor of the Soviet Union from December 1991. It was also evident in the intense interest displayed by Russian leaders – especially President Yeltsin himself – in trying to preserve the exclusive bilateral 'top table' relationship with the US that the Soviet Union had enjoyed during the 'detente' era of the Cold War. Strobe Talbott, who served as President Clinton's chief point man on Russia during the 1990s, has attested in his memoir of that period to Yeltsin's almost obsessive desire to maintain this status, regardless of the overall material condition of US–Russian relations at any given time.[11]

To a significant extent, the US under Clinton was willing to oblige Yeltsin and his government. In his own memoirs, the former US president records that, in the seven years from 1993 to 1999, he had no fewer than eighteen summit meetings with Yeltsin – comfortably more than with any other foreign leader.[12] Perhaps, more significantly, there is some evidence to suggest that, for a brief period at least, the Clinton administration had been prepared tacitly to accept Russia as the leading regional power in Central, Eastern and South-Eastern Europe in return for the latter's support for key American foreign and security policy objectives elsewhere in the world. Such an arrangement would have been based on informal recognition of mutual spheres of interest and influence amongst self-styled Great Powers. This was a notion with which Alexander Gorchakov himself, from his own experiences of European politics in the nineteenth century, would have been both familiar and comfortable.

At one of his earliest meetings with Yeltsin, in Moscow in January 1994, Clinton had stated publicly, in responding to a question about the continuing presence of Russian military units on the territory of other former Soviet states: 'I think there will be times when you will be involved [in these states] and you will be more likely to be involved in some of these areas near you, just like the United States has been involved in the last several years in Panama and Grenada near our area.'[13] These remarks, coupled with Clinton's generally respectful demeanour towards Yeltsin at their summit, suggested that there was some American interest in an informal mutual understanding whereby Russia and the US between them would ascribe to each other unique responsibilities for managing particular regions of the world.

The situation was certainly interpreted in that way by some of Clinton's domestic critics. Former National Security Adviser Zbigniew Brzezinski accused the president of effectively offering the Russians *carte blanche* for military intervention in other post-Soviet states, thus *de facto* limiting the latter's sovereignty.[14] Other critics argued in a similar vein.[15] These criticisms were, to a large extent, overplayed. Brzezinski's, for example, was based on selective use of Clinton's statement quoted above. He omitted to mention that the president had gone on to state: 'The thing I think that we have to try to do [is to ensure that] where there is an involvement beyond the borders of the nation, that it is consistent with international law and, wherever possible, actually supported through other nations either through the United Nations or through some other instrument of international law.'

Nevertheless, the criticisms evidently did have an effect, and the Clinton administration soon began to back away from hints of *de facto* recognition of a Russian sphere of interest in Europe. Its revised stance was most evident in growing support for the enlargement of NATO's membership to embrace the Soviet Union's erstwhile allies in Central Europe (and, eventually, some of the ex-Soviet states themselves). This revised posture was maintained in spite of consistent and sometimes truculent opposition from Russian leaders across the political spectrum, and NATO enlargement began with the accession of the Czech Republic, Hungary and Poland in March 1999.

The rapid and substantial deterioration in US–Russian relations brought about by NATO enlargement[16] illustrated the essential fragility of the new bipolarity. Basically, to the extent that it existed at all, it was dependent primarily on American indulgence. Once the Clinton administration began, under domestic pressure, to move away from notions of preserving some kind of special bipolar relationship with Russia, in 1994 and 1995, there was little that the Russian government could do to prevent it.

Primakovian multipolarity

Sensing that attempts to preserve some kind of bipolarity had failed, the Yeltsin government shifted towards support for a more multipolar configuration of international relations. This was both symbolized and confirmed in the changeover from Andrei Kozyrev to Yevgeny Primakov as foreign minister at the beginning of 1996.[17] Primakov was responsible for effectively abandoning the previous official interest in trying to preserve a bipolar relationship with the US as the basis of Russia's role and status in the international arena. In its place, he attempted to define a more 'balanced' international order, based on 'partnerships' between Russia and several other leading actors. These included, but were not limited to, the United States.

The development of a 'strategic partnership' between Russia and China was perhaps the most important achievement of Primakov's multi-vector approach during his time in office. This has, however, been widely viewed by detached observers as being at least as much a reactive and essentially defensive move against the perceived threat of US domination as a creative and proactive means of advancing Russia's own national interests.[18] Russian ministers and officials on occasion did not even take the trouble to hide this essentially instrumental motivation. In speaking of the emerging Sino-Russian 'partnership' in late 1995, for example, the then defence minister, Pavel Grachev, had openly depicted it as a reaction to the American-inspired moves to enlarge NATO's membership. He was quoted as saying: 'If NATO looks east then we will also look east and find allies with whom we can solve security problems.'[19]

Primakov's overall concept suffered from significant limitations. The fact that it was founded on an essentially negative premise – rather than any positive idea of cooperation – in itself limited its scope for development. The Sino-Russian relationship has never become an alliance, and neither side has permitted it to shape or limit their freedom of action in the international arena in any significant way. As a result, its impact on international affairs in general – and American policy and attitudes in particular – has been limited.

In this context, it is noteworthy that successive Russian governments have made little obvious effort actively to co-opt China into supporting their international stances, even on issues of key importance to the former. Such was the case during the Kosovo crisis in 1998–9, for example. As noted in chapter 7, the Russian government was resolute in its determination to prevent the UN Security Council from even contemplating authorizing possible NATO military action against Serbia. It made no evident effort, however, to solicit support for this stance from its Chinese partner as a possible basis for a counterbalancing coalition in opposition to the US and NATO. China was essentially a passive actor throughout the Kosovo crisis, even after its Belgrade embassy was hit during a NATO bombing strike in May 1999.

Similarly, no apparent attempt was made by the Putin government to try and cement China into an international coalition against the George W. Bush administration's drive to war in Iraq in 2002–3. Perhaps most pertinently, at the time of its own war with Georgia in August 2008, as far as is known, the Russian government did not consult, or even inform, its Chinese partner about its decision to use military force. Following a ceasefire, when Russia did seek support in the Shanghai Cooperation Organization (SCO) for the proclaimed 'independence' of the Georgian enclaves of Abkhazia and South Ossetia, neither China nor any of the SCO's Central Asian members were willing to acquiesce. This resulted in a situation which *The Economist* at the time rightly described as showing a 'startling lack of support' for a supposed partner.[20]

There is a suggestion here also of a certain reticence on the part of successive Russian governments about possibly antagonizing the US to the extent that it might consider adopting damaging countermeasures. This is congruent with Robert Legvold's argument – noted in chapter 7 – that, notwithstanding rhetoric to the contrary, Russian leaders have been well aware of their state's relative lack of material, and perhaps also ideational, assets in comparison to the United States. Some Russian analysts have, therefore, argued for a kind of 'hedging' approach, whereby the Russian government develops greater means *potentially* to counterbalance the US, but refrains from actually doing so unless the latter's behaviour is judged to be becoming excessive. Stanislav Kondrashov, for example, has argued along these lines that:

> It is extremely important to be on good terms with America, but we should not lie down and let it walk all over us ... It would be ... natural ... to make overtures to Europe and form a bloc with it when America's pretensions ... become too absolute. We must not forget China and India either.[21]

In similar vein, Alexei Pushkov wrote in 2003 that 'the world is currently in a state of *unequal multipolarity*. But at certain stages of history, given problems of global scope, leadership by one state is sometimes necessary. I am not opposed to American leadership. I am opposed to American military hegemony that disregards the national interests of other states' (emphasis in the original).[22] In practice, suggestions that Russia develop the means to make multipolarity less 'unequal' had appeared unrealistic, at least during the 1990s. This was because of the material and governmental debilitations afflicting the Russian state (and wider society).

Additionally, and importantly in the context of the overall argument of this book, there has been little evidence to suggest that Russian leaders have appreciated the importance of the social dimensions of power in this context, either during the 1990s or since. One indication of this has been the absence of official interest in either the soft or the ideational dimensions of power, as noted in chapter 7. Bobo Lo has also rightly labelled successive Russian governments as being 'reluctant multilateralists at heart'. This has been borne out by the Kosovo, Iraq and Georgia examples noted above. In all three cases, the Russian government at the time made little or no sustained effort to build multilateral diplomatic coalitions, even with states and governments that could plausibly have been expected to be supportive, or at least sympathetic. This contributed directly to Russia's failure to achieve stated goals in both the Kosovo and Iraq cases (no NATO military action in the case of the former, and at least no early US-led action in the latter). It also contributed to the very limited international sympathy and support for its preferred outcome of the conflict in Georgia (i.e., recognition of the independence of Abkhazia and South Ossetia). In this case, apart from Russia itself, only three other states had recognized the independence of Abkhazia and South Ossetia by the summer of 2011, three years on from the Russian war with Georgia.

As Lo has also usefully reminded us: 'Genuine multilateralism, as opposed to multipolarity and pseudo-multilateralism, involves many parties in collective decisionmaking.'[23] He makes the important – but often unstated – point that multipolarity and multilateralism are not automatically coterminous. The first term describes a pattern of power distribution amongst actors, often assumed to be determined primarily by material assets and resources. The second captures processes and structures for social interaction amongst them. This is what counts in helping effectively to operationalize power in its social dimensions. It can be argued that a multipolar world order is more likely to facilitate the development of multilateralism than is a unipolar one. This is because some negotiation is likely to be necessary in order to secure preferred outcomes in a world where it is less likely that any single actor could successfully attempt simply to force its will on others. There is nothing preordained or inevitable about this, however. Multilateralism, rather, requires conscious political and diplomatic effort.

Post-Cold War Russian governments, it would appear, have never really appreciated this. They have often been interested in seeking the *ends* of multipolarity as a means of stopping, or at least slowing, the development of a US-dominated unipolar world. On the other hand, however, they have been much less consistently willing to submit themselves to the multilateral *means* which may have facilitated progress towards that desired goal.

Competitive multipolarity

From 2000, the governments dominated by Vladimir Putin seemed to promise the kind of domestic 'concentration' that Alexander Gorchakov had earlier suggested was necessary for Russia to consolidate and revive as a Great Power, following particularly trying or traumatic experiences. As discussed in chapter 7, domestic consolidation was the clear focus of Putin's original 1999 manifesto *Russia at the Turn of the Millennium*, which effectively presaged his subsequent approach to developing 'sovereign democracy'. This document bore clear traces of neo-Gorchakovian thinking, although the latter's name was not explicitly invoked in it.

The Putin government was rhetorically committed to advancing multipolarity in the international arena from the start of its time in office. In January 2000, Foreign Minister Igor Ivanov stated that 'the objective tendency in the development of civilization is toward multipolarity, to which there is no reasonable alternative'.[24] Six months later, the Russian government released a new *Foreign Policy Concept* document. This affirmed multipolarity as the declared basis of the Russian approach to international affairs. It reflected the view that the US was becoming overly dominant (French hypothesizing about 'hyperpower' was another contemporary manifestation of these concerns, as discussed in chapter 4), and therefore tacitly accepted that the Yeltsin–Primakov approach to promoting multipolarity had failed. With this in mind, the Russian *Foreign Policy Concept* stated that:

> A trend is growing towards the establishment of a unipolar world structure that would be dominated by the US economically and through force. There is a focus on restricted-membership Western institutions and fora in addressing fundamental issues of international security, with a weakening role of the UN Security Council. The strategy of unilateral actions can destabilize the international situation, provoke tensions and an arms race, and exacerbate the contradictions between states and national and religious strife...Russia will seek to achieve a multi-polar system of international relations that would genuinely reflect the diversity of the contemporary world with its varied interests.[25]

Subsequently, the events of 9/11 may have helped to create the conditions, in the minds of some Russian leaders, for moving beyond a neo-Gorchakovian selective approach to international affairs.[26] In 2003, for example, Mikhail Margelov, chairman of the Foreign Policy Committee of the Federation Council (the upper house of the Russian Parliament), evoked a sense of post-9/11 and post-Iraq invasion flux as affording opportunities for the kind of 'pragmatic' foreign policy which Putin claimed to be pursuing. Margelov further suggested that Russia went beyond neo-Gorchakovian self-limiting prescriptions, and pursued an approach which would be almost Soviet in the apparent scope of its international ambition:

> Russia must offer rapid reactions to events or even foresee them, using every window of opportunity that may open in the international arena. It must make scores wherever possible, and not

sniff at small achievements. The one who cannot knock out others has to develop maneuverability.[27]

This approach evidently saw the international arena as being essentially a competitive environment. Here, it was up to Russian leaders to 'make scores' on behalf of their state, and to advance Russia's interests on a wide spectrum of issues and with a variety of interlocutors. It was not necessarily a confrontational stance, however. Instead, Margelov was suggesting that Russia could and should advance its interests mainly through diplomatic dexterity and flexibility. In similar vein, Foreign Minister Sergei Lavrov argued in March 2007: 'It is [international] competition, and not confrontation, that determines the essence of today's developments in the world.'[28] In 2009, Alexander Lukin, of the Moscow State Institute of International Relations, argued that the economic and financial crisis affecting the US and many of its allies in Western Europe at the time gave Russia the opportunity to advance the cause of what he called 'genuine multipolarity'. Lukin defined this as 'not only the plurality of political centers of power, but also the plurality of development models'.[29]

During the 2000s, such views, envisaging the evolution of essentially peaceful but competitive forms of multipolarity, became increasingly prevalent in the Russian debates. Formulations such as Margelov's and Lukin's suggested that Russia could and should act as a free-standing player in a several-sided international competition, in which the US would also be a principal player, but not the only one – or even necessarily the single most important on all issues.

This worldview can be seen as a logical outgrowth of the domestic concept of sovereign democracy, which Putin and his advisers were developing at the time. Inherent in this concept is the view that only a handful of international actors actually meet the key criterion for being truly sovereign – i.e., not relying for their security on others to the extent that their freedom of action becomes significantly constrained. Using this as a basis, it could be argued that only the US, Russia, China, India and, perhaps, the European Union qualified as being fully sovereign. Since 2000, Russian views of competitive multipolarity have often envisaged world politics and international relations being shaped primarily by peaceful competition amongst these principal actors.

Some have suggested that, in this kind of international environment, the leading actors are unlikely to develop strong or deep alliances or partnerships with other states, or at least with the other leading ones. Dmitri Trenin, for example, has argued that, 'as a major country, Russia must be an independent actor. By definition, it can have no natural friends or sponsors. Instead, it has partners who are also competitors. Virtually anyone can be a partner, and practically anyone can be an opponent.'[30]

In essence, therefore, this would be a world recognizable to realists. This is not to say that partnerships of any kind would be impossible in such a world. Those that do develop, however, are unlikely to do so to the extent that they will constrain the important national interests of the participants, and most especially those of the leading states. A good example of a limited international arrangement of this kind can be seen in the Sino-Russian 'partnership', discussed earlier.

Competitive multipolarity might seem likely to be attractive to Russian leaders. It presupposes that the US is not the singularly dominant international actor. It also seems to reinforce Russia's own inherent place amongst the leaders as a truly 'sovereign democracy'. Perhaps somewhat surprisingly, therefore, this kind of thinking appears gradually to have lost ground as the Putin era has progressed. In the view of many sceptics, this development occurred because Russia does not possess the necessary material power resources, and concomitant international status and leverage, to make competitive multipolarity actually work in its own interests.

Some, indeed, have feared that its relative weaknesses might even call into question Russia's ability to survive as a sovereign actor in a world order in which a premium is placed on competition amongst states. In 2005, for example, the Russian analyst Sergei Kortunov argued:

> The idea of a 'multipolar world order'...is actually extremely dangerous for Russia. In its present condition, it falls far short of the status as one of the 'poles' in this construction. Given Russia's irreversible demographic decline, its territory will be literally torn to pieces by the more dynamic 'poles'.[31]

Many of the critics in this regard chose to hark back and criticize Yevgeny Primakov during his time as Russian foreign minister in the late 1990s. The critics did have a point when they argued that, given Russia's relative weakness and consequent lack of 'stopping power' *vis-à-vis* the US, the Primakov approach to multipolarity had sometimes fallen back on embarrassing or counterproductive gesture politics, such as the ultimately futile efforts to block UN authorization for the Kosovo war.[32]

As suggested earlier, largely absent from the Russian debates about multipolarity to date has been any clear idea of the importance of international social networks as a factor of power. By definition, attempts to revive bipolarity in the 1990s had focused primarily on just one relationship – that with the United States. Even when this gave way to conceptions of a more multipolar international order, Russia's other international relationships still tended to be seen, in comparison to that with the US, as being instrumental rather than essential. Their relative importance and value was determined mainly by the extent to which they could help Russian governments to develop and advance their core agendas *vis-à-vis* the US. Meaningful alliances and partnerships with other states, or international associations such as the EU, figured relatively little in conceptions of competitive multipolarity developed during the Putin era.

The low priority imputed to the potential value of international networks has been reflected in Russian foreign policy on important issues. In chapter 7, it was shown how the Yeltsin government was left effectively isolated at the time of the Kosovo crisis. This was due in significant part to its failure actively to try and develop international alliances in opposition to what it saw as NATO's provocative and aggressive stance towards Serbia. Rather, the Russian government simply asserted that it would veto any attempt to secure UN approval for military action, and left it at that. Not only did this fail to stop the US and its NATO allies from proceeding with their air campaign, but Russia itself was blamed by some for the fact that they did so without a UN mandate.

Although Russian governments in the Putin era generally sought to avoid attempting to play a similar 'spoiler' role on key international issues, they also tended to evince little sustained interest in cultivating international support for Russia's stance on important issues. This was evident, for example, in the almost complete failure to secure international recognition for the breakaway statelets of Abkhazia and South Ossetia in the years since the Russo-Georgian war of August 2008.

Concert-based multipolarity

There has occasionally been interest amongst senior Russian leaders in the possibility of developing more cooperative and inclusive forms of multipolarity. In 2006, Foreign Minister Lavrov tried to capture this with the metaphor of 'a global "orchestra" of the leading powers'. 'This orchestra', Lavrov argued, 'would be able to consolidate the collective principles in global politics and put an end to the practice of creating various kinds of balances of forces in the world.' In short, it would provide 'collective leadership' in international affairs.[33]

Lavrov suggested that Russia's historical and geographical heritage as a 'cultural and civilizational bridge' equipped it to play a unique role in the international orchestra.[34] Similar views had been expressed – perhaps surprisingly – by Russian military leaders. In 2003, for example, General Anatoly Kvashnin, then chief of the general staff, described Russia as an 'interregional state and one of the centers of the world community'. He argued that establishing partnerships with five 'world power centres' should be a key 'strategic objective' of Russian foreign policy. The five he had in mind were the US, the EU, China, India and 'the Mideast oil-producing countries'.[35] If such an approach were to be pursued, it would imply greater attention being devoted by the Russian government to developing significant international networks of power and influence.

Some non-Russian analysts have apparently been persuaded that the Putin-dominated governments have been seriously interested in cooperative forms of multipolar world order. In this context, Eugene Rumer, for example, has argued that:

> Russia is not a revolutionary power . . . Russian leaders talk about a multipolar world, about the balance of power and interest, not a unipolar world revolving around Russia. Russia is still seeking recognition as a major power, a star in the constellation, and its leaders are hardly intent on destroying that constellation.[36]

To the (limited) extent that it has been evident, the Putin approach to concert-based multipolarity has rested – as have the other approaches examined here – fundamentally on an understanding that the United States remains the pivotal actor in contemporary world affairs. Russian governments have also consistently stressed that cooperation with the Americans can take place 'solely on the basis of equality and mutual respect'.[37] As discussed earlier, this was the basis of the Yeltsin–Kozyrev approach to trying to maintain an essentially bipolar relationship with the US during the 1990s, and it did not ultimately work out. For some, however, a globalizing world order makes this an increasingly realistic aspiration, if only because the US has allegedly lost the ability to dominate to the extent that it formerly did. It was in this context that Yevgeny Primakov, for example, argued in retirement in 2003 that 'there are no "superpowers" remaining in the world today: the USSR has ceased to exist and the USA has lost this status.'[38]

Putin and 'multipolarity' in practice

In practice, official Russian attempts to advance multipolarity in the international arena have not amounted to much, even in the Putin era. Vladimir Putin grandiloquently declared, in February 2003, that the emergence of an informal Franco-German-Russian diplomatic coalition, in opposition to the early use of military force by the US against Iraq, marked 'the first contribution to the building of a multipolar world' since the end of the Cold War.[39] Care was evidently taken not to portray Russia as leading the opposition to the US on this issue. Putin thus 'credited' France with being the driving force behind the dissenting coalition. Evidently, this posture reflected Putin's aversion to seeing Russia tagged as being a potential spoiler. He said as much publicly: 'It would have been impossible to accomplish anything like this in Moscow...we would immediately have been accused of trying to spoil relations between Europe and America.'[40] In similar vein, then Foreign Minister Ivanov said that the Franco-German-Russian position should not be seen as a challenge to the US, but rather viewed as 'an invitation to jointly seek a resolution of the crisis'.[41]

Several Russian leaders and commentators had argued at the time for their government to position itself to try and play a role as an 'honest broker', and seek to extract maximum diplomatic prestige and benefit from doing so. Georgy Bovt, for example, suggested that the best role for Russia would be as 'a broker that would be respected equally by all the parties to the conflict, but nevertheless remain slightly above the fray'.[42] Vladimir Lukin, deputy speaker of the State Duma, argued, with a neo-Gorchakovian touch:

> We now have a unique opportunity to act as a mediator. France and Germany have quarrelled with the US 'at the highest level', and so their dialogue with Washington is greatly impeded. Great Britain is regarded in Europe as a foreign policy 'appendage' of the US. We can take something close to the European antiwar position while preserving opportunities for dialogue with both America and Europe. The aim of this dialogue should not be to play Europe and the US off against each other or to artificially emphasize Russia as an alternative 'pole' in a 'multipolar' world. Rather, the aim should be to create a decision-making system within the Euro-Atlantic community that is more acceptable to our country, and hence to preserve peace on our borders. This will give Russia the 20 to 30 years of security needed for the indispensable modernization of our country.[43]

In the event, of course, Russian – and all other – diplomacy failed to prevent the US-led invasion of Iraq. It is not clear that the Russian government had any serious expectation that it would and could do so. It seemed more interested in showing that Russia had a distinctive view – opposed to early military action in Iraq, although not necessarily to an eventual military option *per se* – on the leading international issue of the day. Having established that, the Putin government was evidently not interested in pursuing its arguments to the point that it risked seriously antagonizing the Bush administration in the US.

In this latter context, the Russian approach did yield an important political dividend. Despite its government's stated scepticism about an early invasion of Iraq, the country's reputation in the United States was not traduced in the way that France's was in late 2002 and early 2003. Given Putin's evident desire to avoid seeing Russia identified as being a spoiler, this mattered. Subsequently, following the launch of the Iraq invasion in March 2003, Russian leaders and officials repeatedly made clear that they did not intend to allow disagreements over Iraq to undermine their country's overall relations with the United States.[44]

More pertinently to these discussions, this episode suggested that the Russian government, under Vladimir Putin, was basically content to allow a domestic debate to develop, suggesting that it favoured some kind of multipolar world order, without following through by systematically developing and promoting policies designed to give effect to this in the international arena. This reticence may reflect lessons learned from the failures of Yeltsin, Kozyrev and Primakov to give practical effect to their own visions of international order during the 1990s. Perhaps more importantly, it probably also reflects an essentially defensive mindset *vis-à-vis* perceptions of the relative material advantages of the US, coupled with concerns – occasionally expressed openly by participants in its domestic debates – that Russia is not strong enough to survive as a leading power centre in any multipolar order that might actually come into being. In this context, Thomas Ambrosio, in one of the few existing book-length analyses of the Russian approach to multipolarity, argues convincingly that it has been 'inherently defensive in nature'. In Ambrosio's words: 'The ultimate aim of multipolarity is to resist American domination of the international system so that Russia is not placed in the role of a junior partner in its relationship with the United States nor would the United States be able to dictate unilateral outcomes which affect Russian security interests.'[45]

Overall, if one thing is clear from the analysis in this chapter, it is that 'multipolarity' has been confined largely to the realms of domestic debates in Russia, rather than forming the basis for any agreed or systematic vision or plan for actually recasting the existing world order. This reflects enduring Russian perceptions of their state's own relative weaknesses, leavened, however, by periodic indications of a neo-Gorchakovian belief – or perhaps merely a hope – that this situation will not prove to be permanent.

9

China: 'Rising Power' or 'Constrained State'?

During the past decade, it has effectively become a truism to describe China as a 'rising power' in the international arena. Often this proposition has been accepted with relatively little critical evaluation of China's alleged power assets and resources. Kenneth Waltz, for example, simply asserted in 2000 that 'China will emerge as a great power even without trying so long as it remains politically united and competent.'[1]

The analysis in this chapter, and in the one that follows, will attempt to offer a more considered and developed view. It will assess both hard and soft power resources. Particular attention will be paid to what may be described as China's key relationships – with the United States and with its Asian neighbours – and how it has been perceived and engaged with by the states concerned.

The overall objective of this chapter is to identify and evaluate the bases and validity of the arguments for viewing contemporary China as an increasingly important – and perhaps also threatening – international power. Given the emphasis in this book on the importance of ideas in debates about power, the discussions in chapter 10 will then focus on the notion of 'harmony'. This has increasingly become a key concept – with both domestic and international ramifications – for the Chinese government.

China's military power resources

Since the mid-1990s, a lively debate has developed amongst Western analysts about the extent to which the Chinese government has actively been seeking to develop the country's military capabilities and, if it has, to what end. The majority view accepts that there is evidence of efforts being made to develop them, but that the emphasis thus far has remained on enhancing area defence and regional military projection rather than developing significant longer-range capacities. In addition to the work of prominent academic specialists,[2] this perspective has been evident in official American appraisals of Chinese military capabilities.[3]

Consistently the most significant security issue for the Chinese government has been the unfinished business of 'reunification' with the island of Taiwan. This is officially viewed as an internal rather than an external matter, because it is seen as intimately bound up with China's sovereignty and territorial integrity. Secondly, and viewed in a similar way, are regions on the Chinese mainland where there have been long-standing ethnic and religious tensions, and occasional outbreaks of violence. Internationally, the 'Tibetan Autonomous Region' is probably the best known of these, followed by Xinjiang Province. Finally, China, together with other states in North-East and South-East Asia, has various contested claims to maritime and territorial rights in the South and East China Seas.[4]

Developments in China's military spending, and also in specific military equipment programmes, are increasingly discussed amongst Western analysts. At the beginning of 2011, for example, there was a considerable amount of rather excited speculation in the US and Europe about the potential impact of a newly revealed programme by the Chinese air force to develop a 'stealth' jet fighter capability.[5] Less commonly cited is evidence to suggest that the Chinese armed forces remain a significant distance away from being able to threaten the US and its key global and regional interests directly, even if that were the intention of the Chinese government.

In 2009, the last full year for which figures were available at the time of writing, the Chinese government claimed an annual defence budget of the equivalent of $70.3 billion, compared with $690.3 billion for the US. The latter dwarfs every other state in the world, and, indeed, the American defence budget is routinely described as being nearly as large as the rest of the world's defence spending put together. In terms of key military force projection capabilities, in 2009 the US possessed fourteen ballistic-missile carrying submarines, compared with China's three, and eleven squadrons of long-range bomber aircraft, compared with China's five regiments, with aircraft of a more limited range. The US also maintained eleven aircraft carriers and associated support vessels ('carrier battle groups'), whereas China had none.[6]

In June 2011, senior military officers announced that China was in the process of developing what would be its first aircraft carrier, albeit one apparently being constructed on a Cold War-era Soviet hull. This would still leave China considerably behind the United States, as the latter assigns no fewer than six of its own carriers to potential operations in the Asia-Pacific region.[7] The Chinese government knows the strategic and political impact that carrier battle groups can have. In March 1996, in response to rising tensions between China and Taiwan, the Clinton administration deployed two of its Asia-Pacific carrier groups close to the Taiwan Strait. The US action was widely seen as having dissuaded the Chinese government from escalating tensions and attempting to intimidate the Taiwanese.[8] Given this demonstration of the potency of carrier deployments, it is perhaps surprising that the Chinese government had waited fifteen years before announcing a programme to develop its own capability. This suggested that it had not, thus far, been seeking to enter into a competitive arms-race dynamic with the United States.

Having said that, it is apparent that China *is* spending more on its armed forces and striving to increase their capabilities, although thus far largely within regional parameters.[9] To what end are these developments taking place? Thomas Christensen, a former senior US State Department official with responsibility for Asia-Pacific affairs, has argued persuasively that China will not directly challenge the US in the Asian region, or elsewhere. On the other hand, its military modernization programmes – particularly the development of longer-range missile and anti-satellite capabilities – will make it increasingly difficult for the US to safeguard its own security interests in the Asia-Pacific. Christensen has thus argued that China can still potentially 'pose problems without catching up' with it.[10]

In this context, China's well-publicized destruction of one of its own communication satellites in January 2007 was interpreted by some as a high-profile warning to the United States. The 'message', allegedly, was that China was developing technologies that could potentially threaten American space-based intelligence, reconnaissance and communication capabilities, and thus prospectively 'blind' US forces operating in the Asia-Pacific during a crisis.[11]

All of this suggests that the Chinese government's motivation for its military build-up has been mainly defensive, driven by a concern not to allow the US credibly to threaten to coerce China into reaching accommodations against its perceived interests. This may well have been the main lesson that the Chinese government took from the 1996 Taiwan Strait crisis.

Hegemonic conflict with the US?

Does China's 'rise' in the military sphere nonetheless increase the possibility of 'hegemonic war' with the United States, at least in the Asia-Pacific? It may be recalled from the discussions in chapter 3 that this term has been

used in reference to an armed conflict fought when an established hegemonic state is confronted with a rising challenger, potentially seeking to
displace it. American perceptions are – by definition – an important factor
in this equation. There have been some indications of a tendency amongst
American political and military leaders to over-interpret China's military
development as being potentially threatening to core American interests.
This has been particularly apparent since the turn of the century. In 2000,
for example, Congress mandated the Defense Department to prepare and
publish an annual report on *The Military Power of the People's Republic of
China.* No comparable congressional mandate exists for any other state in
the world. This suggests that, for some American lawmakers at least, China
is considered to pose a unique military risk.

Controversies over Sino-American relations became particularly prominent from 2001 during the George W. Bush administration. Initially, the
administration's views seemed to be coloured by so-called China threat
thinking, which has tended to view a rising China as being both inevitable
and at least potentially hostile.[12] Operating at the outer reaches of this
China threat school of thought has been a small group of analysts advocat-
ing that the US should prepare for – if not actually seek – a (preventive)
hegemonic war with China.[13]

In the early 2000s, the Bush administration switched from officially
regarding China as a 'strategic partner' (as had been the case during the
Clinton presidency) to viewing it as a 'strategic rival'. The Defense
Department was, perhaps, the most important institutional player in
shaping this policy at that time. Deputy Defense Secretary Paul Wolfowitz,
in particular, had previously evinced sympathy with those who argued that
a rising China would inevitably be competitive, and perhaps also conflictual, with the US.[14] The then defense secretary, Donald Rumsfeld, meanwhile, appeared to need little persuading of the view that China was more
a rival than a partner. In a 2005 speech, Rumsfeld stated:

> Since no nation threatens China, one must wonder: Why this
> growing investment? Why these continuing large and expanding
> arms purchases? Why these robust deployments? Though
> China's economic growth has kept pace with its military spend-
> ing, it is to be noted that a growth in political freedom has not
> yet followed suit. With a system that encouraged enterprise and
> free expression, China would appear more a welcome partner
> and provide even greater economic opportunities for the
> Chinese people.[15]

Rumsfeld's final statement showed another element consistently stressed by members of the China threat school: that, if its government sincerely wants to develop better bilateral relations, China should become more like the United States. Aside from the conceit evident here, it is also noteworthy that the questions Rumsfeld asked about the potential purpose of increased Chinese military spending and procurement could just as easily have been asked, by non-Americans, about the United States itself!

With this kind of thinking in the ascendancy, there was a risk of a 'security dilemma' developing in Sino-American relations during the 2000s. This can happen when the leaders of two or more states develop their military capabilities in order (as they see it) to enhance their defensive and deterrent capacities. The other state(s) involved may perceive such programmes as being potentially offensive and hostile, however, thus perhaps stimulating a mutual arms race and raising the possibility of conflict, albeit perhaps of an inadvertent kind.[16]

Fortunately, perhaps, not all senior members of the Bush administration subscribed to Rumsfeld's and Wolfowitz's views. Alternative opinions arguably found their most pertinent expression in a speech given by then Deputy Secretary of State Robert Zoellick, also in 2005. Zoellick argued that the Chinese government should be actively encouraged to adapt its behaviour in ways conducive to US interests, rather than being threatened, or expected somehow to 'see the light' on its own. This approach should, Zoellick suggested, focus on encouraging China to develop a role as a 'responsible stakeholder' in the international system.[17] Zoellick did not simply envisage China being socialized into the system as a passive actor. By arguing that, 'as a responsible stakeholder, China would be more than just a member – it would work with us to sustain the international system that has enabled its success', he accepted that China would expect – and indeed should be given – a leading role in shaping the future evolution of the system.

From 2009, the Obama administration ostensibly premised its own policy towards China on a continuation of this basic approach. It accepted that it was unlikely to succeed if the US gave the impression that its leaders simply expected the Chinese government to fit into established structures and processes. Thus, the Obama Defense Department, under then Defense Secretary Robert Gates, stated: 'The United States welcomes the rise of a stable, peaceful, and prosperous China, and encourages China to participate responsibly in world affairs by taking on a greater share of the burden for the stability, resilience, and growth of the international system.'[18] On a visit to China in November 2009, Obama himself suggested that the two states share 'the burden of leadership', adding that 'there are very few global challenges that can be solved unless the US and China agree'.[19] The president thus appeared to be proposing to his Chinese interlocutors an idea which had been circulating in academic circles for some months previously. This envisaged a reformed international economic and financial system becoming increasingly centred on a so-called G2 partnership between China and the United States.[20]

Yet, notwithstanding Obama's relative emphasis on cooperative, multilateral approaches, there remained an implicit sense that China might still pose a threat to the US and its interests. In this context, it was striking how often assumptions were made by American and other Western officials and analysts about the importance of retaining US military 'superiority' or 'supremacy' over any potential challenger, with little apparent regard for how this might be seen by other states. Thomas Christensen, for example, has argued that 'US military superiority [in Asia], properly considered, is an integral part of [a] broader engagement strategy and makes diplomatic engagement itself more effective.'[21] Jonathan Holslag, meanwhile, has suggested that the US can actually prevent China's rise from turning 'aggressive' by itself acting in a seemingly aggressive manner – specifically 'by maintaining a supreme [military] position along China's economic lifelines'.[22]

The importance of maintaining military superiority has continued to figure in statements of American government policy. Even whilst welcoming the rise of 'a stable, peaceful, and prosperous China', the Obama administration still maintained – in its 2010 *National Security Strategy* document – that it was essential for the US to retain 'superior capabilities to deter and defeat adaptive enemies and to ensure the credibility of security partnerships that are fundamental to regional and global security'.[23] This was not explicitly directed at China, but it might, nonetheless, have been reasonably interpreted in those terms by many Chinese leaders and officials.

Obama did little to dispel such impressions by continuing a periodic tendency of American leaders to respond to perceived Chinese challenges by falling back on Cold War analogies. He gave a number of speeches in which he evoked what he called a '*Sputnik* moment' for the US. This was a reference to the Soviet Union's launching in the late 1950s of the earth orbiting satellite *Sputnik*. It achieved this feat ahead of the US, causing much *angst* amongst American leaders at the time over the prospect of falling behind in developing vital civil/military technologies. In the modern era, Obama declared, the challenge to Americans was not to fall dangerously behind China economically, commercially and technologically.[24] Whilst his underlying message was a perfectly reasonable one in itself, Obama's use of the *Sputnik* metaphor was rightly criticized for implying that China could be seen as a similar kind of 'enemy' as the Soviet Union during the Cold War.[25]

Overall, the risk of hegemonic war between China and the US is currently low, if it is viewed as most likely occurring as a consequence of a Chinese bid for international primacy. The risk of inadvertent conflict occasioned by a developing security dilemma is, however, potentially higher. Even if the Chinese government is motivated mainly by defensive considerations *vis-à-vis* the US in military terms, it might nonetheless be provoked into responding militarily to what its leaders may judge to be aggressive or provocative American moves, even if these, in turn, were intended by American leaders as essentially defensive.[26]

Economic, financial and commercial issues

Chinese economic growth rates since the 1980s have been a principal foundation for almost all of the claims that China has become the world's most significant rising power. This was, for example, evident in August 2010, when China became 'the second largest economy in the world' after the United States. The two statistics most often cited as measurements of China's economic prowess are, firstly, the overall size and relative strength of its economy, which is usually expressed in terms of Gross Domestic Product. GDP can, however, be measured in different ways, and not all of them show China at number two. The second statistic often cited is the annual economic growth rate. Most estimates place China's at around 9 per cent year on year, which makes it one of the highest – if not *the* highest – in the world.[27]

The structures and processes of the 'world economy' continue to be based substantially around the US. This, indeed, is a key element of the enduring liberal hegemonic system. This system, established by the US after the Second World War, was as much economic and commercial as it was military. This is not to say, of course, that the US has been the *only* important actor within it. Yet official Chinese attitudes and approaches have been significantly coloured by the government's wish to accede to key elements of the system – acknowledging that this would hardly be possible without American support.

The impact of this could perhaps be seen most clearly at the end of the 1990s, when the Chinese government agreed to make significant concessions to American demands in order to gain accession to the World Trade Organization (WTO). As one observer noted: 'When China joined the World Trade Organisation in late 2001, it was for the first time in its history agreeing voluntarily to open its markets according to a set of rules and principles set down by an extraterritorial body' – and one whose norms and rules had been shaped to a significant extent by the United States.[28] The concessions granted were politically risky for Chinese leaders. The WTO endgame coincided with the NATO bombing of the Chinese embassy in Belgrade during the Kosovo conflict. This provoked substantial (if ultimately short-lived) anti-American demonstrations inside China, and it was not certain at the time that popular anti-American sentiment had been brought fully under control by the government. American diplomacy on the WTO issue has also been described as maladroit and insensitive to Chinese concerns, allegedly owing to the Clinton administration's focus on the concerns of domestic American interest groups.[29] Yet, despite this unpromising backdrop, the Chinese government essentially agreed to the American terms.

In accounting for their government's interest in joining established international economic and commercial institutions, Chinese officials argued that it was a conscious and positive choice to break with the failed and costly attempts at national autarky pursued under Mao Tse-tung in the 1950s and 1960s.[30] Whatever the motivation, the willingness of Chinese leaders to make significant concessions in order to do so is congruent with the characteristics of a liberal hegemonic system. It was suggested in chapter 3 that an important feature of such a system is its openness. This can be defined not only as the openness of the system to potential new members but also the extent to which the leaders of states seeking participation are persuaded of the desirability of opening up previously closed or restrictive national systems in order to join, and to maximize the benefits of their membership once they do.

Population and demographics

Population size is sometimes assumed to be a factor of power – often without closer definition, as noted in chapter 2. China is currently the most populous state in the world, with upwards of 1.3 billion people. In this context, it is noteworthy how often Chinese leaders have emphasized, in public statements, the extent to which China's population size is at least as much of a burden as an asset to its development. This has been pithily expressed by Zheng Bijian, a senior Communist Party ideologist, as the 'multiplication and division' problem.

Zheng argues that 'any problem of economic or social development' will appear daunting when 'multiplied by 1.3 billion'. On the other hand, when divided by the same figure, 'China's financial and material resources, no matter how abundant they are, will be at extremely low per capita levels.'[31] Official Chinese analyses of population issues have repeatedly suggested that China's supposed economic strengths should not be quantified in overall aggregate terms, but rather assessed on a per capita basis. Because per capita measurements, by definition, offer a *disaggregated* picture, this, it is argued, gives a fairer and more realistic sense of China's relative strengths and weaknesses.

Data prepared by the US Central Intelligence Agency suggested that, in 2010, the Chinese economy was ranked third in the world (after the EU and the US) in terms of GDP, measured by purchasing power parity.[32] Measured in per capita terms, however, China's GDP ranking dropped to 125th in the world. This placed it behind, *inter alia*, Grenada, Palau and Belize.[33] Yet, Chinese leaders often preferred to draw attention to this type of statistic.[34] They generally did so in the course of arguing that China remains a developing country, and one where widespread poverty still exists. In April 2009, for example, Fu Ying, China's then ambassador to the UK (and subsequently a vice foreign minister), noted that 'people outside China tend to see the big and strong aspects...while inside China, people are more aware of its weakness and challenges'.[35]

There are three possible explanations for this evident official reticence, which contrasts markedly with the tendency of Russian leaders to talk up their state's perceived strengths and advantages, as noted in chapter 7. Firstly, it could be some kind of ruse, designed to lull the US and others into believing that China is less strong and potentially threatening than it actually is. The official playing down of China's strengths often takes place in conjunction with assertions that it is engaged in a 'peaceful rise' internationally.[36] Those fearing future hegemonic competition, and even conflict, might view this concept as being essentially a ruse designed to buy China time to develop its economic and military strengths without serious interference, until its leaders feel strong enough to mount a more overt and confident challenge to the established international order.

A second possible explanation is that China's leaders really are keenly concerned about their domestic economic and social problems. In this context, it has been argued that China's population is becoming increasingly unbalanced, with fewer people of working age available to support progressively large numbers of retired persons. These demographic factors are by no means unique to China; similar trends are evident in many European societies, for example. In the Chinese case, however, the situation is arguably exacerbated by the communist government's so-called one child policy. This was first introduced in 1978 as a means of trying to constrain overall population growth, and the consequent social and economic demands that this would pose, at a time when the early post-Mao government under Deng Xiaoping was seeking to kick-start economic and industrial development.

Regardless of whether the demographic effects of this policy are seen as being generally positive, negative or mixed,[37] it has clearly had the effect of politicizing demographics to a significantly greater extent than in many other societies. In consequence, the Chinese government has come to see its own ability to continue to govern the country effectively as being closely bound up with demographic trends, which it has actively sought to shape and control for over thirty years. Official statements about demographic challenges do therefore, on this reading, reflect genuine concerns, rather than constituting some kind of tactical ruse designed primarily for overseas consumption.

A third possible explanation, related to the second, sees official sensitivity to demographic factors, and a tendency to view China's demographics as being as much a potential liability as an asset, as being closely related to the Chinese government's concerns about its own domestic legitimacy. Legitimacy, as already noted, is an important factor of power in its own right. It is therefore appropriate to turn our attention to it in the Chinese context here.

Domestic legitimacy and fragility

The essentially bifurcated nature of the Chinese state – combining substantial economic and financial freedoms with continuing political authoritarianism – rests on an implicit bargain. The Chinese people effectively consent to the maintenance of the Communist Party's monopoly of political control, in exchange for the expanding material and social benefits of continued significant economic growth.[38] Should the latter falter, or perceptions develop that its benefits are not being sufficiently equitably shared around the country, then the domestic legitimacy of the government could be called into question. Despite the existence of the Communist Party's well-developed apparatus for monitoring and controlling internal dissent, some analysts argue that its domestic legitimacy – and prospects for maintaining political control – are, therefore, perpetually fragile and ultimately uncertain.

This fragility can be seen in the levels of ongoing – and apparently rising – social and political protest and unrest inside the country. These have taken the form of demonstrations and protests of various kinds – mainly against alleged abuses or corruption by local party or state officials. Even allowing for China's population size, the numbers of such protests documented – by both governmental and other sources – are noteworthy. They would probably be seen in the US and many European states as evidence of serious underlying societal and governmental malaise. In 2004, 74,000 protests were reportedly recorded, with 'more than' 80,000 reported for both 2005 and 2006. There were reportedly 100,000 protests in 2008 and 180,000 in 2010.[39] Detailed research by Murray Scot Tanner, of the American RAND Corporation, has suggested that the incidence of protest throughout China has been rising steadily since at least the early 1990s.[40] In 2009, Bao Tong, a prominent Chinese dissident, claimed that 'every four minutes there is a protest of more than 100 people' in China.[41]

What is noteworthy here is not just the rising number of protests, but also the extent to which the government seems to have accepted that they are effectively a fact of life. This in itself does not necessarily suggest system-threatening social and political fragility. In an interesting article published in 1996, Kevin O'Brien traced the evolution of a social process, which he called 'rightful resistance', from its roots amongst rural populations in imperial China. O'Brien defined rightful resistance as an officially sanctioned and regulated right to protest, in order to demand redress in the face of abuses of authority by local or regional state officials.[42] From a government's point of view, the problem, as O'Brien acknowledged, is that this kind of semi-tolerated, semi-regulated, social cum political process almost by definition contains the potential for escalating into a more serious and widespread challenge to the existing social and political order *per se*.[43] An example of this could be seen in early twentieth-century tsarist Russia, when protesters, having been motivated initially to seek redress from the tsar for grievances against local and regional officials, joined what in 1905 became a major (although only partially successful) revolutionary challenge to the established monarchical system.

The contemporary Chinese government has been highly sensitive to the possibility of officially tolerated protests escalating into something which might potentially threaten its continued rule. To this end, the one child policy, discussed earlier, has been most rigorously enforced in towns and cities. Alongside economic and developmental rationales, it is likely that there has also been an important *political* consideration behind this in view of the emphasis placed in Marxist theory on the growth of a mass, disaffected, urban proletariat as the key revolutionary force in society.

The Chinese government has been consistently sensitive to the perceived risks of the successful popular overthrowing of other rulers and regimes possibly helping to inspire or ignite similar efforts at home. This was apparent, for example, in its response to the events of the Arab spring in early 2011. Major efforts were made to prevent public gatherings of any kind in urban environments, and surveillance and detention of known dissidents was increased. Sustained attempts were also made to control the availability of non-official sources of information about developments in the Arab world. These included designing programs to filter out potentially 'dangerous' words, such as 'Tunisia', 'Egypt' and 'jasmine',[44] from the search engines serving internet users inside China.[45]

A feeling of political and societal fragility is further suggested by the Chinese government's sensitivity to any hint of ethnic tension or unrest, as shown in the emphasis given to the dangers of 'splittism' in Communist Party ideology. This is a revealing choice of terminology, suggesting as it does that significant official fears exist about the possibility of the Chinese state itself potentially breaking up. Such fears were on display, for example, in the official response to short-lived ethnic disturbances in Xinjiang Province in July 2009. An editorial in the *People's Daily* (the Communist Party's principal media organ) portrayed what had been sporadic and quickly contained outbreaks of violence as a threat to the very 'idea of national unity'. This, in turn, was described as 'the basic foundation for the safety of all ethnic people, and... also the great power that keeps Chinese civilization going on and on'.[46] Individual Chinese leaders weighed in with dramatic calls to 'build a steel wall for stability' and construct a 'Great Wall of ethnic unity' to counter any danger of splittism taking hold.[47]

Soft power

The domestic legitimacy problems examined above have important implications for China's ability to operationalize soft power in the international arena. The view that China does, in fact, possess a significant – and growing – soft power capability has become increasingly fashionable amongst analysts in recent years, to the extent that it sometimes seems to go virtually unchallenged. The genesis of this view can, in significant part, be traced back to a short book published by Joshua Cooper Ramo in 2004. Ramo argued that a new 'Beijing consensus' was emerging internationally – in the economic, financial and commercial arenas in particular. This was, in Ramo's view, beginning to challenge established American-led international institutions and the norms of liberal hegemony (sometimes called the 'Washington consensus'). In doing so, it was effectively giving China an increasingly important international role as a pole of attraction to developing states in particular, offering an alternative model of development to that both followed and prescribed by the US and its traditional allies in Europe and Asia.[48]

Since 2004, the view that China is developing significant soft power capabilities has been discussed with increasing regularity by both Western and Chinese observers. Zheng Bijian has explained to Chinese audiences that his 'peaceful rise' concept is a useful means of increasing China's 'discourse power' in the international arena, by presenting its advances in an attractive and non-threatening way to other states and societies.[49] Others have developed this idea further. Two Chinese scholars – Luo Shou and Wang Guifang – have defined 'discourse power' as being based on 'the dissemination of China's unique cultural values [which] will influence the world's discourse environment – cultivating influence over the world's direction of development within the realm of culture and values and, as a result, obtaining universal world respect'.[50] Looking behind this rather pompous language, it appears that Luo and Wang were concurring with the view advanced by Ramo: that China is engaging essentially in a contest of ideas with the US and its allies and offering an alternative – and increasingly attractive – development model. Expressing concern that this may indeed be occurring, in January 2010 *The Economist* in London suggested that a reported decline in the number of functioning democratic states in the world could be attributed in part to a 'fascination', amongst developing countries, 'with copying China's trick' of combining economic liberalism and political authoritarianism.[51]

Some have suggested that China has increased its international attractiveness – especially amongst its Asian neighbours – mainly by demonstrating its credentials as a 'responsible country'. These observers often highlight China's performance during the 1997–8 Asian financial crisis, when its government was widely perceived to have responded helpfully in trying to prevent further financial turmoil in the region. The Chinese government's prompt and relatively generous disaster relief response to the 2004 Asian tsunami has also been cited in this context.[52] The suggestion has also been made, with regard to the former, that the Chinese government was able to capitalize on perceived American reluctance to become significantly involved in supporting vulnerable Asian economies, other than in the case of its South Korean ally. The American government may indeed have come to regret this. In his memoirs, Bill Clinton, who was president at the time, wrote that not intervening sooner and more generously with economic and financial support in Asia in 1997–8 had been a significant policy error on the part of his administration.[53]

A Chinese soft power strategy?

Notwithstanding what has been noted above, if there has indeed been a deliberate Chinese soft power strategy in the international arena, as some have been suggesting, then the evidence for its effectiveness has thus far been rather limited. To begin with, there are, as usual, questions about whether the approaches that have been adopted really deserve to be regarded as examples of soft power. Joshua Kurlantzick, who has compiled a detailed study of China's alleged soft power capabilities, has been quick to dismiss any resemblance between the Chinese approach and Joseph Nye's original concept:

> For the Chinese, soft power means anything outside of the military and security realm, including not only popular culture and public diplomacy but also more coercive economic and diplomatic levers like aid and investment and participation in multilateral organizations . . . Indeed, Beijing offers the charm of a lion, not of a mouse.[54]

The failure of the Chinese government to operationalize soft power on the basis of real and meaningful attraction is having important real-world effects. An argument has been made that China's current drive to improve relations, and gain commercial opportunities, with states in Africa and South America has been based on, and aided by, the effective operational-ization of soft power. Partly, it is argued, this has come in the form of financial and technical aid, generally given without the conditionality sometimes imposed by Western governments or international financial institutions. This is closer to Joseph Nye's own articulation of soft power – i.e., based on attraction rather than bribes – and it has also been suggested that Chinese leaders have sought to use a self-ascribed designation of China as the world's largest developing country in order to position it as the natural leader of the developing and 'anti-imperialist' world.[55] Proponents of the efficacy of Chinese soft power often point to the effects which the country's financial and business investments are having in Africa and South America. Joshua Cooper Ramo, for example, has argued that these programmes are the harbinger of the new 'Beijing consensus' about international development, and indeed the conduct of international relations more generally.[56]

Yet, by adopting an increasingly high-profile role in exploiting key resources such as African oil, China risks coming to be seen itself as a new foreign 'imperialist', notwithstanding its government's routine anti-imperialist rhetoric.[57] Its willingness to give aid largely without conditions to local elites might also undermine its reputation and image, should this come to be seen locally as propping up repressive and unpopular regimes. There is, indeed, some evidence of an emerging backlash against the Chinese business presence in parts of Africa. In autumn 2009, for example, rebels in the Delta region of Nigeria issued a warning against Chinese oil firms setting up there and described them as 'locusts who will ravage any farmland in minutes'. At the same time, unnamed African Union officials were quoted in the British press as expressing concerns about potential Chinese 'neo-colonialism' in Africa.[58]

These examples illustrate an important truism about efforts actively to operationalize soft power in the developing world. Those who do so run the risk of being seen to act as neo-imperialists, almost to the same degree as if they had used or threatened military coercion. This is as true for China as it is for the United States or any other state. In the Chinese case, it has been compounded, as suggested above, by its government's focus on elite-level transactions. Given established inequalities and corruption amongst ruling elites in many recipient states, far from endearing China to the populations at large, if anything its investment policies may be more likely to have the opposite effect.[59]

These setbacks to China's image and reputation are helping to usher in a more nuanced and realistic appraisal of its international attractiveness in some quarters. Some recent analyses have been relatively more circumspect in suggesting that some kind of Chinese model of international development is being successfully developed and exported.[60] This is an area where fragile domestic legitimacy may be having a dissuasive effect internationally. Whilst aggregate Chinese economic growth rates may be attractive to many in the developing world, the essential concomitant to these, in any 'Chinese model', is an authoritarian domestic political system. This, after all, is what most clearly distinguishes China from the United States. Such a system might still be viewed as a potentially attractive option in some quarters, providing that it was seen to be secure and effective. The inherent domestic fragilities discussed earlier, however, significantly undermine its potential attractiveness in this respect.

Detailed opinion poll research, published in 2009 by the Chicago Council on Global Affairs, suggested that China's soft power capacities were limited, and were having relatively little effect even on its own neighbours. This was notwithstanding the Chinese government's efforts to cast it as a 'responsible country' in the Asia-Pacific region. Nor did public opinion in Asia appear to have been significantly influenced in a positive direction by government attempts to emphasize China's cultural attractiveness – a campaign which has seen a revival of official Chinese interest in the virtues of Confucianism.[61]

The fact that the government had chosen to reach back deep into China's imperial history, rather than emphasizing the country's present-day social and political order, is in itself revealing of an implicit recognition of the latter's comparative lack of international appeal. Even with the official emphasis on culture rather than politics, however, the Chicago Council's polling led it to conclude that 'China is not considered much of a cultural soft power by citizens of the major powers [in Asia] even though there is a general perception that China possesses a rich cultural heritage.'[62]

A poll of wider international opinion, conducted for the BBC World Service in London in the following year, recorded similar findings. In particular, it found that positive views of the United States had increased significantly in many countries since the election of Barack Obama as president in 2008. Positive views of China and its role in the world were, on the other hand, 'stuck in neutral' at best, and lower than those recorded for the US.[63]

Several interesting points emerge from this polling evidence. Firstly, it supports the view that soft power is mainly innate rather than instrumental. It either exists or it does not. Secondly, the evidence discussed here suggests that some states are innately more 'soft powerful' than others. The Chinese experience suggests that soft power is relatively more difficult to operationalize for certain states, depending on the perceptions held by others of the nature and character of their domestic system of governance. As Joshua Kurlantzick puts it: 'China cannot offer average people a comprehensive, inspiring vision of how to build a free, rights-oriented political system and economy, a vision that remains popular in many parts of the world.'[64]

The United States, on the other hand, would appear to have innate soft power strengths in comparison with China. These are by no means indestructible, as the decline in US international poll ratings during much of George W. Bush's presidency suggests. The relative American soft power strengths do, however, appear to possess an underlying robustness. In 2009, the Chicago Council survey found, after eight years under Bush, that the US still outscored China in soft power terms.[65] This may have been due in part to the effects of the Bush administration's increasingly more multilateral approach to international affairs, evident during its second term. The 2010 BBC poll, meanwhile, suggested that positive appraisals of the US role in the world increased significantly after Barack Obama assumed office.

Overall, the evidence discussed here suggests, therefore, that the specific policies and actions of governments can diminish a state's international soft power attractiveness, but without destroying it altogether. It remains latent and thus with the potential to be resuscitated when policies or governments change. On the other hand, soft power is difficult – if not impossible – to create or acquire by government *fiat*.[66]

China's leaders are, perhaps, coming to recognize this. In public at least, they have shown only periodic interest in soft power since the term was first used by President Hu Jintao in 2007.[67] They have, it is true, shown rather more interest in the concept than their Russian counterparts – although that is not saying much, as the latter's level of interest has been close to zero. Chinese leaders have also occasionally decried their relative soft power limitations *vis-à-vis* the US.[68] All told, however, it is apparent that China's leaders have been sufficiently aware of the lack of appeal of a 'China model' internationally as to have not invested so far in *systematic* efforts to explore the possibilities of operationalizing soft power more effectively.

China as a constrained state

The cumulative impact of the issues and factors discussed in this chapter has been to leave the Chinese government in a significantly (self-)constrained position internationally. The main reason for this is that it has consistently had to focus its energies and attention on domestic social, political and ethnic challenges. This has left relatively little political energy for foreign affairs, unless the government has judged that the latter directly impinge on China's core interests – as do relations with the United States and its regional security concerns in Asia. Outside of these, however, the

Chinese government has been relatively little involved in the global arena. China was, for example, a largely passive actor during the major international crises over Kosovo in 1998–9, Iraq in 2002–3 and Libya in 2011.

Chinese leaders have been candid in stressing the primacy of domestic affairs. In spring 2006, for example, the *New York Times* reported that Hu Jintao had told his then counterpart George W. Bush that 'fighting political corruption, rural unrest, a widening wealth gap and severe pollution' took up nearly all his time. This report added that Hu had also told Bush that 'domestic problems left China with neither the will nor the means to challenge America's dominance in world affairs'.[69] Bush corroborated elements of this story in his memoirs. He recalled that Hu had identified his top priority as being 'creating twenty-five million new jobs a year' to cope with continuous population increases in China. Bush also wrote that he concluded from their conversation that Hu 'was a practical leader focused inward, not an ideologue likely to stir up trouble abroad'.[70]

China has certainly increased its presence internationally since the 1990s, most especially in Africa and South America. This has been driven primarily by commercial and resource interests, however, and there has been little evidence thus far of the Chinese government using it to try and develop wider international spheres of influence or a more assertive global presence generally.

10

China, 'Anti-Hegemonism' and 'Harmony'

As noted in the previous chapter, contemporary Chinese governments have often stressed the supposedly 'peaceful' nature of their country's rise as an international power. A second concept has also come to feature increasingly prominently in their official discourse: that of 'harmony'. This is certainly not a new idea in Chinese culture, and it can be traced back to the body of semi-religious philosophy commonly known as Confucianism.

The discussions in this chapter will explore the harmony concept and its usage by Chinese leaders in the contemporary domestic and international contexts. Following on from the discussions in chapter 9, attention here will focus in particular on the possible motivations of Chinese leaders in using this concept, and the extent to which it can be said to be assuming the status of an important quasi-ideology shaping official Chinese attitudes and policy in the post-Cold War world.

Confucianism

The body of thought and belief known as Confucianism derives principally from interpretations of the sayings attributed to the sixth-century BC teacher and thinker 'Master Kong' (Confucius), and others regarded as his followers or as working within a similar tradition of thought. Of the latter, the best known is probably the philosopher Mencius. The *Analects of Confucius* are widely regarded as the foundation text of this philosophical tradition.

It becomes clear from a reading of the *Analects* that Confucianism, in terms of the organization of a social entity, is essentially about developing and reflecting upon 'the good way'. Central to this good way is the development and use of 'moral force' – as opposed to physical force – whenever possible. According to the *Analects*, Confucius said that 'he who rules by moral force is like the pole-star, which remains in its place while all the lesser stars do homage to it'.[1]

A second key element evident in the *Analects* is an emphasis upon hierarchy and deferring to superiors. This is a – perhaps indeed the – key factor underpinning a 'harmonious' social and political order. This deference is not seen as being one-sided, however. It is apparent that an effective and harmonious hierarchy depends crucially upon those at the top behaving in ways that engender the 'respect' and even the 'affection' of their subjects.[2] This latter aspect is developed in particular in sayings, attributed to Mencius, which stress the desirability of 'benevolence' in rulers and are also markedly anti-militaristic. A consistent theme in the *Sayings of Mencius* is that the use of military force is not only generally ineffective in securing a ruler's interests, but is likely to be counterproductive, in leading to frustrations and sorrows of various kinds.[3]

In this context, there are important similarities between the ideas and concepts developed by thinkers in ancient Greece – as discussed in chapter 2 of this book – and those attributed to Confucius and Mencius. In particular, a distinction similar to that drawn between *hegemonia* (equating to Confucian moral force) and *arkhe* (physical force) can be seen in Confucius and Mencius, as can scepticism about the utility of the latter. Confucian ideas also bear comparison with the insights into hegemony offered by Antonio Gramsci. It may be recalled that Gramsci argued 'that account be taken of the interests and the tendencies of the groups over which hegemony is to be exercised' in order for this type of power relationship to be sustainable and effective.

Having thus briefly introduced core elements of Confucian thinking, attention in the rest of this chapter will be focused on examining potential motivations behind the evident contemporary official Chinese interest in it. As was noted in chapter 9, the institutions and processes of governance in contemporary China are essentially bifurcated. A market-based and capitalistic economic and financial system co-exists with, and indeed is effectively directed by, an authoritarian political structure. The latter is still nominally based on a version of Marxist ideas and principles.

In reality, however, it is apparent to many observers that Marxism in China has increasingly become an essentially empty ideological shell. As it has done so, this argument suggests, contemporary Chinese leaders have consciously reached back to the social and cultural history of imperial China, and sought to revive and also remould Confucianist ideas in ways that might serve core interests of the Chinese state today. It has been suggested that among the main such interests are, firstly, contributing to domestic societal and thus state consolidation and cohesion. Secondly, it has been argued that Confucianism also provides a useful ideological basis for promoting positive notions and views of China in the international arena.[4] These arguments will be examined below.

A unifying domestic ideology?

On one level, the appeal of 'harmony', given the contemporary Chinese domestic context described in chapter 9, should be clear. It was noted in that chapter that there is a substantial – and apparently increasing – trend towards widespread popular protest in China. Thus far, this has been directed mainly at perceived corruption and misgovernment at the local and regional levels. Chinese leaders have also, it was suggested there, been worried about the possibility of ethnic tensions spilling over into open conflict.

Taken as a whole, the evidence suggests, however, that the revival of official interest in Confucianism has not, so far, reflected a serious effort to develop an ideological counter to these trends. A central tenet of traditional Confucian thinking is, as noted, the idea of *mutual* obligation between rulers and ruled and the equally important idea of governance by consent. It cannot be said that either of these exist at the national level in contemporary China. Essentially, the response to domestic unrest and protest has often taken the form of a combination of accommodation of local demands, together with increased surveillance and policing methods designed to try to ensure that the protests do not spread. If they do, more overt repression may be employed – the best-known example of the latter being, of course, the violent suppression of the protests in Tiananmen Square in Beijing in June 1989.

Overall, it can therefore be argued that, since the early 1980s, and especially since the discrediting of Marxism in light of the collapse of communist governments in Eastern Europe and the Soviet Union in 1989–91, the Chinese state has, domestically, effectively been without a core operational ideology. To the extent that the government has itself periodically felt the need to identify one, it has generally referred to 'socialism with Chinese characteristics'. This, however, in practice appears to be little more than an official circumlocution. It has been used to provide at least thin cover for the introduction of capitalist-type economic methods and reforms since the late 1970s, whilst simultaneously maintaining a nominally Marxist system of centralized political control.

This does not in itself mean that socialism with Chinese characteristics is politically unimportant. It has been formulated in large part to try to underpin the continued legitimacy of the Chinese Communist Party. The party's main stated *raison d'être* is to lead the way in building 'socialism' in China. With this in mind, it can be argued that, in the domestic social and political context, the official revival of Confucian ideas by party ideologists and officials does not seem intended to play a fundamental role. To the extent that this has a domestic rationale at all, it appears designed mainly to fulfil limited, tactical objectives, and not to signal any significant ideological refinements – still less fundamental shifts.

A soft power resource?

In chapter 9 it was argued that, notwithstanding periodic official interest in the concept, the Chinese government has not so far been very effective in attempting to operationalize soft power. It has been suggested that its efforts have been significantly hampered by the demise of Marxism as an ideological system with any real remaining claim to global relevance.[5] With this in mind, can the revival of Confucianism be seen in part as being motivated by an attempt to develop an 'idea of China' with potentially greater international appeal? Shaun Breslin, for example, has assessed the official utility of Confucianism in these terms, although his analysis suggests that it has been circumscribed and limited in its effects. According to Breslin, Confucianist ideas may, at best, help to promote an image of China in the world which, whilst it might 'not... attract, then at least perhaps... might not repel'.[6]

This is an obviously limited objective. So much so, in fact, that it is doubtful whether it is appropriate to consider it in a soft power context at all – at least if Joseph Nye's definition of soft power based on attraction is used. The limited horizons suggested by Breslin might at least be realistic, however. The polling evidence discussed in chapter 9 suggested that attempts to 'sell' China as a positive presence and actor in Asia – in part on the basis of its cultural and philosophical traditions – have made little impact on political and popular opinion in the region. In general, China does not possess significant innate soft power resources. Attempts by its government to harness Confucianism seem, thus far, to have made little apparent difference in this respect.

'Anti-hegemonism'

The notion of 'anti-hegemonism' has become established as a key *leitmotif* in the ideology of the Chinese Communist Party. It was, for example,

clearly reflected in the historic 'Shanghai Communiqué', the joint statement issued at the end of President Richard Nixon's path-breaking visit to
China in February 1972. This document averred that 'China will never be
a superpower and it opposes hegemony and power politics of any kind.'
Elsewhere in the statement, both sides pledged that 'neither should seek
hegemony in the Asia-Pacific region and each is opposed to efforts by any
other country or group of countries to establish such hegemony.'[7]

As a result of statements such as these, it has been argued that a contemporary tendency amongst critics of American and Western approaches
to international relations – to use 'hegemony' as an essentially negative
descriptor, akin to 'imperialism' – owes much to this long-standing usage
of the term by the Chinese communists. Their views had come increasingly to the attention of Western observers following the US–China thaw
of the early 1970s.[8]

For both the Chinese government and many Chinese analysts, the
concept of hegemony remains closely associated with essentially negative
notions of coercion and subjugation of the weak by the strong.[9] This
entrenched worldview can be accounted for, in part, with reference to the
presence of some residual impact of Marxist theory on official Chinese
thinking. Perhaps more pertinent, in the contemporary context, has been
the long-term legacy of the Sino-Soviet split of the late 1950s and early
1960s. Chinese anti-hegemonism was not originally developed primarily
with the United States in mind. There was little doubt as to the identity of
the 'other country' that the Chinese and American governments both
viewed as a potential 'hegemonic' threat to Asia in their 1972 communiqué.
David Shambaugh, a noted analyst of contemporary China, has traced the
origins of official anti-hegemonism specifically to the Chinese government's response to the Soviet-led military intervention in Czechoslovakia
in 1968, to crush the so-called Prague spring.[10] Others have traced essentially negative Chinese conceptions of hegemony much further back in the
country's history – to the era of the so-called unequal treaties. These were
essentially unilateral arrangements, imposed on the decaying late imperial
Qing Dynasty by various Western states, including the US. This period is
usually reckoned to have lasted approximately one hundred years, from the
1840s to the founding of communist China in 1949.[11]

Some observers have detected an element of hypocrisy in contemporary
Chinese opposition to hegemony, in view of imperial China's own long
history as a recognizably hegemonic state and society. Those arguing from
this perspective often point to the so-called tributary system, practised
by successive imperial dynasties over several thousand years. Under this

system, the rulers of smaller, neighbouring territories were expected to pay tribute of various kinds and to varying degrees to the Chinese emperor, often according to a system of prescribed and elaborate rituals. The governments of stronger and more distant states were also often expected to participate in the system to a lesser extent, as the price of gaining and maintaining commercial links with the imperial Chinese state.[12]

The key point about the tributary system, in the context of the discussions here, is that it was, by definition, unequal and effectively obligatory for the smaller and weaker participants. For some observers, these characteristics are sufficient to qualify it as an example of 'negative' hegemony, of the kind which contemporary Chinese leaders routinely deplore. Others have argued against this perspective, however. These analysts have suggested that the traditional system reflected Confucian notions of hierarchy of the kind discussed earlier. Under this sort of system – which more closely reflects the understanding of 'hegemony' developed and used in this book – both superiors and subordinates were expected to undertake prescribed mutual responsibilities. These were necessary in order to underpin the key objective of the whole Confucian system: the preservation of social and political harmony. Related to this, it has been argued that the tributary system tended to be strongest in practice when the imperial Chinese state had tangible rewards and incentives to offer to its interlocutors.[13] It was not, therefore, based simply, or even mainly, on the practice or threat of coercion.

The potential cost to an emperor of failing to honour the reciprocal basis of the system could be serious, involving the loss of the 'mandate of heaven' on which his right to rule – i.e., legitimacy – was based. This was indeed a real sanction. One analyst has noted historical occasions when, 'if a ruler became tyrannical, armed forces of other states who invaded to depose the unpopular ruler were given praise for having served a just cause'.[14] Retribution might also come from within. Stefan Halper has observed pithily that, if a ruler was perceived to have lost the mandate of heaven, and hence legitimacy, 'then Chinese peasantry have a heritage for bottom-up rebellion that is almost unrivalled in history'.[15]

These examples suggest that the Confucian philosophical tradition is not straightforwardly pacifist in attitudes to the potential use of physical force. In this context, several noted contemporary analysts have pointed to the existence, in ancient Chinese texts, of the notion of 'righteous war', whereby the use of physical force was considered permissible, and even laudatory, providing that it was undertaken against 'unrighteous' rulers.[16] The origins of the concept of rightful resistance, as posited by Kevin

O'Brien and discussed in chapter 9, can also be traced in part to this strand of Confucianist thinking.

Overall, David Shambaugh has offered a useful summary evaluation of the nature of the imperial Chinese tributary system. He argues that it was:

> characterized by a combination of patron–client ties; economic interdependence; security protection for those closest to China (especially Korea); cultural assimilation into Confucian customs...political ritual...and benevolent governance....The tribute system may have been hegemonic, but it was not based on coercion or territorial expansionism.[17]

China's 'peaceful rise'

How is this relevant in the contemporary context? To begin with, it has been argued persuasively that the legacy of the 'century of humiliation' from the 1840s is still a factor in shaping Chinese attitudes and policy today. This is the case with regard both to China's own role in the world and to its relations with other leading contemporary states. With this in mind, Shambaugh has noted that:

> Chinese across the professional spectrum regularly claim that because of China's past horrific encounters with foreign imperialism and hegemony, it will never exert the same on others...There has been a strong continuity in Chinese articulations about the impact of this historical experience, China's preferred...order, and...future place in it.[18]

The contemporary Chinese concept of peaceful rise is overtly predicated on China's self-restraint in the international arena. In his public formulations of this notion, Zheng Bijian has emphasized this repeatedly. In one of his earliest statements on the concept, in December 1997, Zheng rejected the idea that imperial China had been some kind of benevolent hegemon. Instead, he argued that 'China's arrogance in the past, when it looked down upon foreign countries as "barbarians", was mocked and penalized by history.' Contemporary China should not and would not repeat that mistake, Zheng asserted.[19] Later, in April 2004, he argued that 'our biggest achievement is to have realized that peace and rise, which look quite contradictory, can actually be integrated. In the past, the rise of a big power often involved toppling the international order and threatening peace.

China breaks this rule.'[20] Zheng also made frequent references to the importance of China's rise taking place in tandem with – not opposition to – 'economic globalization'.[21] In official Chinese parlance, this phrase is often used to refer to the institutions and processes of the established international economic, commercial and financial systems such as the World Trade Organization, which China had finally joined in 2001.

China and Asia

As suggested in chapter 9, some have seen the official emphasis on peaceful rise since the mid-1990s (more recently often supplanted in official state-ments by the term 'peaceful development') as being essentially a ruse. Used in such a manner, it might help to mollify and thus circumscribe potential international opposition, whilst China emerges as a 'new superpower'. Having thus risen, China could then, if its leaders so chose, challenge the existing international order in potentially threatening ways.[22]

Evidence in support of such views can, on the face of it, be adduced from what some perceive to be an increasingly assertive – if not indeed aggressive – posture by the Chinese government towards China's neigh-bours in Asia. This, it is argued, can be seen in particular with reference to its relations with smaller neighbours – such as Taiwan, Vietnam, Malaysia and the Philippines – with whom it has territorial disputes and/or disputes regarding control over some or all of the Spratly and Paracel Islands in the South China Sea. These straddle key shipping lanes and are rich in fish stocks and also, potentially, deposits of oil and gas. There have been growing concerns, expressed in the Western media, that the various con-tested claims over some or all of these islands are contributing to worsen-ing relations overall between China and a number of neighbouring states.[23]

These disputes – fractious though they may be – do not necessarily reflect or portend a more aggressive Chinese posture in the Asia-Pacific region overall. To begin with, Taiwan is – for all Chinese leaders – a special case and, indeed, not an international issue at all. Rather, it is seen as an *internal* matter, bound up with the historic 'reunification of the mother-land'. The focus on Taiwan has, perhaps, also distorted the Chinese govern-ment's overall regional posture – especially in the South and East China Seas. In this context, former US Secretary of State Madeleine Albright recalled in her memoirs the extent of the Chinese government's apparent obsession with the Taiwan issue – to the detriment, she suggested, of other, equally important, challenges.[24] The arguably distorting priority given to the island of Taiwan may help to explain why the Chinese government has shown a willingness to negotiate compromise agreements on many (though not all) of its territorial and border disputes with its neighbours on land, but not to the same extent with regard to contested territorial jurisdictions in the South and East China Seas.[25]

This is no small matter as, traditionally, disputes over territory and borders have been major flashpoints for armed conflict. As cases in point, China itself fought a brief war with India over competing territorial claims in 1962, and came close to one with the Soviet Union over their (then) contested border seven years later. In addition to strategic concerns over shipping lanes and the possibility of securing control over potential future energy sources, the relative Chinese intransigence over ongoing maritime disputes can be explained by reference to its government's long-standing and seemingly absolute determination to avoid conceding anything that could compromise its future ability to 'reunify' with Taiwan – by force if necessary.

This posture clearly represents at least a potential threat to Taiwan's current *de facto* existence as a quasi-state. It is less clear, however, that it reflects a broader Chinese intention to threaten or intimidate other Asian states. Nor, notwithstanding recent speculation in Western media about the alleged deterioration of relations between China and its neighbours, has this process yet reached the extent to which most of them are actively considering countermeasures, such as the formation of stronger military alliances, to try to balance Chinese military capabilities and a growing sense of threat.[26] Regional security structures and institutions in Asia are famously weak and relatively underdeveloped – at least when compared with those which evolved in Europe during the Cold War years. There is still no comparable Asian equivalent of either NATO or the EU, and none looks in prospect for the foreseeable future. Although there has been no shortage of regional meetings to discuss security issues (one survey counted over 270 such meetings in 2007 alone),[27] these have generally been ritualistic and formulaic, rather than binding and substantive, in nature. As a result, they have had little meaning or effect on the overall balance of military power in the Asia-Pacific region.

The absence, thus far, of clearer indications of regional balancing against China does not mean that neighbouring states and societies have been happy to trust its government's assurances that it is engaged in a peaceful rise. Local threat perceptions have so far been blunted, rather, because it is apparent that, to a significant extent, China is a constrained state. In chapter 9, this concept was discussed primarily in the domestic context. Here, it can be argued that it is also evident in the Asian regional context.

China is constrained from developing regional primacy, firstly, by the existence of both India and Japan as significant poles of power in their own right. Moreover, neither of these states has traditionally enjoyed good relations with communist China. Territorial disputes between China and India remain unresolved, and there are also ongoing maritime disputes with Japan in the East China Sea, together with unresolved political, social and cultural animosities dating from the Japanese military conquest and occupation of swathes of Chinese territory in the 1930s and 1940s.

In the contemporary context, both India and Japan could become potentially formidable rivals to, and competitors with, China in the Asia-Pacific. This is an especially sensitive Chinese concern with regard to Japan because of its ability to project naval force – in conjunction with the United States – into the Taiwan Strait. Because of its significant and enduring maritime and land force presence in the Asia-Pacific region, the United States is, indeed, a crucial third element in this overall constraining equation.[28]

A 'more harmonious world'

Taking the above points into account, and viewed in the Asian regional context, Chinese leaders' public articulations of the concepts of peaceful rise/peaceful development may thus reflect a wish on the part of the Chinese government to avoid provoking possible developments unfavourable to China's core interests – primarily those bound up with Taiwan. Concerns about domestic political and social fragility are also relevant here. Several observers have noted the connection often made or assumed in official Chinese thinking between perceived domestic vulnerabilities and potential threats from outside.[29] This has been reflected in the linkages frequently made in contemporary Chinese government statements between promoting harmony at home and a more 'harmonious world' internationally.

Official thinking in this area was consolidated in a major policy statement issued by the Chinese government as a 'White Paper' in December 2005. Although a common feature of the political process in many Western states, the release of a public White Paper is a relatively rare event in China. This suggested that the Chinese government regarded the issues which it covered as being especially relevant and important. The White Paper's main theme was summarized thus:

> China persists in its pursuit of harmony and development internally while pursuing peace and development externally; the two

> aspects, closely linked and organically united, are an integrated whole, and will help to build a harmonious world of sustained peace and common prosperity.

The paper was also candid in its description of China as a state with 'a large population, a weak economic foundation and unbalanced development'. In short, it stated that China remained 'the largest developing country in the world'.

There was a notable Confucian flavour throughout the text, most especially in the invocation of Chinese history: 'The Chinese nation has always been a peace-loving one. Chinese culture is a pacific culture. The spirit of the Chinese people has always featured their longing for peace and pursuit of harmony.' Overall, the link between security and stability abroad and development at home was a key theme of the paper. For a major policy statement on behalf (as some might see it) of an emerging superpower, this White Paper's general tenor was notably (and presumably intentionally) self-effacing.[30]

Does the Chinese government's stated commitment to promoting harmony in world politics have substance? One way of measuring its practical impact is to look at China's increasing participation in international organizations and institutions. In this context, probably the most significant event in recent times was its accession to the WTO in 2001, although the 'joining process' can be traced back to the late Mao era. Also pivotal, somewhat earlier, had been China's accession to the United Nations (in place of Taiwan), which accompanied the *rapprochement* with the US in the early 1970s.[31] China's participation in the institutional structures and processes of the international system generally was highly circumscribed during the Mao era, at least from the late 1940s to the early 1970s. It has increased substantially since Deng's time, however. Research by Chenghong Li has shown that, between the early 1970s and the late 1990s, China's membership of international state-based organizations increased from twenty-one to fifty-two, and of international non-governmental organizations from seventy-one to 1,163.[32] China's increasing levels of support for, and participation in, UN peacekeeping and related operations since the 1980s has also been well documented – and analysed in essentially positive terms.[33]

Despite this raw data suggesting a greater willingness on the part of the Chinese government to participate in the existing international system, there has remained some scepticism amongst informed observers about the nature and extent of China's *normative* commitment to its institutions and processes. In a 2001 article, for example, David Shambaugh contended that 'China accepts multilateralism in form, but not in essence'. He cited Chinese passivity, or indeed opposition, 'when it comes to forging or enforcing rules, particularly those that involve punitive sanctions or enforcement inside national borders'.[34]

Over time, however, the balance of opinion amongst analysts has shifted progressively towards the view that the Chinese government has been giving clear indications of an increasing interest in multilateral institutions and processes. This has been coupled with a willingness at least to acquiesce in the outcomes of multilateral negotiations in which other leading states have established and identified important stakes.[35]

Support for these views can be adduced, firstly, from the role played by China in the six-party talks over North Korea's nuclear weapons programmes. Despite occasional self-deprecating remarks by Chinese officials,[36] since 2003 the Chinese government has, on occasion, played a key instrumental role in exerting behind the scenes pressure on its North Korean counterpart to remain within the talks and accept constraints on its nuclear programmes.[37] Few observers contend that the Chinese government has done this for anything other than hard-headed reasons of its own perceived national interests,[38] but that is not the point at issue here. The interesting point, from the perspective of these discussions, is that the Chinese government has increasingly shown a willingness to work with and through a developing multilateral process – and one suggested and promoted by the United States.

A former George W. Bush administration official, Thomas Christensen, has suggested that evolving Chinese attitudes on the North Korean issue may in part be due to that administration's 2005 proposal that China should increasingly act – and in turn be rewarded as – a 'responsible stakeholder' in the international system.[39] Related to this, it is possible to see the evolving Chinese stance as developing both in response to, and in further encouragement of, the Bush administration's own more positive approach to multilateral processes during its second term. This was evidenced, amongst other things, in its support for the six-party framework for North Korea, as discussed in chapter 6.

In another significant development, at the end of 2008, the Chinese government authorized the sending of ships from its navy to join an *ad hoc* international flotilla conducting counter-piracy operations off the coast of Somalia. These operations took place under the authority of the UN Security Council. Of particular importance in this case was the Security Council's authorization to UN member states to use force, if necessary, within Somalia's territorial waters for the purposes of countering piracy.

The Chinese government's support for – and indeed participation in – these operations represented an important departure from what had been a cardinal principle of its attitudes to international relations hitherto: the non-interference by states in the 'internal affairs' of other states (including within their territorial waters).

The fact that China was seeking to protect its own national interests – i.e., the safety of Chinese vessels and nationals in the Gulf of Aden and surrounding waters, and its broader economic and commercial interests in Africa – was not denied. At the same time, official statements argued that the deployment of vessels from the Chinese navy made a practical contribution to the development of a 'more harmonious world'. It was, therefore, something to be welcomed, and not feared, by other states. When the deployment was announced in December 2008, for example, a commentary in the *China Daily* (an English-language state-run newspaper) reflected these twin agendas. It stated: 'China's military participation sends a strong political message to the international community, that a China with its improved economic and military strength is willing to play a larger role in maintaining world peace and security.' At the same time, it was contended that the deployment offered a useful opportunity to test the Chinese navy's developing capabilities, which were of increasing importance as China developed and pursued its own interests in the Asia-Pacific security arena.[40]

A similar message was offered by the *People's Daily* at the time of the sixtieth anniversary of the founding of the Chinese navy in 2009:

> The protection offered by the...fleet safeguards the national interests of China and projects a favourable image of China to the world.... This mission indicates that as a responsible power of the international community, China is fulfilling its promise to advance the construction of a harmonious world, and is taking actions to uphold world peace and boost mutual development. At the same time it is demonstrating to the world that China, currently in the course of peaceful development, is utilizing its own military power to provide 'public goods' to the international community. China is neither pursuing 'gunboat diplomacy' to invade other nations, nor resorting to military power to seek hegemony and expansion.[41]

In explaining their state's increasing engagement with and in multilateral structures and processes, Chinese observers have also argued that this is required in order to mitigate the impact of relative resource weaknesses, especially in comparison with the US. In this context, in 2005, for example, Wang Jisi, a leading Chinese scholar, argued that, notwithstanding 'the tremendous gap between the two countries in national power and international status', the overall commercial, diplomatic and strategic 'pattern of interactions' with the US nonetheless constituted 'a relationship between equals' as far as China was concerned.[42]

These explanatory evaluations are of interest here because of indications that the evolving official attitudes towards international 'interference' with a state's sovereignty, evident in the Somalia operation, might presage a more general and enduring shift in official Chinese thinking and policy. This was suggested in March 2011, when China abstained on, and therefore did not block, the UN Security Council Resolution authorizing the use of military force to prevent and stop the Gaddafi regime from attacking civilians in the context of the Libyan revolutionary war. The Chinese government adopted this stance in spite of the fact that the UN resolution was permissive in sanctioning potential armed action at sea, in the air, and against regime military targets on Libyan territory itself – excluding only the possible deployment of a 'foreign occupation force'.[43]

Harmony and peaceful rise as strategic requirements

The Libya example, following from the Chinese stance on counter-piracy operations off Somalia, raises the question as to whether it can justifiably be argued that a process of socialization in official attitudes and policy is currently under way. This might explain why the Chinese government is apparently becoming increasingly willing, over the longer term, to forsake previously apparently entrenched positions on such issues as the inviolability of state sovereignty, and also to participate constructively in multilateral engagement on a variety of issues. Recently, some analysts have indeed started to advance tentative suggestions along these lines.[44] At the time of writing, however, it would still take a bold observer to assert such a proposition with a significant degree of confidence.[45]

Having said that, the contemporary Chinese concepts of 'harmony' and 'peaceful rise' should not be dismissed out of hand as mere propaganda tools or tactical expedients. It perhaps makes more sense to view them instead as what might be called strategic requirements. The arguments developed in this chapter, together with those advanced in chapter 9, suggest that the Chinese government is sincerely interested in promoting a more 'harmonious world', not out of altruism but because it is in its own interests to do so.

This is the case, in the first instance, because China needs a stable international environment in which to pursue and develop its increasingly global economic, financial and commercial interests, and to secure reliable supplies of energy resources. These discussions also suggest that the Chinese government has perceived a clear link between global harmony (i.e., an international environment of greater stability and reduced risk) and stability at home. The discussions in chapter 9 suggested that, politically and socially, China is a significantly fragile state. Its government cannot risk, therefore, the prospect of instability and disorder in the international arena spilling over into China itself.

This consideration, coupled with China's position as a regionally constrained state, for the reasons discussed earlier, also explains, finally, why it is not probable that the Chinese government will intentionally provoke instability and possible conflict in Asia. This is likely to remain the case, notwithstanding its currently unresolved territorial and maritime disputes with many of its neighbours.

Conclusions: The US, Russia and China in a Changing World

Having explored in the preceding chapters important dimensions of international power, conceptually and in practice, since the end of the Cold War, what can be said in conclusion about the overall nature of power, and the power capacities and relations amongst the three states which have been analysed in this book? In this final section, the key overall findings that have emerged from the research here will be presented and briefly discussed.

The social dimensions of power

The central argument throughout the book has been that power is primarily a social construct. This dimension of power has been relatively neglected in much of the international relations and world politics literature to date. Notable, and welcome, exceptions to the general rule in this respect have been the works of Anne-Marie Slaughter and Martha Finnemore, discussed in chapter 1 and chapter 3, respectively. Slaughter has put forward the interesting idea of 'networked' power as a means of better understanding how it works in an increasingly globalized world. This idea, in turn, has drawn upon older notions of 'structural' power, which were suggested, amongst others, by Susan Strange in the 1980s and 1990s.

Simply occupying a central position in the core structures of international life is not, in itself, sufficient to guarantee power. The position needs to be used in order to orchestrate and facilitate effective bargaining, agreement and consequent action. This will likely involve intensive – and, perhaps, frustrating – diplomatic efforts on the part of the state seeking to operationalize effective social power.

As the discussions in chapter 5 suggested, these were neglected by the George W. Bush administration during much of its first term – to its cost in terms of undermining its ability to operationalize effective (or 'superior') power on key issues. The administration's approach to international politics at that time appeared to be premised on a belief that a combination of material strength (particularly in the military sphere), righteous indignation and widespread international sympathy in the wake of 9/11 should have been sufficient to enable it to act in the international arena effectively as it saw fit. Subsequent experience showed that this was not the case. Indeed, the administration's approach ensured that international sympathy and support were, in fact, quite quickly undermined and dissipated after 2001.

The Bush administration's key mistakes in this respect were, firstly, to premise its post-9/11 campaign overtly on a series of 'take it or leave it' propositions – telling potential partners bluntly that 'you are either with us or with the terrorists', and asserting that its interpretations of core human values were 'non-negotiable'. Even more importantly, the administration seemingly wilfully neglected established international institutions and processes in waging its war on terror: these included NATO, in the case of the early stages of the campaign in Afghanistan in 2001–2, and the UN, in the build-up to the decision to launch the invasion of Iraq in 2003.

The delicate multilateralist balance

The Bush administration did not act without partners in either Afghanistan or Iraq, and in his memoirs Bush appeared irked at suggestions, in view of this fact, that he had acted unilaterally. Indeed, he used uncharacteristically intemperate language in stating that allegations of unilateralism had 'pissed me off'.[1] In both the early Afghan and the Iraqi case, however, the depth and durability of his international support proved to be limited and brittle. This was because his administration had chosen not to invest the time, effort and political capital in the diplomatic give and take that would have been necessary to develop stronger and more genuinely supportive international coalitions.

This reminds us that meaningful multilateralism is not simply about lining up numbers of nominal supporters. It is really about consultation and engagement with other leaders and states (who might not be supporters at the outset) and, through these, engendering a sense of collective agreement on, and stakes in, securing desirable outcomes. In this context, Anne-Marie Slaughter has rightly noted that international social networks 'are not directed and controlled as much as they are managed and orchestrated'.[2] The George W. Bush administration seemed to have little appreciation of this during its early years, although, to its credit, it gave evidence of learning from – and seeking to correct – its mistakes from around 2004–5, as discussed in chapter 6.

The emphasis given in this book to the social dimensions of international power does not mean that its structural aspects are irrelevant. From 2001, the United States was expected to lead the response to the events of 9/11, and not only because its cities had been the targets of the terrorist attacks. Its established central position in the economic, financial and security structures of the international system was instrumental in ensuring that many other states took their own cues from what the US chose to do. The arguments developed here, however, do suggest that the nature and extent of international support for the US is substantially dependent upon the extent to which American leaders, in turn, have shown themselves to be willing to engage in multilateral negotiation and leadership.

The Obama administration and the Libya crisis

Striking the right balance in multilateral institutions and processes is often difficult. The George W. Bush administration undoubtedly erred too far in one direction, by giving the impression that it was not sincerely interested in soliciting the ideas, views and support of others. More recently, however, the Obama administration received criticism in the case of the NATO-led air and naval campaigns against the forces of the Gaddafi regime during the Libyan revolutionary war of 2011 for, allegedly, moving too far in the *opposite* direction. This administration was criticized from amongst its own European NATO allies, both for a perceived reluctance to commit more American strike assets to the air campaign and, more fundamentally, to assume overall strategic and political leadership of the NATO effort. In this context it was accused, allegedly by one of its own senior officials, of 'leading from behind'.[3]

This example suggests that, in practice, effective multilateralism does not necessarily presuppose a relationship of equals. In the Libya case, the US was expected by its allies to lead, as it had been at the time of the Bosnia and Kosovo crises during the 1990s. This expectation held not just amongst its NATO allies, but amongst the international community more generally – as evidenced, in the Libya case, by the absence of opposing votes (including from Russia and China) in the UN Security Council when the authorizing resolution was passed in March 2011. The Libya example also suggests that, when the incumbent American administration is perceived to be failing to fulfil this role, it can be criticized almost as severely as when it is seen to be acting essentially unilaterally.

Of the case studies discussed in this book, the closest that American leaders have probably come to striking the right balance was during the Kosovo crisis of 1998–9, assessed in chapter 4. In this case, the US was, militarily, clearly the dominant player in the NATO air campaign – flying three-quarters of all the strike missions. The Clinton administration also provided overall political and strategic direction, although not without some initial confusion and hesitation. Throughout the campaign, the US worked through NATO command and planning structures – in a lead role, but accepting that compromises would be necessary on issues such as targeting strategy. This closely involved American leadership role was precisely what seemed to critics to be absent from the Libya campaign twelve years later.

The enduring unipolar moment

In 1990, Charles Krauthammer predicted that the post-Cold War 'unipolar moment', which he had proclaimed, would last for at least a generation. Thus far, his foresight has held good. In structural terms – measured both by capabilities and by its central role in the international system – it remains difficult to envisage the US being effectively counterbalanced to the degree and extent necessary to signal a clear shift to a recognizably bipolar, or multipolar, configuration of international power.

A Russian challenge?

Of the two potential challengers considered in this book, it may, at first sight, seem possible that Russia could seek to challenge the US at some point in the future. The arguments developed in chapter 7 suggest that, since the turn of the century, the focus of the Russian government has been on domestic consolidation. The neo-Gorchakovian worldview, discussed subsequently in chapter 8, postulates that, when this process is judged to have strengthened the Russian state sufficiently, it might form the basis for an attempt to relaunch Russia as a more assertive – and potentially truculent – international actor.

This is by no means inevitable, however. To begin with, the Russian state might not be able to develop the resource base necessary to give its leaders sufficient confidence to believe that such a challenge were possible. In this context, it is worth recalling the noteworthy reticence that many Russian officials and analysts have shown towards even the most important element of its current resource base – the export of oil and gas. There is little sense, domestically, of Russia being an 'energy superpower', which suggests a distinct and enduring lack of confidence in the true strength of Russia's material capacities.

Russian leaders have also consistently shown little interest in developing a more important or proactive role for their state in key international networks. Neither have they shown much regard for the value of multilateralism. This has been the case even in organizations and institutions that they themselves have helped to establish. A pertinent example in this context is the Shanghai Cooperation Organization, the members of which were not consulted or even kept informed by Russia during the build-up to its war with Georgia in 2008, and who failed to support its recognition of Abkhazia and South Ossetia thereafter.

Overall, there have, thus far, been few clear signs that Russia is 'concentrating' in the sense in which Foreign Minister Gorchakov used that term in the mid-nineteenth century – i.e., regenerating its strengths prior to launching a determined bid to reclaim former glories. Evidence discussed in chapters 7 and 8 here suggests that, since the 1990s, Russian governments have generally avoided actively frustrating the US on key international issues such as the invasion of Iraq. If Russia was seeking to play a more assertive international role, it is likely that the opposite would have been the case.

The core Putinist concept of 'sovereign democracy' rests on the premise that Russia should develop as one of a handful of truly sovereign states in the international arena, in the sense that it becomes capable, in the final analysis, of looking after itself without undue reliance on others. This approach may, therefore, be predicated on equipping Russia to pursue a strategy of international autarky. This would entail limited engagement internationally, mainly to ensure that Russia's core interests are not seriously threatened.

These interests lie mainly in ensuring the continued territorial integrity of the patchwork quilt that is the Russian Federation and, closely related in Russian minds, establishing and maintaining a Russian sphere of influence over most – if not all – of the other post-Soviet states. The two occasions on which Russian leaders have resorted to the use of armed force since the end of the Cold War have both been local and defensively motivated. The first was the series of campaigns against violent separatist movements in the southern Russian republic of Chechnya during the 1990s. The second was the military intervention in Georgia in August 2008. This latter took place shortly after an apparently clear statement from the

US and its NATO allies that envisaged Georgia (and Ukraine) joining NATO. The Russian government was, in consequence, seeking to give the clearest possible warning that there were regional 'red lines' that the US and NATO should not attempt to cross.

In this context, Andrei Shleifer and Daniel Treisman have advanced the interesting and persuasive argument that contemporary Russia is *already* autarkic to a large extent *vis-à-vis* the United States. This is the case because the US and Russia share few international interests, and because the US offers little that Russia actually wants – other than an understanding that it will not interfere in Russia's domestic sovereign affairs or within its regional sphere of influence. Russian leaders, therefore, are likely to be content with *regional* primacy in the former Soviet area in exchange for not seriously interfering with important US stakes and interests elsewhere in the world.[4]

A Chinese challenge?

China is also unlikely to make a serious challenge to American international primacy in the foreseeable future. This is fundamentally because, whatever its leaders might wish, China is, as argued in chapters 9 and 10, a constrained state. Indeed, there are several levels of effective constraints which prevent China from acting more assertively in the international arena.

The first is domestic, and the constant requirement to focus on the enduring fragilities and instabilities of the social and political order at home. The second is regional, with China being effectively hemmed in by continuing problems in its bilateral relations with both Japan and India, and also by the continuing American military presence in the Asia-Pacific region.

A final self-constraining factor is the desire of Chinese leaders, increasingly evident since the 1970s, to enhance their state's participation in the institutions and processes of the established international system. As this has occurred, they have shown themselves willing to make specific compromises, for example, in order to gain admission to the World Trade Organization in 2001. More generally, there is evidence that China's leaders are modifying their traditional stances on key international issues.

Since the end of the Cold War, an evolving understanding has become evident on what has come to be called the 'Responsibility to Protect' (R2P) – codified by the UN General Assembly in 2005. Under R2P, the UN Security Council may decide to authorize an international intervention, including by military force, if it determines that a state is failing to prevent significant violations of the human rights of its own citizens. Its decision not to block the March 2011 UN resolution authorizing what was, effectively, an R2P action in Libya suggests that the Chinese government may have begun to accommodate itself to an emerging and important international norm in this key area.

In a similar context, it has been suggested that China's leaders have begun responding to the George W. Bush administration's 2005 'invitation' to take up a role as a 'responsible stakeholder' in the established international system.[5] The suggestion, made public by then Deputy Secretary of State Robert Zoellick, was for China effectively to support the US-centred system of liberal hegemony in exchange for taking up an increasingly important and influential role within it.

In practice, and given their legacy of substantial self-imposed international isolation during much of the Mao era, contemporary Chinese leaders have thus far remained noticeably reticent about developing such a role. Hence, China has often seemed a comparatively passive and uninvolved international actor, even in response to major crises such as those over Kosovo, Iraq and Libya. The Maoist legacy has, therefore, been another important self-constraining influence, although perhaps not one that will endure to the same extent over the longer term.

The United States in a continuing unipolar world

In a continuing unipolar world, the US, as noted earlier, is expected to give a lead in responding to important international challenges. In 2010, Secretary of State Hillary Clinton argued that such challenges 'cannot be solved unless a nation is willing to accept the responsibility of mobilizing action', adding that 'the United States is that nation'.[6] The negative consequences of the United States' perceived failure to do that effectively in the case of Libya in the following year suggests that Clinton was right in this respect.

The key challenge for the US should not, therefore, be deciding whether or not to lead on such matters, but *how* to do so. If unipolarity is considered, as Martha Finnemore convincingly suggests that it should be, as at least as much a social construct as a material one, this becomes a vital question. The evidence discussed in this book strongly suggests that the kind of dismissive unilateralism practised by the George W. Bush administration during its first term weakens American power. On the other hand, failing to give a clear lead, as in the case of Obama and Libya, can have the same effect. Hence, American leaders are faced with the constant challenge of striking a delicate balance. Responding effectively entails working through multilateral processes and mechanisms, whilst at the same time acting as the main facilitator, coordinator and leader of international discussions and subsequent action.

The American leadership record since the early 1990s has been uneven. Thus, there have been examples where it has proved to be relatively effective (the 1991 Iraq War, the Bosnia civil war from 1995 and the 1999 Kosovo conflict), those where it has been deficient (the 2003 Iraq War) and those in which the evidence thus far is inconclusive (the intervention in Afghanistan from 2001). The primary task for the United States in the post-Cold War world has not been – and probably will not be – to fend off challengers to its international primacy. Rather, it is to try, preferably through intentional policy or, failing that, a timely process of pragmatic corrective learning, to find better and more effective ways of making unipolar multilateral leadership work, both in its own interests and in those of the international community generally.

Notes

Introduction

1 Michel Foucault, *Power* (*Essential Works of Foucault 1954–1984*, Vol. 3), ed. James Faubion (London: Penguin, 2002), p. 17.
2 Joseph Nye, *Bound to Lead: The Changing Nature of American Power* (New York: Basic Books, 1990), p. 25.
3 Paul Kennedy, *The Rise and Fall of the Great Powers: Economic Change and Military Conflict from 1500 to 2000* (London: Fontana, 1988), p. 290.
4 John Mearsheimer, *The Tragedy of Great Power Politics* (New York: Norton, 2001), p. 55.
5 John Rothgeb, *Defining Power: Force and Influence in the Contemporary International System* (New York: St Martin's Press, 1993), p. 17.
6 For an early articulation of this view in the international relations literature, see A. F. K. Organski, *World Politics* (New York: Knopf, 1960), p. 305.

Chapter 1 Understanding Power

1 Talcott Parsons, *Politics and Social Structure* (New York: Free Press, 1969), ch. 14.
2 These types of criticism of the power/money comparison have been put forward by, *inter alia*: David Baldwin, Stefano Guzzini and Joseph Nye. See David Baldwin, 'Power analysis and world politics: new trends versus old tendencies', *World Politics* 31/2 (1979), pp. 165–6; Stefano Guzzini, 'The concept of power: a constructivist analysis', in Felix Berenskoetter and M. J. Williams, eds, *Power in World Politics* (Abingdon: Routledge, 2007), p. 35; and Joseph Nye, *The Future of Power* (New York: PublicAffairs, 2011), pp. 3–5.
3 Parsons, *Politics and Social Structure*, p. 205.
4 Max Weber, *Economy and Society: An Outline of Interpretive Sociology*, ed. Guenther Roth and Claus Wittich (Berkeley: University of California Press, 1978), I, 1.
5 In Weber's view, 'action is "social" insofar as its subjective meaning takes account of the behavior of others and is thereby oriented in its course.' Ibid.
6 On the importance of mutuality in Max Weber's analysis of money, see ibid., II, 6.
7 See Stephen Krasner, *Sovereignty: Organized Hypocrisy* (Princeton, NJ: Princeton University Press, 1999).
8 This Article both prohibits 'the threat or use of force' by any state against another and forbids UN intervention in 'matters which are essentially within the domestic jurisdiction' of any state. See *Charter of the United Nations and Statute of the International Court of Justice* (New York: United Nations, 1945).
9 Hans Morgenthau, *Politics among Nations: The Struggle for Power and Peace* (brief edn, New York: McGraw-Hill, 1993), p. 29.
10 Jaap Nobel, 'Morgenthau's struggle with power: the theory of power politics and the Cold War', *Review of International Studies* 21/1 (1995), p. 63.
11 See Morgenthau, *Politics among Nations*, ch. 16.

12 Torbjørn Knutsen, *The Rise and Fall of World Orders* (Manchester: Manchester University Press, 1999), p. 2.
13 See the series of articles published in a special issue of the journal *International Organization* 36/2 (1982).
14 Hedley Bull, *The Anarchical Society: A Study of Order in World Politics* (Basingstoke: Macmillan, 1977).
15 Dan Snow, 'Syria's uprising will not be a rerun of Tunisia', *The Times*, 20 April 2011. See also 'The protest network', *The Times*, 2 February 2011.
16 Robert Keohane and Joseph Nye, 'Power and interdependence in the information age', *Foreign Affairs* 77/5 (1998), p. 94.
17 Anne-Marie Slaughter, 'America's edge: power in the networked century', *Foreign Affairs* 88/1 (2009), pp. 94–113.
18 Dennis Wrong, *Power: Its Forms, Bases, and Uses* (New Brunswick, NJ: Transaction, 2004), p. xxii.
19 See, *inter alia*, William Wohlforth, 'Unipolar stability: the rules of power analysis', *Harvard International Review*, 8 July 2007, http://hir.harvard.edu/print/a-tilted-balance/unipolar-stability (accessed January 2011).
20 Steven Lukes, *Power: A Radical View* (2nd edn, Basingstoke: Palgrave, 2005), p. 70.
21 Antonio Gramsci, *Selections from the Prison Notebooks of Antonio Gramsci*, ed. Quintin Hoare and Geoffrey Nowell Smith (London: Lawrence & Wishart, 2005), p. 171.
22 C. Wright Mills, *The Power Elite* (London: Oxford University Press, 1956), p. 9.
23 Hans Morgenthau, 'From great powers to superpowers', in Brian Porter, ed., *International Politics 1919–1969* (London: Oxford University Press, 1972), p. 129.
24 Klaus Knorr, *Power and Wealth: The Political Economy of International Power* (Basingstoke: Macmillan, 1973), esp. pp. 14ff. Nearly twenty years later, in 1990, Joseph Nye grappled with the same issue – what he called the problem of 'power conversion' – when introducing his concept of 'soft power'. See Nye, *Bound to Lead: The Changing Nature of American Power* (New York: Basic Books, 1990), p. 27.
25 Michael Barnett and Raymond Duvall, 'Power in international politics', *International Organization* 59/1 (2005), p. 46.
26 For a brief but helpful discussion of the complicating impact of will on attempts to define power, see Susan Strange, *The Retreat of the State: The Diffusion of Power in the World Economy* (Cambridge: Cambridge University Press, 1996), pp. 17–20.
27 Bertrand Russell, *Power: A New Social Analysis* (London: George Allen & Unwin, 1938), p. 35.
28 Nye, *The Future of Power*, p. 7.
29 See, *inter alia*, Lukes, *Power: A Radical View*, p. 70.
30 Nye, *The Future of Power*, p. 7.
31 Wrong, *Power: Its Forms, Bases, and Uses*, p. xxi.

Chapter 2 Power Resources

1 Robert Dahl, *Who Governs? Democracy and Power in an American City* (2nd edn, New Haven, CT: Yale University Press, 2005), p. 226.
2 Ibid., p. 271.
3 Hans Morgenthau, 'From great powers to superpowers', in Brian Porter, ed., *International Politics 1919–1969* (London: Oxford University Press, 1972), p. 133.
4 Inis Claude, *Power and International Relations* (New York: Random House, 1962), p. 6.
5 See John Mueller, *Retreat from Doomsday: The Obsolescence of Major War* (New York: Basic Books, 1990).
6 See, *inter alia*, A. F. K. Organski, *World Politics* (New York: Knopf, 1960), pp. 197–8.

7 For Kennedy's treatment of this issue, see *The Rise and Fall of the Great Powers: Economic Change and Military Conflict from 1500 to 2000* (London: Fontana, 1988), pp. 255ff. See also Ronald Tammen et al., *Power Transitions: Strategies for the 21st Century* (New York: Chatham House, 2000), pp. 18–19.

8 See Colin Gray, *Hard Power and Soft Power: The Utility of Military Force as an Instrument of Policy in the 21st Century* (Carlisle, PA: Strategic Studies Institute, US Army War College, 2011).

9 This can be measured in terms of statistical preponderance, such as percentage share of global Gross Domestic Product, control and direction over specific commodities such as oil and gas, or a state's position in global financial and currency markets.

10 Susan Strange, *The Retreat of the State: The Diffusion of Power in the World Economy* (Cambridge: Cambridge University Press, 1996), p. 53.

11 Tammen et al., *Power Transitions*, p. 16.

12 Joseph Nye, *Soft Power: The Means to Success in World Politics* (New York: PublicAffairs, 2004), p. x.

13 Ibid., p. ix.

14 Jeffrey Hart, 'Three approaches to the measurement of power in international relations', *International Organization* 30/2 (1976), pp. 291–2.

15 Talcott Parsons, *Politics and Social Structure* (New York: Free Press, 1969), p. 335.

16 Steven Lukes, *Power: A Radical View* (2nd edn, Basingstoke: Palgrave, 2005), p. 27.

17 Ibid., pp. 35–7.

18 Martin Wight, *Power Politics* (Harmondsworth: Penguin, 1986), p. 27. See also Klaus Knorr, *Power and Wealth: The Political Economy of International Power* (Basingstoke: Macmillan, 1973), ch. 1.

19 David Baldwin, 'Power analysis and world politics: new trends versus old tendencies', *World Politics* 31/2 (1979), pp. 183–6.

20 Joseph Nye, 'Notes for a soft-power research agenda', in Felix Berenskoetter and M. J. Williams, eds, *Power in World Politics* (Abingdon: Routledge, 2007), p. 162. For examples of media commentary taking an inclusive view of soft power, see, *inter alia*, Simon Tisdall, 'Soft power can crack hard cases', *The Guardian*, 6 May 2005; and Will Hutton, 'Soft power can be a match for hard men', *The Observer*, 8 April 2007.

21 For a similar critique, see Gray, *Hard Power and Soft Power*, pp. 28–39.

22 Problems of operationalizing and measuring soft power are amongst the major underlying themes of many of the essays in Berenskoetter and Williams, *Power in World Politics*.

23 See, *inter alia*, Ian Clark, 'Legitimacy in a global order', *Review of International Studies* 29 (2003), p. 78; and Herfried Münkler, *Empires: The Logic of World Domination from Ancient Rome to the United States* (Cambridge: Polity, 2007), p. 133.

24 Hutton, 'Soft power can be a match for hard men'.

25 See Mills's essay 'On knowledge and power', reprinted in *Power, Politics & People: The Collected Essays of C. Wright Mills*, ed. Irving Louis Horowitz (Oxford: Oxford University Press, 1967), pp. 599–613.

26 Wendt's most important published elaboration of social constructivist thinking is his *Social Theory of International Politics* (Cambridge: Cambridge University Press, 1999); the quotation cited appears on p. 135. See also Robert Cooper, *The Breaking of Nations: Order and Chaos in the Twenty-First Century* (London: Atlantic Books, 2003), pp. 127–38.

27 Torbjørn Knutsen, *The Rise and Fall of World Orders* (Manchester: Manchester University Press, 1999). See also the comparable analysis of Robert Pastor, who in 1999 argued that 'the power to define norms may be as important in the next century as the power to draw the boundaries of colonies was in the last'. Robert Pastor, 'The Great Powers in the twentieth century', in Pastor, ed., *A Century's Journey: How the Great Powers Shape the World* (New York: Basic Books, 1999), p. 18.

28 Particularly insightful discussions of legitimacy in the international context can be found in Ian Clark, *Legitimacy in International Society* (Oxford: Oxford University Press, 2005); and Andrew Hurrell, 'Legitimacy and the use of force: can the circle be squared?', *Review of International Studies* 31 (2005), pp. 15–32.

29 Barry Hindess, *Discourses of Power: From Hobbes to Foucault* (Oxford: Blackwell, 1996).

30 Dennis Wrong, *Power: Its Forms, Bases, and Uses* (New Brunswick, NJ: Transaction, 2004), p. 122.

31 Max Weber, *Economy and Society: An Outline of Interpretive Sociology*, ed. Guenther Roth and Claus Wittich (Berkeley: University of California Press, 1978), I, 16.

32 Ibid., X, 3.

33 The three are summarized ibid.

34 Russell, *Power: A New Social Analysis*, p. 39 and ch. VI.

35 Parsons, *Politics and Social Structure*, p. 371; C. Wright Mills, *Power, Politics & People: The Collected Essays of C. Wright Mills*, ed. Irving Louis Horowitz (Oxford: Oxford University Press, 1967), p. 23. See also Harold Lasswell and Abraham Kaplan, *Power and Society* (New Haven, CT: Yale University Press, 1950), pp. 133ff.

36 Martin Wight, *International Theory: The Three Traditions*, ed. Gabriele Wright and Brian Porter (Leicester: Leicester University Press, 1991), p. 99.

37 Wendt, *Social Theory of International Politics*, p. 208.

38 Stanley Hoffmann, *Force, Legitimacy, and Order* (Washington, DC: Brookings Institution, 2005).

39 David Beetham, *The Legitimation of Power* (Basingstoke: Macmillan, 1991), p. 8.

40 Mills, *Power, Politics & People*, p. 23.

41 Clark, *Legitimacy in International Society*, p. 186.

42 The Brezhnev Doctrine was not formally stated by then Soviet leader Leonid Brezhnev himself. Its premises were first set out by a relatively junior party official in the newspaper *Pravda* in September 1968. See *Pravda*, 26 September 1968; trans. in *The Current Digest of the Soviet Press* XX/39 (1968), p. 10.

43 For further discussion, see Paul Latawski and Martin A. Smith, *The Kosovo Crisis and the Evolution of Post-Cold War European Security* (Manchester: Manchester University Press, 2003).

44 Beetham, *The Legitimation of Power*, p. 35.

45 See Richard Ned Lebow and Robert Kelly, 'Thucydides and hegemony: Athens and the United States', *Review of International Studies* 27/4 (2001), pp. 593–609.

46 Richard Ned Lebow, 'The power of persuasion', in Berenskoetter and Williams, *Power in World Politics*, p. 133.

47 Thucydides, *The History of the Peloponnesian War*, trans. Richard Crawley (London: Longmans, Green, 1874), V, 89.

48 For a persuasive elaboration of this interpretation, see David Bedford and Thom Workman, 'The tragic reading of the Thucydidean tragedy', *Review of International Studies* 27/1 (2001), pp. 51–67. See also Lebow and Kelly, 'Thucydides and hegemony', pp. 596–603.

49 Thucydides wrote that his account of the various speeches and dialogues was not intended to be read as a straightforward verbatim narrative: 'My habit has been to make the speakers say what was in my opinion demanded of them by the various occasions, of course adhering as closely as possible to the general sense of what they really said.' Thus the *History* can be read as a kind of morality play, based on real-life events but scripted so as to draw out what the author considered to be essential truths. Thucydides, *The History of the Peloponnesian War*, I, 22.

50 Ibid., I, 120.

51 Ibid., III, 10–11.

52 For an example of this, see ibid., I, 95–7.

53 Ibid., V, 95.

54 Lebow and Kelly, 'Thucydides and hegemony', p. 603.

55 'Do international relations precede or follow (logically) fundamental social relations?' Gramsci asked rhetorically, adding: 'There can be no doubt that they follow.' Gramsci, *Selections from the Prison Notebooks of Antonio Gramsci*, ed. Quintin Hoare and Geoffrey Nowell Smith (London: Lawrence & Wishart, 2005), p. 176.

56 Foremost amongst these scholars has been Robert Cox. For an introduction to his thinking in this area, see 'Gramsci, hegemony and international relations: an essay in method', *Millennium: Journal of International Studies* 12/2 (1983), pp. 162–75.

57 Gramsci, *Selections from the Prison Notebooks*, p. 161.

58 See the editor's introduction in Lynne Lawner, ed. and trans., *Antonio Gramsci: Letters from Prison* (London: Jonathan Cape, 1975), p. 42.

59 Gramsci, *Selections from the Prison Notebooks*, pp. 169–70.

60 See Cox, 'Gramsci, hegemony and international relations', pp. 171ff.

61 Michel Foucault, *Power (Essential Works of Foucault 1954–1984*, Vol. 3), ed. James Faubion (London: Penguin, 2002), p. 341. The essay from which this quotation is taken offers perhaps the best general introduction to Foucault's various efforts to conceptualize power. It is reprinted in full as 'The subject and power', ibid., pp. 326–48.

62 Michel Foucault, *Discipline and Punish: The Birth of the Prison* (London: Penguin, 1991), p. 194. See also Foucault, *Power*, p. 120.

63 See Foucault, *Power*, pp. 206–7.

64 Foucault's articulation and development of this concept is reprinted ibid., pp. 298–311.

Chapter 3 Hegemony, Unipolarity and the US

1 Charles Kindleberger, *The World in Depression 1929–1939* (London: Allen Lane, 1973).

2 Useful introductions to the debates about hegemonic stability generally can be found in Robert Keohane, *After Hegemony: Cooperation and Discord in the World Political Economy* (Princeton, NJ: Princeton University Press, 1984); and Duncan Snidal, 'The limits of hegemonic stability theory', *International Organization* 39/4 (1985), pp. 579–614.

3 Robert Gilpin, 'The theory of hegemonic war', *Journal of Interdisciplinary History* 18/4 (1988), pp. 591–613.

4 Walter Lippmann, *US Foreign Policy* (London: Hamish Hamilton, 1943), pp. 5–6.

5 William Fox, *The Super-Powers: The United States, Britain and the Soviet Union: Their Responsibility for Peace* (New York: Harcourt, Brace, 1944).

6 *Charter of the United Nations* (New York: United Nations, 1945), Article 24.

7 For an example of such use, see, *inter alia*, Samuel Huntington, 'Coping with the Lippmann gap', *Foreign Affairs* 66/3 (1987–8), pp. 453–77.

8 Paul Kennedy, *The Rise and Fall of the Great Powers: Economic Change and Military Conflict from 1500 to 2000* (London: Fontana, 1988), p. 81.

9 Ibid., p. 193.

10 Ernst Haas, 'The balance of power: prescription, concept, or propaganda?', *World Politics* 5/4 (1953), pp. 442–77.

11 Quoted in Deepak Lal, *In Praise of Empires: Globalization and Order* (Basingstoke: Palgrave, 2004), p. 211. Lal cites G. Schwarzenberger as the original source of the phrase.

12 Eric Robinson, 'American empire? Ancient reflections on modern American power', *Classical World* 99/1 (2005), p. 47.

13 Charles Maier, *Among Empires: American Ascendancy and its Predecessors* (Cambridge, MA: Harvard University Press, 2006), p. 63.

14 John Mearsheimer, *The Tragedy of Great Power Politics* (New York: Norton, 2001), p. 40.

15 Ibid., p. 41.
16 Ibid., p. 170.
17 Thucydides, *The History of the Peloponnesian War*, trans. Richard Crawley (London: Longmans, Green, 1874), I, 120.
18 See, *inter alia*, John Ikenberry, 'Liberalism and empire: logics of order in the American unipolar age', *Review of International Studies* 30/4 (2004), pp. 609–30; and Ikenberry, 'Power and liberal order: America's postwar world order in transition', *International Relations of the Asia-Pacific* 5/2 (2005), pp. 133–52.
19 Thucydides, *The History of the Peloponnesian War*, V, 89.
20 Christopher Layne, 'The "poster child for offensive realism": America as a global hegemon', *Security Studies* 12/2 (2002–3), pp. 131–2.
21 Chalmers Johnson, *The Sorrows of Empire: Militarism, Secrecy, and the End of the Republic* (London: Verso, 2006), p. 188.
22 See ibid. For discussion specifically in the NATO context, see also Dan Smith, *Pressure: How America Runs NATO* (London: Bloomsbury, 1989).
23 Ikenberry, 'Power and liberal order', p. 140.
24 This phrase was coined by Geir Lundestad. See his 'Empire by invitation? The United States and Western Europe, 1945–1952', *Journal of Peace Research* 23/3 (1986), pp. 263–77. See also John Ikenberry, 'Rethinking the origins of American hegemony', *Political Science Quarterly* 104/3 (1989), pp. 375–400.
25 See, *inter alia*, *Foreign Relations of the United States 1948* (Washington, DC: US Government Printing Office, 1974), III, pp. 11, 287.
26 *Foreign Relations of the United States 1949* (Washington, DC: US Government Printing Office, 1975), IV, pp. 485, 491–3.
27 See Earl Ravenal, 'Europe without America: the erosion of NATO', *Foreign Affairs* 63/5 (1985), p. 1026.
28 William Fox, 'The super-powers then and now', *International Journal* 35 (1980), p. 434.
29 Cees Wiebes and Bert Zeeman, ' "I don't need your handkerchiefs": Holland's experience of crisis consultation in NATO', *International Affairs* 66/1 (1990), pp. 98–9.
30 Ibid., p. 101.
31 Dirk Stikker, 'NATO and its smaller members', *Orbis* 13/1 (1969), p. 328. Stikker was secretary-general of NATO in the early 1960s.
32 Denis Healey, *The Time of my Life* (London: Penguin, 1990), pp. 431–2.
33 Helmut Schmidt, 'Saving the Western alliance', *New York Review of Books*, 31 May 1984, pp. 25–7.
34 For an example of such a view see Smith, *Pressure*.
35 The key work in this respect is Thomas Risse-Kappen, *Cooperation among Democracies: The European Influence on US Foreign Policy* (Princeton, NJ: Princeton University Press, 1995).
36 Quoted in *Department of State Bulletin* 69/1792 (1973), p. 529. See also Richard Ned Lebow, 'The power of persuasion', in Felix Berenskoetter and M. J. Williams, eds, *Power in World Politics* (Abingdon: Routledge, 2007), pp. 133–4.
37 John Gerard Ruggie, 'Multilateralism: the anatomy of an institution', in Ruggie, ed., *Multilateralism Matters: The Theory and Praxis of an Institutional Form* (New York: Columbia University Press, 1993), p. 11.
38 David Calleo, 'NATO's middle course', *Foreign Policy* 69 (1987–8), p. 144.
39 For an excellent analysis of Western European views and influence on the US during the Cuban crisis, see Risse-Kappen, *Cooperation among Democracies*, ch. 6.
40 There is a huge literature on the 1980s nuclear debates. For the author's own analysis of NATO decision-making on this issue, see Martin A. Smith, *NATO in the First Decade after the Cold War* (Dordrecht: Kluwer Academic, 2000), ch. 2.

41 Interview with Chňoupek, in Gabriel Partos, *The World that Came in from the Cold* (London: Royal Institute of International Affairs/BBC World Service, 1993), p. 117.
42 John Lewis Gaddis, *We Now Know: Rethinking Cold War History* (Oxford: Oxford University Press, 1997), p. 219.
43 Stephen Walt, *The Origins of Alliances* (Ithaca, NY: Cornell University Press, 1987), pp. 289–91.
44 William Wohlforth, 'The stability of a unipolar world', *International Security* 24/1 (1999), p. 9.
45 Samuel Huntington, 'The lonely superpower', *Foreign Affairs* 78/2 (1999), pp. 35–49.
46 Huntington used this formulation in testimony before the US Senate Committee on Foreign Relations in November 1990. See Senate Foreign Relations Committee, *Relations in a Multipolar World*, 101st Congress, Second Session (Washington, DC: US Government Printing Office, 1991), p. 185.
47 Stephen Brooks and William Wohlforth, 'American primacy in perspective', *Foreign Affairs* 81/4 (2002), p. 21.
48 Charles Krauthammer, 'The unipolar moment revisited', *The National Interest* 70 (2002–3), p. 6.
49 Charles Krauthammer, 'The unipolar moment', *Foreign Affairs* 70/1 (1990–1), pp. 23–33. Krauthammer's title was rather misleading, as he actually assumed that the so-called moment was likely to last for 'another generation or so'.
50 Harold Lasswell and Abraham Kaplan, *Power and Society* (New Haven, CT: Yale University Press, 1950), p. 255.
51 See Kenneth Waltz, *Theory of International Politics* (New York: McGraw-Hill, 1979); and Waltz, 'Structural realism after the Cold War', *International Security* 25/1 (2000), pp. 5–41.
52 Torbjørn Knutsen, *The Rise and Fall of World Orders* (Manchester: Manchester University Press, 1999), p. 210.
53 Martha Finnemore, 'Legitimacy, hypocrisy, and the social structure of unipolarity', *World Politics* 61/1 (2009), pp. 58–61.
54 Wohlforth, 'The stability of a unipolar world', p. 7.
55 Ibid., p. 9.
56 Finnemore, 'Legitimacy, hypocrisy, and the social structure of unipolarity', p. 68.
57 John Lewis Gaddis, 'Grand strategy in the second term', *Foreign Affairs* 84/1 (2005), p. 6.

Chapter 4   The Multipolar Moment?

1 Charles Krauthammer, 'The unipolar moment', *Foreign Affairs* 70/1 (1990–1).
2 See, *inter alia*, John Mueller, 'A new Concert of Europe', *Foreign Policy* 77 (1989–90), pp. 3–16; Charles Kupchan and Clifford Kupchan, 'Concerts, collective security, and the future of Europe', *International Security* 16/1 (1991), pp. 114–61; Richard Rosecrance, 'A new concert of powers', *Foreign Affairs* 71/2 (1992), pp. 64–82; and Philip Zelikow, 'The new Concert of Europe', *Survival* 34/2 (1992), pp. 12–30.
3 Robert Jervis, 'From balance to concert: a study of international security cooperation', *World Politics* 38/1 (1985), p. 59.
4 Kenneth Waltz, 'The stability of a bipolar world', *Daedalus* 43/3 (1964), pp. 881–909.
5 See Kenneth Waltz, 'The emerging structure of international politics', *International Security* 18/2 (1993), pp. 44–79; and Waltz, 'Structural realism after the Cold War', *International Security* 25/1 (2000), pp. 5–41.
6 Ronald Steel, *Temptations of a Superpower* (Cambridge, MA: Harvard University Press, 1995).

7 David Calleo, 'NATO's middle course', *Foreign Policy* 69 (1987–8), p. 144.
8 See 'On top of the world?', *The Economist*, 9 March 1991, p. 15.
9 Krauthammer, 'The unipolar moment', p. 25.
10 'Why it should matter to Americans that their actions get a Security Council nod from, say, Deng Xiaoping and the butchers of Tiananmen Square is beyond me', he wrote, before adding: 'but to many Americans it matters.' Ibid., p. 26.
11 Resolution 1441 (2002), www.unhcr.org/refworld/docid/3dda0f634.html (accessed May 2011).
12 Krauthammer, 'The unipolar moment', p. 25.
13 George H. W. Bush and Brent Scowcroft, *A World Transformed* (New York: Knopf, 1998), pp. 399–400.
14 'US strategy plan calls for insuring no rivals develop', *New York Times*, 8 March 1992.
15 'Pentagon drops goal of blocking new superpowers', *New York Times*, 24 May 1992. See also Alberto Coll, 'America as the grand facilitator', *Foreign Policy* 87 (1992), p. 51.
16 Poos quoted in 'War in Europe', *The Economist*, 6 July 1991, p. 11; and Delors in Noel Malcolm, 'The case against "Europe"', *Foreign Affairs* 74/2 (1995), p. 68.
17 Christopher quoted in 'Bosnia: now for the hard part', *Independent on Sunday*, 8 October 1995; Perry in 'Clinton team starts Congress troops plea', *Financial Times*, 18 October 1995; and Clinton in *Weekly Compilation of Presidential Documents* 31/48 (1995), p. 2062.
18 See Tim Judah, *Kosovo: War and Revenge* (New Haven, CT: Yale University Press, 2000), p. 269; and Jan Hoekema, *NATO Policy and NATO Strategy in Light of the Kosovo Conflict*, North Atlantic Assembly Defence and Security Committee, www.nato-pa.int/archivedpub/comrep/1999/as252dsc-e.asp (accessed October 2011).
19 'Alliance general cleared to bomb at will', *The Times*, 3 April 1999. See also Robert Jordan, 'NATO as a political organization', in S. Victor Papacosma, Sean Kay and Mark R. Rubin, eds, *NATO after Fifty Years* (Wilmington, DE: Scholarly Resources, 2001), p. 96.
20 P. Rudolf, 'Germany and the Kosovo conflict', in P. Martin and M. Brawley, eds, *Alliance Politics, Kosovo, and NATO's War: Allied Force or Forced Allies?* (Basingstoke: Palgrave, 2000), p. 138.
21 See James Thomas, *The Military Challenges of Transatlantic Coalitions*, Adelphi Paper no. 333 (London: International Institute for Strategic Studies, 2000), pp. 47–8.
22 On France, see 'Kosovo air chief says French put pilots in danger', *Daily Telegraph*, 22 October 1999; and 'USA claims France hindered raids', *Jane's Defence Weekly*, 27 October 1999, p. 3. On the UK, see House of Commons Select Committee on Defence, *Lessons of Kosovo*, Vol. 2: *Minutes of Evidence* (London: The Stationery Office, 2000), para. 90.
23 Quoted in House Armed Services Committee, *United States Policy toward Federal Republic of Yugoslavia*, 106th Congress, First Session (Washington, DC: US Government Printing Office, 1999), p. 40.
24 For Cook, see 'Former peacenik Cook warms to heat of battle', *The Times*, 30 March 1999; and for McCain, 'America's hawks go into hiding', *Sunday Times*, 4 April 1999.
25 *Kosovo/Operation Allied Force After-Action Report* (Washington, DC: Department of Defense, 2000), p. 1.
26 Despite the suggestions during the 2000 campaign that the US would cease to contribute militarily in Kosovo, US troops were deployed there throughout the Bush administration's two terms. In 2011, nearly 800 American troops remained committed to NATO's Kosovo Force. See http://www.nato.int/kfor/structur/nations/placemap/kfor_placemat.pdf (accessed October 2011).
27 Quoted in Anton La Guardia, '1,000 US troops to leave Bosnia', *Daily Telegraph*, 16 March 2001, www.telegraph.co.uk/news/worldnews/northamerica/usa/1326680/1000-US-troops-to-leave-Bosnia.html (accessed May 2011).
28 See *The Military Balance 2011* (London: International Institute for Strategic Studies, 2011), pp. 67–8.

29 See 'To Paris, U.S. looks like a "hyperpower"', *International Herald Tribune*, 5 February 1999.
30 Clinton set the trend by using the phrase twice in key speeches in the first month of his second term. See *20.01.97 Text: President Clinton's Inaugural Address* and *04.02.97 Text: Clinton's State of the Union Address* (both texts supplied to the author by the Reference Center at the US Embassy in London).
31 Quoted in David Calleo, *Follies of Power: America's Unipolar Fantasy* (Cambridge: Cambridge University Press, 2009), p. 8 n. 15.

Chapter 5 A New Era?

1 In an address to a joint session of Congress ten days after the 9/11 attacks, Bush declared that, 'on September the 11th, enemies of freedom committed an act of war against our country'. He further asserted: 'From this day forward, any nation that continues to harbor or support terrorism will be regarded by the United States as a hostile regime.' Address to a joint session of Congress and the American People, 21 September 2001, http://merln.ndu.edu/archivepdf/afghanistan/WH/20010920-8.pdf (accessed October 2011).
2 See Ivo Daalder and James Lindsay, *America Unbound: The Bush Revolution in Foreign Policy* (Washington, DC: Brookings Institution, 2003).
3 See John Newhouse, *Imperial America: The Bush Assault on the World Order* (New York: Knopf, 2003). See also David Calleo, *Follies of Power: America's Unipolar Fantasy* (Cambridge: Cambridge University Press, 2009).
4 Anne Deighton, 'The eleventh of September and beyond: NATO', in Lawrence Freedman, ed., *Superterrorism: Policy Responses* (Oxford: Blackwell, 2002), pp. 119–20.
5 Quoted in Ivo Daalder, 'The end of Atlanticism', *Survival* 45/2 (2003), p. 155.
6 John Kampfner, *Blair's Wars* (London: Free Press, 2003), p. 117.
7 Philip Gordon, 'NATO after 11 September', *Survival* 43/4 (2001–2), p. 92.
8 The first of these – Operation Active Endeavor – remains ongoing. The second – Operation Eagle Assist – was ended in May 2002.
9 David Brown, '"The war on terrorism would not be possible without NATO": a critique', in Martin A. Smith, ed., *Where is NATO Going?* (Abingdon: Routledge, 2006), pp. 28–9.
10 Gordon, 'NATO after 11 September', p. 93.
11 The North Atlantic Treaty, reprinted in *NATO Facts and Figures* (Brussels: NATO, 1989), p. 377.
12 Address to a joint session of Congress and the American People, 21 September 2001.
13 Quoted in Rebecca Johnson and Micah Zenko, 'All dressed up and no place to go: why NATO should be on the front lines of the war on terror', *Parameters* (2002–3), p. 51.
14 Center for Security Policy 'Keeper of the Flame' award dinner, remarks as delivered by Secretary of Defense Donald A. Rumsfeld, Washington, DC, 6 November 2001, www.defenselink.mil/speeches/speech.aspx?speechid=464 (accessed February 2008).
15 I am grateful to my colleague David Brown for suggesting and articulating this concept in various conversations.
16 Francis Fukuyama, *After the Neocons: America at the Crossroads* (London: Profile Books, 2006), p. 173.
17 Martha Finnemore, 'Legitimacy, hypocrisy, and the social structure of unipolarity', *World Politics* 61/1 (2009), p. 68.
18 Secretary Rumsfeld briefs at the Foreign Press Center, 22 January 2003, www.defense.gov/transcripts/transcript.aspx?transcriptid=1330 (accessed October 2011).

19 President Bush delivers graduation speech at West Point, 1 June 2002, http://
    georgewbush-whitehouse.archives.gov/news/releases/2002/06/20020601-3.html
    (accessed October 2011).

20 *The National Security Strategy of the United States of America* (Washington, DC: White
    House, 2002), p. 3.

21 Ibid., p. 17.

22 Michael Hirsh, 'Bush and the world', *Foreign Affairs* 81/5 (2002), p. 26.

23 Robert Fisk, *The Great War for Civilisation: The Conquest of the Middle East* (London:
    Harper Perennial, 2006), p. 1235.

24 See, *inter alia*, Zbigniew Brzezinski, *Second Chance: Three Presidents and the Crisis of
    American Superpower* (New York: Basic Books, 2007), ch. 5; Peter Beinart, *The Icarus
    Syndrome: A History of American Hubris* (New York: HarperCollins/Council on Foreign
    Relations, 2010), ch. 18; Michael Mann, *Incoherent Empire* (London: Verso, 2003), p. 252;
    Chalmers Johnson, *The Sorrows of Empire: Militarism, Secrecy, and the End of the Republic*
    (London: Verso, 2006), p. 152; Jeffrey Record, 'The limits and temptations of America's
    conventional military primacy', *Survival* 47/1 (2005), pp. 39–42; and Nathan Freier,
    'Primacy without a plan?', *Parameters* 36/3 (2006), pp. 7–8.

25 In the immediate aftermath of the Iraq invasion in May 2003, Deputy Defense Secretary
    Wolfowitz – one of the strongest and most consistent advocates of overthrowing
    Saddam Hussein – stated publicly: 'For reasons that have a lot to do with the US govern-
    ment bureaucracy, we settled on the one issue that everyone could agree on [i.e., WMD]
    as the core reason.' Deputy Secretary Wolfowitz interview with Sam Tannenhaus of
    Vanity Fair, 9 May 2003, www.defense.gov/transcripts/transcript.aspx?transcriptid=2594
    (accessed October 2011).

26 Quoted in Ron Suskind, 'Without a doubt', *New York Times*, 17 October 2004.

27 Douglas MacDowell, 'Hybris in Athens', *Greece and Rome* 23 (1976), p. 21.

28 Douglas Cairns, 'Hybris, dishonour, and thinking big', *Journal of Hellenic Studies* 116
    (1996), p. 31.

29 In this context, Richard Ned Lebow has rightly noted that Thucydides' work 'is not just
    about the growth and decline of empires but, more generally, how success spawns
    excessive ambition, overconfidence, and self-destructive behavior'. See Lebow, *Coercion,
    Cooperation, and Ethics in International Relations* (Abingdon: Routledge, 2007), p. 358.

30 Hans Morgenthau, *Politics among Nations: The Struggle for Power and Peace* (brief edn,
    New York: McGraw-Hill, 1993), p. 171.

31 Christian Reus-Smit, *American Power and World Order* (Cambridge: Polity, 2004); Calleo,
    Follies of Power; and Barry Buzan, 'A leader without followers? The United States in
    world politics after Bush', *International Politics* 45/5 (2008), pp. 554–70.

32 The best articulation of this argument is Thomas Ricks, *Fiasco: The American Military
    Adventure in Iraq* (London: Penguin, 2006). See also George Packer, *The Assassins' Gate:
    America in Iraq* (New York: Farrar, Straus & Giroux, 2005).

33 This argument is developed in detail in Michael Gordon and Bernard Trainor, *Cobra II:
    The Inside Story of the Invasion and Occupation of Iraq* (New York: Pantheon, 2006).

34 See Jonathan Steele, *Defeat: Why America and Britain Lost Iraq* (London: I. B. Tauris,
    2008).

35 Daalder and Lindsay, *America Unbound*, pp. 150–1, 155–6, 196.

36 David Beetham, *The Legitimation of Power* (Basingstoke: Macmillan, 1991), p. 220.

37 Ian Clark, *Legitimacy in International Society* (Oxford: Oxford University Press, 2005),
    p. 227.

38 John Ikenberry and Charles Kupchan, 'Liberal realism: the foundations of a democratic
    foreign policy', *The National Interest* 77 (2004), p. 46.

39 Henry Kissinger, 'America at the apex: empire or leader?', *The National Interest* 64 (2001),
    p. 11.

40 *A Smarter, More Secure America* (Washington, DC: Center for Strategic and International Studies, 2007), p. 33.

41 For a useful debate on these and other relevant issues, see Robert Kagan, 'America's crisis of legitimacy', *Foreign Affairs* 83/2 (2004), pp. 65–87; and the rejoinder by Robert Tucker and David Hendrickson, 'The sources of American legitimacy', *Foreign Affairs* 83/6 (2004), pp. 18–32.

42 John R. Bolton, under secretary for arms control and international security, ' "Legitimacy" in international affairs: the American perspective in theory and operation', remarks to the Federalist Society, Washington, DC, 13 November 2003, www.mtholyoke.edu/acad/intrel/bush/legit.htm (accessed October 2011).

43 In this context, Ikenberry and Kupchan have appropriately described international legitimacy as 'the "social capital" of the international system, the normative consensus that binds states together and generates the trust and respect needed to tame anarchy and enable cooperation to flourish'. Ikenberry and Kupchan, 'Liberal realism', p. 45.

44 Fukuyama, *After the Neocons*, p. 63.

45 Joseph Nye, *Soft Power: The Means to Success in World Politics* (New York: PublicAffairs, 2004), p. ix.

46 Fukuyama, *After the Neocons*, p. 63.

47 Paula J. Dobriansky, 'US and European cooperation in democracy promotion, human rights, and development', remarks at the European Institute's conference 'The Strategic Use of Soft Power to Improve Global Stability, Security and Goodwill', Washington, DC, 21 November 2006, www.scoop.co.nz/stories/WO0612/S00194.htm (accessed November 2011).

48 President Bush discusses freedom in Iraq and the Middle East, remarks on the twentieth anniversary of the National Endowment for Democracy, US Chamber of Commerce, Washington, DC, 6 November 2003, www.uscirf.gov/component/content/article/159-iraq-anti-semitism/2119-november-6-2003-president-bush-discusses-freedom-in-iraq-and-middle-east.html (accessed October 2011).

49 Herfried Münkler, *Empires: The Logic of World Domination from Ancient Rome to the United States* (Cambridge: Polity, 2007), p. 85.

50 Joseph Nye, 'The decline of America's soft power', *Foreign Affairs* 83/3 (2004), pp. 16–20.

51 Edward Rhodes, 'The imperial logic of Bush's liberal agenda', *Survival* 45/1 (2003), p. 142.

52 Fukuyama, *After the Neocons*, p. 46.

53 See 'The American discovery of democracy', *The Independent*, 23 June 2005.

54 See 'Rice speaks softly in Egypt, avoiding democracy push', *New York Times*, 16 January 2007.

55 Daalder and Lindsay, *America Unbound*, pp. 196–7.

56 Bush announced the deployment of five extra American military brigades to Iraq, and a change in US counter-insurgency strategy there, in a televised address. See 'President's address to the nation', 10 January 2007, http://georgewbush-whitehouse.archives.gov/news/releases/2007/01/20070110-7.html (accessed May 2011).

57 On American perceptions, see, *inter alia*, 'As Bush confers with NATO, US is seen losing its edge', *New York Times*, 28 June 2004; and 'Gates says anger over Iraq hurts Afghan effort', *New York Times*, 9 February 2008.

Chapter 6 Return to Multilateralism?

1 For the text, see 'International Criminal Court: Letter to UN Secretary General Kofi Annan', www.lb9.uscourts.gov/webcites/08documents/Abagninin_bolton.pdf (accessed October 2011).

2 According to detailed analysis by William Schabas, the root of American objections to the ICC lay in the extent to which its prospective subordination to the UN Security Council had been progressively weakened as the negotiations on its statute progressed. See Schabas, 'United States hostility to the International Criminal Court: it's all about the Security Council', *European Journal of International Law* 15/4 (2004), pp. 701–20.

3 Quoted in 'US renounces world court treaty', *BBC News*, http://news.bbc.co.uk/1/hi/world/americas/1970312.stm (accessed February 2008).

4 American Service-Members' Protection Act (Washington, DC: US Government Printing Office, 2002).

5 Schabas, 'United States hostility to the International Criminal Court', pp. 708–9.

6 Resolution 1422 (2002), http://daccess-dds-ny.un.org/doc/UNDOC/GEN/N02/477/61/PDF/N0247761.pdf?OpenElement (accessed February 2008).

7 Carsten Stahn, 'The ambiguities of Security Council Resolution 1422 (2002)', *European Journal of International Law* 14/1 (2003), http://ejil.oxfordjournals.org/content/14/1/85.full.pdf (accessed October 2011).

8 Neha Jain, 'A separate law for peacekeepers: the clash between the Security Council and the International Criminal Court', *European Journal of International Law* 16/2 (2005), p. 254. For a good general discussion of the legal status of the exemption resolutions, see Stahn, 'The ambiguities of Security Council Resolution 1422 (2002)'.

9 Resolution 1593 (2005), http://daccess-dds-ny.un.org/doc/UNDOC/GEN/N05/292/73/PDF/N0529273.pdf?OpenElement (accessed February 2008).

10 'Powell declares genocide in Sudan', *BBC News*, http://news.bbc.co.uk/2/hi/africa/3641820.stm (accessed February 2008).

11 Convention on the Prevention and Punishment of the Crime of Genocide, www.preventgenocide.org/law/convention/text.htm (accessed February 2008).

12 Townterview hosted by CNN and KTN at the University of Nairobi, www.state.gov/secretary/rm/2009a/08/126954.htm (accessed August 2010).

13 'US engagement with the ICC and the outcome of the recently concluded review conference', www.state.gov/s/wci/us_releases/remarks/143178.htm# (accessed August 2010).

14 See, *inter alia*, John Ikenberry and Charles Kupchan, 'Socialization and hegemonic power', *International Organization* 44/3 (1990), pp. 283–315.

15 In their respective memoirs, both Clinton and then Secretary of State Madeleine Albright assert that the option of military strikes was considered during 1994. See Bill Clinton, *My Life* (London: Hutchinson, 2004), p. 591; and Madeleine Albright, *Madam Secretary* (Basingstoke: Macmillan, 2003), p. 456. For a detailed and insightful account of the crisis and the ensuing diplomatic process which produced the 1994 agreement, see Joel Wit, Daniel Poneman and Robert Gallucci, *Going Critical: The First North Korean Nuclear Crisis* (Washington, DC: Brookings Institution, 2004).

16 Clinton, *My Life*, p. 938.

17 Condoleezza Rice, 'Promoting the national interest', *Foreign Affairs* 79/1 (2000), p. 61.

18 'Press availability with Her Excellency Anna Lindh, minister of foreign affairs of Sweden', 6 March 2001, www.usembassy.it/file2001_03/alia/a1030603.htm (accessed October 2011).

19 Remarks by President Bush and President Kim Dae-Jung of South Korea, 7 March 2001, http://georgewbush-whitehouse.archives.gov/news/releases/2001/03/20010307-6.html (accessed October 2011).

20 Remarks by Secretary of State Colin Powell to the Pool, 7 March 2001, http://georgewbush-whitehouse.archives.gov/news/releases/2001/03/20010307-3.html (accessed October 2011).

21 See Richard Lloyd Parry, 'Today's scoreline: George W. Bush 1, Kim Jong Il', *The Times*, 14 February 2007.

22 Selig Harrison, 'Did North Korea cheat?', *Foreign Affairs* 84/1 (2005), pp. 99–110. See also Wit et al., *Going Critical*, ch. 12.

23 Quoted in Jonathan Watts, Julian Borger and Ian Traynor, 'North Korea vows to abandon nuclear weapons project', *The Guardian*, 20 September 2005. Details of the agreement were released by the US State Department in 'Joint statement of the fourth round of the six-party talks', Beijing, 19 September 2005, www.state.gov/p/eap/regional/c15455.htm and 'North Korea–US statement', 19 September 2005, http://merln.ndu.edu/archivepdf/northkorea/state/53499.pdf (accessed September 2005).

24 George W. Bush, *Decision Points* (London: Virgin Books, 2010), pp. 423–4.

25 There is near unanimity on this point amongst informed analysts. See, *inter alia*, James Miles, 'Waiting out North Korea', *Survival* 44/2 (2002), pp. 37–49; and Gary Samore, 'The Korean nuclear crisis', *Survival* 45/1 (2003), pp. 7–24. In 2004, David Kang went so far as to suggest that the North Korean government 'clearly does not wish to go nuclear'. Rather, he argued that it was using the *threat* of developing a nuclear weapons programme to try to leverage a security guarantee from the US. See 'Can North Korea be engaged? An exchange between Victor D. Cha and David C. Kang', *Survival* 46/2 (2004), p. 99.

26 Although the suggestion by former State Department official Mitchell Reiss that, with the six-party format, the US had effectively 'outsourced' its North Korea policy to China does seem exaggerated. See 'A nuclear-armed North Korea: accepting the "unacceptable"?', *Survival* 48/4 (2006–7), p. 101.

27 'Spokesman for DPRK Foreign Ministry on six-party talks', 20 September 2005, www.kcna.co.jp/item/2005/200509/news09/21.htm#1 (accessed February 2008).

28 In May 2003, for example, the North Korean government issued a statement asserting: 'It is the D[emocratic]P[eoples'] R[epublic of] K[orea]'s stand that the DPRK–U.S. talks should be held first and they may be followed by the U.S.-proposed multilateral talks. As there are the issues to be settled between the DPRK and the U.S., the two sides are required to sit face to face for a candid discussion on each other's policies. Only then, is it possible to have multilateral talks and make them fruitful.' 'U.S. urged not to raise format of talks as precondition', 24 May 2005, www.kcna.co.jp/item/2003/200305/news05/26.htm#13 (accessed February 2008).

29 There has recently been some debate amongst China analysts in the US about the extent to which official Chinese attitudes towards such contentious issues as non-interference in a state's 'internal affairs' are being softened. These issues are discussed further in chapter 10.

30 John Ikenberry, 'America's imperial ambition', *Foreign Affairs* 81/5 (2002), p. 56.

31 Christopher Layne, 'America as European hegemon', *The National Interest* 72 (2003), p. 28.

32 The soft balancing debates were started in a series of articles published in *International Security* in 2005. See Robert Pape, 'Soft balancing against the United States', *International Security* 30/1 (2005), pp. 7–45; T. V. Paul, 'Soft balancing in the age of US primacy', ibid., pp. 46–71; Stephen Brooks and William Wohlforth, 'Hard times for soft balancing', ibid., pp. 72–108; and Keir Lieber and Gerard Alexander, 'Waiting for balancing: why the world is not pushing back', ibid., pp. 109–39.

33 Lieber and Alexander, 'Waiting for balancing', p. 109.

34 David Calleo, *Follies of Power: America's Unipolar Fantasy* (Cambridge: Cambridge University Press, 2009), p. 40.

35 James Steinberg, 'Real leaders do soft power: learning the lessons of Iraq', *Washington Quarterly* 31/2 (2008), p. 160.

36 Amy Belasco, *The Cost of Iraq, Afghanistan, and Other Global War on Terror Operations Since 9/11* (Washington, DC: Congressional Research Service, 2011).

Chapter 7 Russia as a 'Continuing' or 'Reviving' Great Power

1 Putin served two terms as Russia's president, from 2000 to 2004 and from 2004 to 2008. From 2008, he was prime minister under the presidency of Dmitry Medvedev. In September 2011 it was announced that Medvedev and Putin had agreed that the latter would stand again for the presidency in elections in spring 2012, and that Medvedev would serve as prime minister if he was elected. Most observers agreed that this deal 'all but guaranteed' that Putin would win a third term as president. See 'Russia's Putin set to return as president in 2012', 24 September 2011, http://www.bbc.co.uk/news/world-europe-15045816 (accessed October 2011).

2 In this context, some analysts preferred to use the term 'continuing state' to describe Russia's post-Soviet position. See Mark Webber, *The International Politics of Russia and the Successor States* (Manchester: Manchester University Press, 1996), pp. 108–9.

3 Quoted in *Nezavisimaya Gazeta*, 1 April 1992; translated in *The Current Digest of the Post-Soviet Press* (hereafter *CDPSP*) 44/13 (1992), p. 4.

4 A partial precedent did, however, exist. This was the UN General Assembly's de-recognition in the early 1970s of the Republic of China (aka Taiwan) in favour of the People's Republic as the legitimate holder of the Chinese permanent seat.

5 See, for example, Andrei Kozyrev, 'Russia: a chance for survival', *Foreign Affairs* 71/2 (1992), pp. 1–16.

6 *Izvestia*, 11 March 1994 – *CDPSP* 46/10 (1994), p. 2.

7 A. F. K. Organski, *World Politics* (New York: Knopf, 1960), p. 102.

8 Torbjørn Knutsen, *The Rise and Fall of World Orders* (Manchester: Manchester University Press, 1999), p. 81.

9 Coral Bell, 'American ascendency and the pretense of concert', *The National Interest* 57 (1999), p. 57.

10 Thomas Graham, 'World without Russia?', Carnegie Endowment for International Peace, 1999, www.carnegieendowment.org/publications/index.cfm?fa=view&id=285 (accessed June 2010).

11 Condoleezza Rice, 'Promoting the national interest', *Foreign Affairs* 79/1 (2000), pp. 58–9.

12 *Rossiiskaya Gazeta*, 22 December 2004 – *CDPSP* 57/1–2 (2005), p. 7.

13 Robert Legvold, 'Russia's unformed foreign policy', *Foreign Affairs* 80/5 (2001), p. 62.

14 *Izvestia*, 7 October 1998 – *CDPSP* 50/40 (1998), p. 14.

15 An anecdotal account (but one that essentially rings true, given what is known from other sources) attributed to Richard Holbrooke, a senior US official involved in trying to broker a settlement between the Serbs and ethnic Albanians in Kosovo, gives a sense of this Russian rigidity. Holbrooke described an informal discussion in October 1998 between the then German foreign minister, Klaus Kinkel, and Ivanov: 'Ivanov said: "If you take it [the issue of using force] to the UN, we'll veto it. If you don't we'll just denounce you." Kinkel says he wants to take it to the Security Council, as do the British and French...So, Kinkel says: "Let's have another stab at it." But Ivanov says: "Fine, we'll veto it." And Kinkel asks again and Ivanov says: "I just told you Klaus, we'll veto it." ' Quoted in Tim Judah, *Kosovo: War and Revenge* (New Haven, CT: Yale University Press, 2000), p. 183.

16 For an example of the use of the term 'spoiler' in this context, see Bobo Lo, *Axis of Convenience: Moscow, Beijing, and the New Geopolitics* (Washington, DC: Brookings Institution, 2008), p. 88.

17 Independent International Commission on Kosovo, *Kosovo Report* (Oxford: Oxford University Press, 2000), p. 161.

18 'Secretary-General presents his annual report to General Assembly' (Press Release SG/SM/7136GA/9596), 20 September 1999, www.un.org/News/Press/docs/1999/19990920.sgsm7136.html (accessed July 2002).

19 Oleg Levitin, 'Inside Moscow's Kosovo muddle', *Survival* 42/1 (2000), pp. 130–40.
20 This analysis draws on Paul Latawski and Martin A. Smith, *The Kosovo Crisis and the Evolution of Post-Cold War European Security* (Manchester: Manchester University Press, 2003), ch. 4.
21 See the interesting comparative analysis in Michael O'Hanlon, 'Winning ugly in Libya: what the United States should learn from its war in Kosovo', *Foreign Affairs*, 30 March 2011, www.foreignaffairs.com/articles/67684/michael-ohanlon/winning-ugly-in-libya?page=show (accessed May 2011).
22 An English-language translation of the document can be found in Richard Sakwa, *Putin: Russia's Choice* (2nd edn, Abingdon: Routledge, 2008), pp. 317–28. I am grateful to Professor Sakwa for drawing my attention to his translation, from which all quotations are taken. For a contemporary Russian press commentary, see *Nezavisimaya Gazeta*, 30 December 1999 – *CDPSP* 52/1 (2000), pp. 7–8.
23 See, *inter alia*, *Noviye Izvestia*, 28 July 2001 – *CDPSP* 53/30 (2001), p. 19; 'Hope gleams anew', *The Economist*, 3 November 2001, pp. 47–8; *Kommersant*, 6 February 2002 – *CDPSP* 54/6 (2002), p. 17; and *Moskovskiye Novosti*, 12–18 February 2002 – *CDPSP* 54/6 (2002), pp. 17–18.
24 For useful background on the Soviet legacy and Russia's Cuba policy in the early 1990s, see Yuri Pavlov, 'Russian policy toward Latin America and Cuba', in Peter Shearman, ed., *Russian Foreign Policy since 1990* (Boulder, CO: Westview Press, 1995), pp. 257–64.
25 *Sevodnya*, 13 and 17 October 1995 – *CDPSP* 47/42 (1995), pp. 6–7.
26 See, *inter alia*, *Vremya Novostei*, 19 October 2001 – *CDPSP* 53/42 (2001), p. 3; and *Nezavisimaya Gazeta*, 19 October 2001 – *CDPSP* 53/42 (2001), p. 4.
27 *Vremya MN*, 26 October 2001 – *CDPSP* 53/43 (2001), p. 5.
28 *Vremya MN*, 25 July 2002 – *CDPSP* 54/31 (2002), pp. 1–2.
29 'Putin tells the nation Russia can be rich and strong again', *Johnson's Russia List* (hereafter *JRL*), 7186, 19 May 2003, www.cdi.org/russia/johnson/7186-1.cfm (accessed June 2010).
30 *Izvestia*, 12 January 2002 – *CDPSP* 54/2 (2002), p. 18.
31 *Vremya MN*, 19 January 2002 – *CDPSP* 54/3 (2002), p. 3. See also Irina Kobrinskaya, 'The multispeed commonwealth', *Russia in Global Affairs* 1 (2004), http://eng.globalaffairs.ru/numbers/6/509.html (accessed June 2010).
32 *Kommersant*, 21 August 2002 – *CDPSP* 54/34 (2002), p. 16.
33 *Vremya Novostei*, 22 November 2002 – *CDPSP* 54/47 (2002), p. 1.
34 *Izvestia*, 4 February 2003 – *CDPSP* 55/5 (2003), p. 4; *Noviye Izvestia*, 5 February 2003 – *CDPSP* 55/5 (2003), p. 4.
35 *Vremya Novostei*, 31 January 2003 – *CDPSP* 55/4 (2003), p. 4.
36 Quoted in *Rossiiskaya Gazeta*, 19 May 2000 – *CDPSP* 52/20 (2000), p. 5.
37 For details, see the articles in *Rossiiskaya Gazeta*, 16 May 2000; *Kommersant*, 19 May 2000; and *Izvestia*, 17 May 2000 – all in *CDPSP* 52/20 (2000), pp. 1–4. See also *Nezavisimaya Gazeta*, 10 October 2000 – *CDPSP* 52/41 (2000), p. 1.
38 *Rossiiskaya Gazeta*, 19 May 2000 – *CDPSP* 52/20 (2000), p. 5.
39 Quoted in Dov Lynch, '"The enemy is at the gate": Russia after Beslan', *International Affairs* 81/1 (2005), p. 153.
40 Putin announced details in a speech to ministers, members of his presidential staff and regional representatives on 13 September 2004. See *Rossiiskaya Gazeta*, 14 September 2004 – *CDPSP* 56/37 (2004), pp. 1–4.
41 *Komsomolskaya Pravda*, 29 September 2004 – *CDPSP* 56/39 (2004), p. 3.
42 *Vremya Novostei*, 29 September 2004 – *CDPSP* 56/39 (2004), p. 5.
43 *Moskovskiye Novosti*, 19–25 March 2002 – *CDPSP* 54/11 (2002), p. 7.
44 *Rossiiskaya Gazeta*, 26 April 2005 – *CDPSP* 57/17 (2005), p. 1. All quotations from the speech in the sections following are taken from this translation (pp. 1–6).
45 *Izvestia*, 13 September 2006 – *CDPSP* 58/38 (2006), p. 7.

46 See, *inter alia*, Andrei Kokoshin, 'What is Russia: a superpower, a great power or a regional power?', *International Affairs* [Moscow] 48/6 (2002), p. 103.

47 *Kommersant*, 11 September 2006 – *CDPSP* 58/38 (2006), p. 6.

48 *Nezavisimaya Gazeta*, 11 May 2006 – *CDPSP* 58/18–19 (2006), p. 12.

49 *Izvestia*, 10 March 2006 – *CDPSP* 58/10 (2006), p. 4.

50 Ironically, even as the gas price crisis with Ukraine was taking hold in December 2005, Vladimir Putin was speaking publicly of the importance of Russia 'reliably supplying the world economy with traditional fuels, and doing so on terms that are acceptable to both the producing countries and the consumers'. *Vremya Novostei*, 23 December 2005 – *CDPSP* 57/51 (2005), p. 9.

51 In 2006, it was estimated that oil and gas accounted for 55 per cent of Russia's total export revenues. See Vladimir Shlapentokh, 'Russia as a newborn superpower: Putin as the lord of oil and gas', *JRL* 18, 19 February 2006, www.cdi.org/russia/johnson/2006-39-18.cfm (accessed June 2010).

52 The concept of monodimensionalism in this context is borrowed from John Lewis Gaddis, who developed it in order to help explain the collapse of the Soviet Union. In Gaddis's view: 'By the 1980s ... Moscow's power had come to rest upon a monodimensional military base, while that of the United States and its allies remained multidimensional; the resulting situation determined which side finally prevailed in the Cold War.' See *The United States and the End of the Cold War* (Oxford: Oxford University Press, 1992), p. 5.

53 *Rossiiskaya Gazeta*, 21 November 2006 – *CDPSP* 58/47 (2006), p. 6.

54 See, *inter alia*, Sergei Karaganov in *Rossiiskaya Gazeta*, 12 January 2005 – *CDPSP* 57/1–2 (2005), p. 10; and Vladislav Inozemtsev in *Vremya Novostei*, 19 May 2006 – *CDPSP* 58/20 (2006), p. 10.

55 For useful discussions of these issues, see Andrew Barnes, *Medvedev's Oil: The Burdens of Great Wealth and the Potential for Coping with Them*, PONARS Eurasia Policy Memo 31 (Washington, DC: Georgetown University, 2008); and Vladimir Popov, *A Curse or a Blessing? What to Expect from a Typical Developing Resource-Abundant State*, PONARS Eurasia Policy Memo 32 (Washington, DC: Georgetown University, 2008).

56 Joseph Nye, *The Future of Power* (New York: PublicAffairs, 2011), p. 99.

57 See, *inter alia*, Andrei Tsygankov, 'If not by tanks, then by banks? The role of soft power in Putin's foreign policy', *Europe–Asia Studies* 58/7 (2006), pp. 1079–99; Nicu Popescu, *Russia's Soft Power Ambitions* (Brussels: Centre for European Policy Studies, 2006); and Fiona Hill, *Energy Empire: Oil, Gas and Russia's Revival* (London: Foreign Policy Centre, 2004).

58 Dmitri Trenin, 'Russia redefines itself and its relations with the West', *Washington Quarterly* 30/2 (2007), p. 95. See also the article by Mikhail Krasnov in *Trud*, 12 August 2000 – *CDPSP* 52/33 (2000), pp. 11, 24.

59 Vladimir Baranovsky, 'Russia: a part of Europe or apart from Europe?', *International Affairs* 76/3 (2000), pp. 444–5; Sergei Karaganov, 'A new epoch of confrontation', *Russia in Global Affairs* 5/4 (2007), pp. 29–31.

60 See Simon Tisdall, 'Putinism could be the next Russian export', *The Guardian*, 21 November 2007; and Tisdall, 'Russia and the US must stop treating this region like a giant playboard', *The Guardian*, 9 April 2010.

Chapter 8 The Russian Multipolarity Debates

1 The essential features of a neo-Gorchakovian approach are outlined in Flemming Splidsboel-Hansen, 'Past and future meet: Aleksandr Gorchakov and Russian foreign policy', *Europe–Asia Studies* 54/3 (2002), pp. 377–96.

2 Quoted by then Foreign Minister Yevgeny Primakov in a lecture to mark the bi-centenary of Gorchakov's birth. See Primakov, 'Russia in world politics: a lecture in honor of Chancellor Gorchakov', *International Affairs* [Moscow] 44/3 (1998), p. 8.

3 Sergei Karaganov, 'Dangerous relapses', *Russia in Global Affairs* 4/2 (2006), p. 81; and Andrei Tsygankov, 'Projecting confidence, not fear: Russia asserts itself', *JRL* 18, 6 February 2006, www.cdi.org/russia/johnson/2006-38-18.cfm (accessed June 2010).

4 For Primakov, see 'Russia in world politics'. For Ivanov, see his article 'The new Russian identity: innovation and continuity in Russian foreign policy', *Washington Quarterly* 24/3 (2001), pp. 8–9.

5 Primakov, 'Russia in world politics', p. 10.

6 Ivanov, 'The new Russian identity', pp. 10–11.

7 Bobo Lo, *Axis of Convenience: Moscow, Beijing, and the New Geopolitics* (Washington, DC: Brookings Institution, 2008), pp. 33–4.

8 Andrei Kozyrev, 'The lagging partnership', *Foreign Affairs* 73/3 (1994), pp. 59–71.

9 Daniel Deudney and John Ikenberry, 'The unravelling of the Cold War settlement', *Survival* 51/6 (2009–10), p. 52. For an earlier Russian assessment which bears some comparison with this view, see the article by Sergey Rogov in *Nezavisimaya Gazeta*, 18 December 2001 – *CDPSP* 53/52 (2001), pp. 4–5.

10 Kenneth Waltz, 'The stability of a bipolar world', *Daedalus* 43/3 (1964).

11 Strobe Talbott, *The Russia Hand: A Memoir of Presidential Diplomacy* (New York: Random House, 2002).

12 Bill Clinton, *My Life* (London: Hutchinson, 2004), p. 504.

13 'Remarks by the president in live telecast to Russian people', 14 January 1994, http://clinton6.nara.gov/1994/01/1994-01-14-presidents-remarks-in-live-telecast-to-russian-people.html (accessed October 2011).

14 Zbigniew Brzezinski, 'The premature partnership', *Foreign Affairs* 73/2 (1994), p. 70.

15 See, *inter alia*, 'Toward the Brezhnev Doctrine', *Wall Street Journal*, 24 January 1994; and 'The West underwrites Russian imperialism', *Wall Street Journal*, 7 February 1994.

16 The course of the increasingly acrimonious relations between Russia, on the one hand, and the US and its NATO allies, on the other, is detailed and analysed in Martin A. Smith, *Russia and NATO since 1991: From Cold War through Cold Peace to Partnership?* (Abingdon: Routledge, 2006).

17 In an interview published in July 2002, Primakov's successor as foreign minister, Igor Ivanov, reflected on this and conceded that it would be impossible for Russia to 'reestablish a bipolar world, or lay claim once more to the role of a power that dictates its own ground rules to others'. He claimed that 'we don't even want to do that, but even if we did, we wouldn't be able to. But we are fully capable of participating in the formation of the new world order.' *Izvestia*, 10 July 2002 – *CDPSP* 54/28 (2002), p. 3.

18 See, *inter alia*, Lo, *Axis of Convenience*; Chikahito Harada, *Russia and North-East Asia*, Adelphi Paper no. 310 (London: International Institute for Strategic Studies, 1997), ch. 2; and 'Russia and China', *The Economist*, 26 April 1997, pp. 21–3.

19 Quoted in 'Russia looks east for allies', *Financial Times*, 16 November 1995.

20 'Cold comfort', *The Economist*, 6 September 2008, p. 31.

21 *Vremya MN*, 17 November 2001 – *CDPSP* 53/46 (2001), p. 6.

22 *Trud*, 27 December 2003 – *CDPSP* 55/52 (2003), p. 7.

23 Lo, *Axis of Convenience*, p. 126.

24 *Nezavisimaya Gazeta*, 20 January 2000 – *CDPSP* 52/3 (2000), p. 9.

25 An English-language translation of the *Foreign Policy Concept of the Russian Federation* was published in *International Affairs* [Moscow] 46/5 (2000), pp. 1–14. The passage quoted appears on p. 3.

26 On this, see John O'Loughlin, Gearóid Ó Tuathail and Vladimir Kolossov, 'A "risky westward turn"? Putin's 9–11 script and ordinary Russians', *Europe–Asia Studies* 56/1 (2004), pp. 3–34.
27 Mikhail Margelov, 'Victory on points: pragmatism in foreign policy', *Russia in Global Affairs* 1/3 (2003), p. 22.
28 Quoted in 'Russia refuses to be a follower in international relations', *JRL* 20, 7 March 2007, www.cdi.org/russia/johnson/2007-56-20.cfm (accessed June 2010).
29 Alexander Lukin, 'Russia to reinforce the Asian vector', *Russia in Global Affairs* 7/2 (2009), p. 85.
30 Dmitri Trenin, *Getting Russia Right* (Washington, DC: Carnegie Endowment for International Peace, 2007), p. 76. See also Ted Hopf, *Russia's Place in the World: An Exit Option?*, PONARS Eurasia Policy Memo no. 79 (Washington, DC: Georgetown University, 2009).
31 Sergei Kortunov, 'Invigorating Russia's foreign policy', *Russia in Global Affairs* 3/4 (2005), p. 29.
32 In this vein, for example, Sergei Karaganov argued that the conduct of foreign policy under Primakov had ensured that, in the international arena, Russia ended the 1990s looking like 'either a bogeyman or a clown'. *Moskovskiye Novosti*, 26 December 2000/2 January 2001 – *CDPSP* 52/52 (2000), p. 7. See also, *inter alia*, Vladimir Frolov in *Vremya MN*, 23 November 2001 – *CDPSP* 53/47 (2001), p. 5; and Viktor Sheinis in *Nezavisimaya Gazeta*, 18 December 2001 – *CDPSP* 54/1 (2002), p. 4.
33 Sergei Lavrov, 'The rise of Asia, and the eastern vector of Russia's foreign policy', *Russia in Global Affairs* 4/3 (2006), p. 76.
34 Ibid., p. 71.
35 *Nezavisimaya Gazeta*, 20 January 2003 – *CDPSP* 55/3 (2003), p. 23.
36 Eugene Rumer, *Russian Foreign Policy beyond Putin*, Adelphi Paper no. 390 (London: International Institute for Strategic Studies, 2007), pp. 52–3.
37 This formulation was used by Putin, *inter alia*, in an address to Russian diplomats in June 2006. *Vremya Novostei*, 28 June 2006 – *CDPSP* 58/26 (2006), p. 4.
38 Yevgeny Primakov, 'A world without superpowers', *Russia in Global Affairs* 1/3 (2003), p. 11. See also Evgeniy Bazhanov, 'A multipolar world is inevitable', *International Affairs* [Moscow] 49/5 (2003), p. 22.
39 *Vremya Novostei*, 13 February 2003 – *CDPSP* 55/6 (2003), p. 2.
40 Ibid.
41 *Noviye Izvestia*, 13 February 2003 – *CDPSP* 55/6 (2003), p. 3.
42 *Izvestia*, 13 March 2003 – *CDPSP* 55/10 (2003), p. 7.
43 *Moskovskiye Novosti*, 11–17 March 2003 – *CDPSP* 55/9 (2003), p. 4.
44 See, *inter alia*, *Kommersant*, 19 March 2003 – *CDPSP* 55/11 (2003), pp. 1–2; *Kommersant*, 22 March 2003 – *CDPSP* 55/12 (2003), p. 2; *Izvestia*, 4 April 2003 – *CDPSP* 55/13 (2003), p. 8; and *Izvestia*, 23 May 2003 – *CDPSP* 55/20 (2003), p. 5.
45 Thomas Ambrosio, *Challenging America's Global Preeminence: Russia's Quest for Multipolarity* (Aldershot: Ashgate, 2005), p. 2.

Chapter 9 China: 'Rising Power' or 'Constrained State'?

1 Kenneth Waltz, 'Intimations of multipolarity', in Birthe Hansen and Bertel Heunlin, eds, *The New World Order* (Basingstoke: Macmillan, 2000), p. 6. See also Waltz, 'The emerging structure of international politics', *International Security* 18/2 (1993), p. 68.
2 See, *inter alia*, M. Taylor Fravel, 'China's search for military power', *Washington Quarterly* 31/3 (2008), pp. 125–41; and Lyle Goldstein, 'China's Falklands lessons', *Survival* 50/3 (2008), pp. 65–82.

3 See *Annual Report to Congress: Military Power of the People's Republic of China 2009* (Washington, DC: US Government Printing Office, 2009).

4 For an official statement of the Chinese government's security concerns, stressing internal and regional priorities, see *China's National Defense in 2008*, http://www.gov.cn/english/official/2009-01/20/content_1210227.htm (accessed September 2010).

5 See, *inter alia*, Jane Macartney and Michael Evans, 'Stealth jet flight is obvious warning to US about Beijing's military ambitions', *The Times*, 12 January 2011; 'Discord', *The Economist*, 15 January 2011, pp. 12–13; and 'Another go at being friends', ibid., pp. 49–50. For a somewhat more considered analysis of this development, see 'China's J-20: future rival for air dominance?', *IISS Strategic Comments* 17/4 (2011).

6 All figures cited are taken from *The Military Balance 2010* (London: Routledge/International Institute for Strategic Studies, 2010).

7 Jonathan Holslag, *Trapped Giant: China's Military Rise* (London: Routledge/International Institute for Strategic Studies, 2010), p. 31.

8 See Robert Ross, 'The 1995–1996 Taiwan Strait confrontation: coercion, credibility, and use of force', *International Security* 25/2 (2000), pp. 87–123.

9 There is a sizeable literature on Chinese military developments since the end of the Cold War. See, *inter alia*, Mark Leonard, *What Does China Think?* (London: Fourth Estate, 2008), pp. 104ff.; David Shambaugh, 'China's military views the world', *International Security* 24/3 (1999/2000), pp. 52–79; Denny Roy, 'China's reaction to American predominance', *Survival* 45/3 (2003), pp. 57–78; and 'The long march to be a superpower', *The Economist*, 4 August 2007, pp. 20–2.

10 Thomas Christensen, 'Posing problems without catching up', *International Security* 25/4 (2001), pp. 5–40.

11 See Ashley Tellis, 'China's military space strategy', *Survival* 49/3 (2007), pp. 41–72.

12 See, *inter alia*, John Mearsheimer, *The Tragedy of Great Power Politics* (New York: Norton, 2001); and Mearsheimer, 'The future of the American pacifier', *Foreign Affairs* 80/5 (2001), pp. 46–61. Also Suraj Sengupta, 'Is China the next superpower?', *Defense & Security Analysis* 19/4 (2003), pp. 389–404.

13 See Bradley Thayer, 'Confronting China: an evaluation of options for the United States', *Comparative Strategy* 24 (2005), pp. 71–98.

14 See Paul Wolfowitz, 'Remembering the future', *The National Interest* 59 (2000), pp. 35–45.

15 'Remarks as delivered by Secretary of Defense Donald H. Rumsfeld, Shangri-La Hotel, Singapore, Saturday, June 4, 2005', www.highbeam.com/doc/1G1-133371061.html (accessed October 2011).

16 The classic academic formulation of the security dilemma concept is John Herz, 'Idealist internationalism and the security dilemma', *World Politics* 2/2 (1950), pp. 171–201.

17 'Whither China: from membership to responsibility?' Remarks to National Committee on US–China Relations, 21 September 2005, www.ncuscr.org/files/2005Gala_RobertZoellick_Whither_China1.pdf (accessed October 2011).

18 *Annual Report to Congress: Military Power of the People's Republic of China 2009*, p. 1.

19 Tania Branigan, 'Obama criticises internet censorship but falls short of attacking China's human rights record', *The Guardian*, 17 November 2009.

20 The concept of the G2 was articulated initially by C. Fred Bergsten, 'A partnership of equals', *Foreign Affairs* 87/4 (2008), pp. 57–69.

21 Thomas Christensen, 'Shaping the choices of a rising China: recent lessons for the Obama administration', *Washington Quarterly* 32/3 (2009), p. 91.

22 Jonathan Holslag, 'Embracing Chinese global security ambitions', *Washington Quarterly* 32/3 (2009), p. 114.

23 *National Security Strategy* (Washington, DC: White House, 2010), pp. 17–18.

24 See 'Remarks by the president on the economy in Winston-Salem, North Carolina', 6 December 2010, http://www.whitehouse.gov/the-press-office/2010/12/06/remarks-president-economy-winston-salem-north-carolina (accessed June 2011).

25 See 'China in the mind of America', *The Economist*, 22 January 2011, p. 56.

26 See Charles Glaser, 'Will China's rise lead to war?', *Foreign Affairs* 90/2 (2011), pp. 80–91.

27 For a useful compendium of economic and financial data on China, see the US Central Intelligence Agency's *World Factbook*, https://www.cia.gov/library/publications/the-world-factbook/geos/ch.html (accessed September 2010).

28 James Kynge, *China Shakes the World: The Rise of a Hungry Nation* (London: Phoenix, 2007), p. 117. See also Mark Beeson, 'Hegemonic transition in East Asia? The dynamics of Chinese and American power', *Review of International Studies* 35/1 (2009), pp. 108–9.

29 See Susan Shirk, *China: Fragile Superpower* (Oxford: Oxford University Press, 2007), ch. 8. Shirk was a senior official in the State Department at the time.

30 Zheng Bijian, 'China's "peaceful rise" to great power status', *Foreign Affairs* 84/5 (2005), p. 20.

31 *China's Peaceful Rise: Speeches of Zheng Bijian 1997–2005* (Washington, DC: Brookings Institution, 2005), pp. 14–15. See also Kynge, *China Shakes the World*, ch. 3.

32 CIA *World Factbook*, https://www.cia.gov/library/publications/the-world-factbook/rankorder/2001rank.html?countryName=China&countryCode=ch&regionCode=eas&rank=3#ch (accessed October 2011).

33 CIA *World Factbook*, https://www.cia.gov/library/publications/the-world-factbook/rankorder/2004rank.html?countryName=China&countryCode=ch&regionCode=eas&rank=128#ch (accessed October 2011).

34 During a visit to the US by President Hu Jintao in January 2011, for example, a senior Chinese diplomat reminded a British newspaper that, 'in terms of per capita GDP, we are still behind over 100 countries'. Julian Borger et al., 'Hard power meets soft power as China is finally granted equal status by US', *The Guardian*, 19 January 2011.

35 'China destined to be a strong country without hegemony, Fu Ying', *People's Daily Online*, http://english.people.com.cn/90001/90780/91342/6650662.html (accessed July 2009).

36 Zheng, 'China's "peaceful rise"', p. 19; Pranab Bardhan, 'China, India superpower? Not so fast!', *Yale Global*, 25 October 2005, http://yaleglobal.yale.edu/content/china-india-superpower-not-so-fast (accessed October 2011); and 'Challenges and opportunities of Chinese foreign and security policy', *People's Daily Online*, http://english.people.com.cn/90001/90780/91342/6655883.html (accessed July 2009).

37 For a useful discussion of China's demographic challenges and the one child policy, see 'The most surprising demographic crisis', *The Economist*, 7 May 2011, pp. 56–7.

38 On this, see Stefan Halper, *The Beijing Consensus: How China's Authoritarian Model Will Dominate the Twenty-First Century* (New York: Basic Books, 2010).

39 2004 figure: 'The dragon comes calling', *The Economist*, 3 September 2005, p. 27; 2005 figure: John Thornton, 'China's leadership gap', *Foreign Affairs* 85/6 (2006), p. 138; 2006 and 2008 figures: Wei Jingsheng, 'A tidal wave of discontent threatens China', *The Times*, 14 January 2009; 2010 figure: Leo Lewis, 'Beijing acts to combat outbreak of "crazy" violence', *The Times*, 14 June 2011.

40 Murray Scot Tanner, 'China rethinks unrest', *Washington Quarterly* 27/3 (2004), pp. 138–40.

41 Quoted in Peter Beaumont, 'Why fearful China stamps out dissent', *The Observer*, 17 January 2010.

42 Kevin O'Brien, 'Rightful resistance', *World Politics* 49/1 (1996), pp. 31–55.

43 Ibid., p. 54.

44 'Jasmine Revolution' was the name popularly given to the wave of protests that overthrew President Ben Ali of Tunisia in January 2011.

45 See, *inter alia*, 'The wind that will not subside', *The Economist*, 19 February 2011, p. 61; Isabel Hilton, 'Tweak of the tiger's tail', *The Guardian*, 26 February 2011; Bill Emmott, 'Libyan tremors will be felt as far away as China', *The Times*, 28 February 2011; 'No awakening, but crush it anyway', *The Economist*, 5 March 2011, p. 61; 'On the defensive', *The Economist*, 9 April 2011, p. 66; and 'China's crackdown', *The Economist*, 16 April 2011, p. 13.

46 'People's Daily: national unity is ultimate interest of ethnic people', *People's Daily Online*, http://english.people.com.cn/90001/90776/90785/6701596.html (accessed July 2009).

47 Steel wall: 'Senior leader calls to build "steel wall" in Xinjiang for stability', *People's Daily Online*, http://english.people.com.cn/90001/90776/90785/6698432.html (accessed July 2009); Great Wall: 'Former NPC vice-chairman: "Great Wall of ethnic unity" remains firm', *People's Daily Online*, http://english.people.com.cn/90001/90776/90785/6700489.html (accessed July 2009).

48 Joshua Cooper Ramo, *The Beijing Consensus* (London: Foreign Policy Centre, 2004).

49 See Daniel Lynch, 'Chinese thinking on the future of international relations: realism as the *ti*, rationalism as the *yong*?', *China Quarterly* 197 (2009), p. 88.

50 Ibid., p. 101.

51 'Crying for freedom', *The Economist*, 16 January 2010, p. 57.

52 See, *inter alia*, Joshua Kurlantzick, *Charm Offensive: How China's Soft Power is Transforming the World* (New Haven, CT: Yale University Press, 2007), pp. 34–6; the comments of Professor Qu Xing in 'China: is it a threat, or an opportunity? (II)', *People's Daily Online*, http://english.people.com.cn/200508/23/print20050823_204165.html (accessed July 2009); Avery Goldstein, 'The diplomatic face of China's grand strategy: a rising power's emerging choice', *China Quarterly* 168 (2001), p. 845; and 'Reaching for a renaissance: a special report on China and its region', *The Economist*, 31 March 2007, pp. 7–10.

53 Bill Clinton, *My Life* (London: Hutchinson, 2004), pp. 806–7.

54 Kurlantzick, *Charm Offensive*, p. 6.

55 Martin Jacques, *When China Rules the World* (London: Allen Lane, 2009), pp. 230–2. For good discussions of the mixed motivations behind China's increasing African engagements, see, *inter alia*, Chris Alden, 'China in Africa', *Survival* 47/3 (2005), pp. 147–63; Ian Taylor, 'China's oil diplomacy in Africa', *International Affairs* 82/5 (2006), pp. 937–59; and Sarah Raine, *China's African Challenges* (London: International Institute for Strategic Studies/Routledge, 2009).

56 Ramo, *The Beijing Consensus*.

57 Jacques, *When China Rules the World*, ch. 8.

58 See, respectively, Tom Burgis, 'Nigerian militants oppose China's oil plans', *Financial Times*, 30 September 2009; and 'Chinese scramble', *The Times*, 13 October 2009. In similar vein, see also 'Rumble in the jungle', *The Economist*, 23 April 2011, pp. 15–16; and Alexei Barrionuevo, 'In Brazil, angst over China's push for land', *New York Times*, 5 June 2011 [article reprinted in *The Observer*].

59 This problem is regularly noted in discussions about China's soft power. See, *inter alia*, Kurlantzick, *Charm Offensive*, pp. 161ff.; Halper, *The Beijing Consensus*, pp. 97–9; and Shogo Suzuki, 'The myth and reality of China's "soft power"', in Inderjeet Parmar and Michael Cox, eds, *Soft Power and US Foreign Policy* (Abingdon: Routledge, 2010), pp. 207–8.

60 See, *inter alia*, Gregory Chin and Ramesh Thakur, 'Will China change the rules of global order?', *Washington Quarterly* 33/4 (2010), p. 123; and Shaun Breslin, 'China's emerging global role: dissatisfied responsible great power', *Politics* 30 (2010), issue supplement, p. 57.

61 *Soft Power in Asia: Results of a 2008 Multinational Survey of Public Opinion* (Chicago: Chicago Council on Global Affairs, 2009), pp. 9, 10, 17–18.

62 Ibid., p. 9.

63 *BBC World Service Poll: Global Views of United States Improve while Other Countries Decline* (London: BBC, 2010), pp. 1–4.
64 Kurlantzick, *Charm Offensive*, p. 229.
65 *Soft Power in Asia*, p. 8.
66 See Shaun Breslin, *The Soft Notion of China's 'Soft Power'* (London: Chatham House, 2011).
67 See 'A wary respect: a special report on China and America', *The Economist*, 24 October 2009, p. 11.
68 In 2008, for example, Hu Jintao publicly bemoaned 'the West's strength and our weakness' in global exchanges of attractive ideas. See 'The Chinese are coming', *The Economist*, 6 March 2010, p. 71.
69 Joseph Kahn, 'In candor from China, efforts to ease anxiety', *New York Times*, 17 April 2006.
70 George W. Bush, *Decision Points* (London: Virgin Books, 2010), p. 427.

Chapter 10 China, 'Anti-Hegemonism' and 'Harmony'

1 Arthur Waley (trans.), *The Analects of Confucius* (London: Allen & Unwin, 1938), II, 1.
2 Ibid., I.
3 *The Sayings of Mencius*, in *Chinese Literature*, www.gutenberg.org/ebooks/10056 (accessed July 2009).
4 For a good introduction to the alleged influence of Confucianism on key aspects of contemporary Chinese life, see Daniel Bell, *China's New Confucianism: Politics and Everyday Life in a Changing Society* (Princeton, NJ: Princeton University Press, 2008). For an articulate argument that Confucian ideas are having an important impact specifically on contemporary Chinese foreign and security policies, see Huiyun Feng, *Chinese Strategic Culture and Foreign Policy Decision-Making* (Abingdon: Routledge, 2007). For the view that Confucianism has historically influenced China's foreign and security policies, in combination with political realism, see Alastair Iain Johnston, *Cultural Realism: Strategic Culture and Grand Strategy in Chinese History* (Princeton, NJ: Princeton University Press, 1995).
5 See, *inter alia*, Avery Goldstein, 'The diplomatic face of China's grand strategy: a rising power's emerging choice', *China Quarterly* 168 (2001), p. 862; and Charles Kupchan et al., *Power in Transition: The Peaceful Change of International Order* (Tokyo: United Nations University Press, 2001), p. 93.
6 Shaun Breslin, *The Soft Notion of China's 'Soft Power'* (London: Chatham House, 2011), p. 10.
7 Joint Communiqué of the United States of America and the People's Republic of China, 28 February 1972, www.taiwandocuments.org/communique01.htm (accessed June 2009).
8 See Robert Vitalis, 'Theory wars of choice: hidden casualties in the "debate" between hegemony and empire', in Charles-Philippe David and David Grondin, eds, *Hegemony or Empire? The Redefinition of US Power under George W. Bush* (Aldershot: Ashgate, 2006), p. 25 n. 12.
9 Thus, for example, in a 2001 analysis by Yong Deng considering Chinese perceptions of US foreign policy, 'hegemons' are portrayed as innately aggressive, and also as scheming and duplicitous in seeking to advance their own interests internationally at the expense of others. See Yong Deng, 'Hegemon on the offensive: Chinese perspectives on US global strategy', *Political Science Quarterly* 116/3 (2001), pp. 343–65.
10 David Shambaugh, *Beautiful Imperialist: China Perceives America, 1972–1990* (Princeton, NJ: Princeton University Press, 1991), p. 78.

11 On this see, *inter alia*, Russell Ong, *China's Security Interests in the 21st Century* (Abingdon: Routledge, 2007), pp. 37–8; and Kenneth Johnson, *China's Strategic Culture: A Perspective for the United States* (Carlisle, PA: Strategic Studies Institute, US Army War College, 2009), pp. 4–5.

12 The classic collection of studies of this system remains John Fairbank, ed., *The Chinese World Order: Traditional China's Foreign Relations* (Cambridge, MA: Harvard University Press, 1968).

13 Chusei Suzuki, 'China's relations with inner Asia: the Hsiung-Nu, Tibet', in Fairbank, *The Chinese World Order*, pp. 183–4.

14 Cho-Yun Hsu, 'Applying Confucian ethics to international relations', in Joel Rosenthal, ed., *Ethics and International Affairs: A Reader* (Washington, DC: Georgetown University Press, 1999), p. 155.

15 Stefan Halper, *The Beijing Consensus: How China's Authoritarian Model Will Dominate the Twenty-First Century* (New York: Basic Books, 2010), p. 150.

16 See, *inter alia*, Alastair Iain Johnston, *Cultural Realism: Strategic Culture and Grand Strategy in Chinese History* (Princeton, NJ: Princeton University Press, 1995), pp. 69ff.; and Shambaugh, *Beautiful Imperialist*, p. 83.

17 David Shambaugh, 'China engages Asia', *International Security* 29/3 (2004–5), p. 95.

18 David Shambaugh, 'Correspondence: China engages Asia? Caveat lector', *International Security* 30/1 (2005), p. 210. See also 'Universalists v exceptionalists' [part of a special report on China], *The Economist*, 25 June 2011, pp. 15–16.

19 *China's Peaceful Rise: Speeches of Zheng Bijian 1997–2005* (Washington, DC: Brookings Institution, 2005), p. 87.

20 Ibid., p. 30.

21 Ibid., pp. 71–2, 83–4.

22 See David Lampton, *The Three Faces of Chinese Power: Might, Money, and Minds* (Berkeley: University of California Press, 2008).

23 See, *inter alia*, 'Friend or foe?' [special report on China's place in the world], *The Economist*, 4 December 2010; 'Carps among the Spratlys', *The Economist*, 12 March 2011, p. 70; Demetri Sevastopulo and Kathrin Hille, 'China defends naval actions', *Financial Times*, 6 June 2011; 'Not littorally Shangri-La', *The Economist*, 11 June 2011, p. 62.

24 Albright wrote: 'During our many official meetings [in the late 1990s], we had an agenda that included nonproliferation, terrorism, human rights, market access, Tibet, religious freedom, the environment, and international crime, as well as Taiwan. I had the impression, however, that the Chinese idea of a perfect meeting would have consisted of a single statement on my part reiterating America's acceptance of Beijing's one China policy. For them, Taiwan was by far the paramount issue.' See Madeleine Albright, *Madam Secretary* (Basingstoke: Macmillan, 2003), p. 432.

25 M. Taylor Fravel, 'Power shifts and escalation: explaining China's use of force in territorial disputes', *International Security* 32/3 (2007–8), pp. 44–83.

26 See Jonathan Holslag, *Trapped Giant: China's Military Rise* (London: Routledge/ International Institute for Strategic Studies, 2010), p. 16.

27 See *The Economist*, 4 December 2010, p. 11.

28 See Joseph Nye, *The Future of Power* (New York: PublicAffairs, 2011), pp. 185–6.

29 See, *inter alia*, *The Economist*, 25 June 2011, pp. 15–16; and Wang Jisi, 'China's search for a grand strategy', *Foreign Affairs* 90/2 (2011), p. 69.

30 Quotations taken from 'Full text: China's peaceful development road', *People's Daily Online*, http://english.people.com.cn/200512/22/print20051222_230059.html (accessed July 2009).

31 This has justly been described as 'a watershed event in Chinese history'. Jing Men, 'Changing ideology in China and its impact on Chinese foreign policy', in Sujian Guo

and Shiping Hua, eds, *New Dimensions of Chinese Foreign Policy* (Lanham, MD: Lexington Books, 2007), pp. 13–14.

32 Chenghong Li, 'Increasing interdependence between China and the US and its implications for Chinese foreign policy', in Guo and Hua, *New Dimensions of Chinese Foreign Policy*, p. 225.

33 See, *inter alia*, Bates Gill and James Reilly, 'Sovereignty, intervention and peacekeeping: the view from Beijing', *Survival* 42/3 (2000), pp. 41–59; Pang Zhongying, 'China's changing attitude to UN peacekeeping', *International Peacekeeping* 12/1 (2005), pp. 87–104; and Bates Gill and Chin-Hao Huang, *China's Expanding Peacekeeping Role: Its Significance and the Policy Implications* (Stockholm: SIPRI, 2009).

34 David Shambaugh, 'China or America: which is the revisionist power?', *Survival* 43/3 (2001), p. 28. See also Shambaugh, 'Coping with a conflicted China', *Washington Quarterly* 34/1 (2011), pp. 17–20.

35 See, *inter alia*, Bates Gill, *Rising Star: China's New Security Diplomacy* (Washington, DC: Brookings Institution, 2007); Alastair Iain Johnston, 'Is China a status quo power?', *International Security* 27/4 (2003), pp. 5–56; Evan Medeiros and M. Taylor Fravel, 'China's new diplomacy', *Foreign Affairs* 82/6 (2003), pp. 22–35; and Yong Deng and Thomas Moore, 'China views globalization: toward a new great power politics?', *Washington Quarterly* 27/3 (2004), pp. 117–36.

36 In 2009, one Chinese official was quoted as saying that all his country could do was 'apply a little oil to the lock' in order to help get negotiations started. See 'The importance of being insincere', *The Economist*, 15 January 2011, p. 53.

37 See John Park, 'Inside multilateralism: the six party talks', *Washington Quarterly* 28/4 (2005), pp. 81–5; and Hui Zhang, 'Ending North Korea's nuclear ambitions: the need for stronger Chinese action', *Arms Control Today* 39 (2009), www.armscontrol.org/act/2009_07-08/zhang (accessed September 2009).

38 See 'Friends like these', *The Economist*, 2 July 2011, p. 53.

39 Thomas Christensen, 'The advantages of an assertive China', *Foreign Affairs* 90/2 (2011), pp. 55–7.

40 'Sailing to strengthen global security', *People's Daily Online*, 26 December 2008, http://english.people.com.cn/90001/90776/90786/6562488.html (accessed July 2009).

41 'Defender of a harmonious ocean', *People's Daily Online*, 24 April 2009, http://english.people.com.cn/90001/90776/90786/6644733.html (accessed July 2009).

42 Wang Jisi, 'China's search for stability with America', *Foreign Affairs* 84/5 (2005), pp. 46–7.

43 Security Council Resolution 1973, 17 March 2011, http://daccess-dds-ny.un.org/doc/UNDOC/GEN/N11/268/39/PDF/N1126839.pdf?OpenElement (accessed July 2011).

44 See, *inter alia*, Gregory Chin and Ramesh Thakur, 'Will China change the rules of global order?', *Washington Quarterly* 33/4 (2010); and Christensen, 'The advantages of an assertive China'.

45 For a recent pessimistic assessment of the prospects of the Chinese government wholeheartedly embracing multilateralism, see Shambaugh, 'Coping with a conflicted China'.

Conclusions

1 George W. Bush, *Decision Points* (London: Virgin Books, 2010), p. 256.

2 Anne-Marie Slaughter, 'America's edge: power in the networked century', *Foreign Affairs* 88/1 (2009), p. 99.

3 See Ryan Lizza, 'The consequentialist: how the Arab spring remade Obama's foreign policy', *New Yorker*, 2 May 2011, http://www.newyorker.com/reporting/2011/05/02/110502fa_fact_lizza?printable=true (accessed July 2011).

4 Andrei Shleifer and Daniel Treisman, 'Why Moscow says no', *Foreign Affairs* 90/1 (2011), pp. 122–38.
5 See Thomas Christensen, 'The advantages of an assertive China', *Foreign Affairs* 90/2 (2011).
6 Hillary Rodham Clinton, 'Leading through civilian power', *Foreign Affairs* 89/6 (2010), p. 13.

Selected Further Reading

It has been a central argument of this book that the concept of power, and its applications in the contemporary international arena, have thus far been relatively under-analysed in the literature on world politics and international relations. With this in mind, readers may find a brief guide to further reading on the main issues and topics raised in these chapters helpful.

Chapters 1 and 2

The relative paucity of international relations literature on the concept of power does not mean that no help is available for those seeking to further their own thinking and understanding in this area. As is suggested in the early chapters of this book, a substantial, relevant and interesting literature has been developed by sociologists and philosophers. In spite of its vintage, Bertrand Russell's 1938 book *Power: A New Social Analysis* (London: George Allen & Unwin) remains a model of brevity, clarity and insightful analysis. Also useful on the core concept of power is the work of the American sociologist Talcott Parsons, collected in his *Politics and Social Structure* (New York: Free Press, 1969). Amongst more recent useful evaluations by sociologists are Dennis Wrong, *Power: Its Forms, Bases, and Uses* (New Brunswick, NJ: Transaction, 2004), and Steven Lukes, *Power: A Radical View* (2nd edn, Basingstoke: Palgrave, 2005).

The argument that there is a relative dearth in conceptual writing on power in the IR literature is not to say that no valuable published discussions exist. A useful early example – still frequently cited – is David Baldwin, 'Power analysis and world politics: new trends versus old tendencies', *World Politics* 31/2 (1979). A 2005 article by Michael Barnett and Raymond Duvall, 'Power in international politics', *International Organization* 59/1, also offers a useful exploration of various dimensions of the concept.

Over the past two decades, Joseph Nye has achieved comfortably more than anybody else in keeping debates about power alive in the international

relations field. His notion of 'soft' power has also achieved the rare acco-
lade – for a scholarly concept – of being frequently used by political leaders,
the media and the informed public. Readers interested in tracing the development of Nye's thinking on the concept may profitably consult, firstly,
his 1990 book *Bound to Lead: The Changing Nature of American Power* (New
York: Basic Books). This introduced soft power in the context of the
winding down of the Cold War and specifically in relation to the United
States. In 2004, Nye suggested, in *Soft Power: The Means to Success in World
Politics* (New York: PublicAffairs), that it could be useful for other states
and leaders too. Finally, in *The Future of Power* (New York: PublicAffairs,
2011), Nye argues for the effectiveness of political approaches judiciously
combining both soft and 'hard' power assets and resources – which he (and
others) have referred to as 'smart' power.

Chapter 3

Given the extensive and lively debates engendered by George W. Bush's
approach to international affairs during his first term in office, it is surprising that the academic literature on American unipolarity (as opposed to
specific aspects of the Bush foreign policy) is not more extensive. Those
seeking to explore the concept may usefully begin with Charles
Krauthammer's provocative article 'The unipolar moment', *Foreign Affairs*
70/1 (1990–1), which has been credited with introducing unipolarity into
the debates about post-Cold War international relations. A decade later,
Krauthammer reaffirmed his thesis in 'The unipolar moment revisited',
The National Interest 70 (2002–3).

The controversies provoked by Bush's foreign policy during the early
2000s produced many polemics suggesting that American unipolarity was
damaging and destructive *per se*. On the other hand, a number of interesting articles were published arguing for the virtues of unipolarity as, relatively, the most stabilizing power arrangement available in the post-Cold
War world. A principal exponent of this view has been William Wohlforth.
See especially his article 'The stability of a unipolar world', *International
Security* 24/1 (1999).

For Wohlforth and others, what counts is the willingness of American
leaders, even under unipolarity, to work cooperatively and multilaterally
with others in pursuit of shared goals. They argue that there is no
intrinsic reason why this should not be possible – and desirable – in a structurally unipolar world. See, *inter alia*, Samuel Huntington, 'The lonely

superpower', *Foreign Affairs* 78/2 (1999), and Wohlforth and Stephen Brooks, 'American primacy in perspective', *Foreign Affairs* 81/4 (2002).

A major problem with the literature on unipolarity has been the tendency to emphasize its structural, rather than social, dimensions. A key exception to this trend has been Martha Finnemore's article 'Legitimacy, hypocrisy, and the social structure of unipolarity', *World Politics* 61/1 (2009). This offers a thoughtful evaluation of the social dimensions of unipolarity and the resources American leaders could devote to making it work in the interests of both the US and the international community generally.

Chapters 4, 5 and 6

Analysis of the record of the George W. Bush administration in international affairs has been largely negative. Doubtless a 'revisionist' view will develop over time, and Bush has defended his approach in his memoirs *Decision Points* (London: Virgin Books, 2010). Cogent general criticisms of the administration's approach, especially during its first term, and its damaging effect on American power can be found in Ivo Daalder and James Lindsay, *America Unbound: The Bush Revolution in Foreign Policy* (Washington, DC: Brookings Institution, 2003); John Newhouse, *Imperial America: The Bush Assault on the World Order* (New York: Knopf, 2003); and David Calleo, *Follies of Power: America's Unipolar Fantasy* (Cambridge: Cambridge University Press, 2009).

Francis Fukuyama's 2006 critique *After the Neocons: America at the Crossroads* (London: Profile Books) is especially interesting because he wrote as someone who had shared many of the premises on which the Bush foreign policy was based. Fukuyama argued that the administration undermined its objectives by over-emphasizing the utility of military force and under-emphasizing the importance of support from allied and friendly states. Similar criticisms are offered in Christian Reus-Smit, *American Power and World Order* (Cambridge: Polity, 2004), and Barry Buzan, 'A leader without followers? The United States in world politics after Bush', *International Politics* 45/5 (2008).

Other Bush critics based their case on his administration's ignorance or neglect of the importance and utility of soft power and the related concept of international legitimacy. An 'eminent persons' commission established by the Center for Strategic and International Studies in Washington, DC, and co-chaired by Joseph Nye, published in 2007 *A Smarter, More Secure America*, which can be credited with popularizing the notion of smart power. Similar criticisms were offered in 2008 by James Steinberg, in 'Real leaders do soft power: learning the lessons of Iraq', *Washington Quarterly* 31/2. Steinberg went on to serve as deputy secretary of state in the Obama administration. Readers seeking to access the debates on the impact of the Bush approach on American legitimacy can profitably begin with Robert Kagan, 'America's crisis of legitimacy', *Foreign Affairs* 83/2 (2004), and the rejoinder by Robert Tucker and David Hendrickson, 'The sources of American legitimacy', *Foreign Affairs* 83/6 (2004).

Chapters 7 and 8

Readers seeking access to contemporary thinking and debates about Russia's power and place in the world have three excellent English-language sources available. Two are academic journals and fairly widely available in university libraries: *International Affairs* [Moscow] and *Russia in Global Affairs*. Both regularly feature articles by prominent Russian leaders and officials as well as academics. Notwithstanding the reported enervation of critical opinions during the Putin era, both journals have, thus far, continued to publish articles offering a variety of views – some sharply critical – of Russia's foreign policy. The weekly translations of articles from a variety of daily and periodical publications, collected and published in *The Current Digest of the Post-Soviet Press*, is an invaluable research resource.

Amongst Western-based analysts, the work of Dmitri Trenin stands out for being well informed and perceptive, in particular 'Russia leaves the West', *Foreign Affairs* 85/4 (2006); 'Russia redefines itself and its relations with the West', *Washington Quarterly* 30/2 (2007); and *Getting Russia Right* (Washington, DC: Carnegie Endowment for International Peace, 2007).

Considering the importance of multipolarity in Russian domestic debates on international affairs, there is a surprising dearth of Western academic literature on this topic. An important exception is Thomas Ambrosio, *Challenging America's Global Preeminence: Russia's Quest for Multipolarity* (Aldershot: Ashgate, 2005). Overall, however, multipolarity – both in its Russian manifestations and more generally – remains a neglected area in Western academic debates.

Chapters 9 and 10

The general perception in Europe and the US of China as a 'rising superpower' – and perhaps also an emerging threat to Western interests – has ensured that an extensive literature has developed on aspects of this alleged rise and its likely consequences. Military developments have been thoroughly evaluated, and readers seeking a sense of the main issues can profitably consult David Shambaugh, 'China's military views the world', *International Security* 24/3 (1999–2000); Denny Roy, 'China's reaction to American predominance', *Survival* 45/3 (2003); 'The long march to be a superpower', *The Economist*, 4 August 2007; and Jonathan Holslag, *Trapped Giant: China's Military Rise* (London: Routledge/International Institute for Strategic Studies, 2010).

Thoughtful analysis of the extent to which Chinese military developments may challenge American interests in Asia, and also the security of China's smaller neighbours, can be found in Thomas Christensen, 'Posing problems without catching up', *International Security* 25/4 (2001); David Shambaugh, 'China engages Asia', *International Security* 29/3 (2004–5); and M. Taylor Fravel, 'Power shifts and escalation: explaining China's use of force in territorial disputes', *International Security* 32/3 (2007–8). The official Chinese concept of 'peaceful rise' – still apparently influential in leadership circles – was developed in a series of speeches by Zheng Bijian from the late 1990s. They have been collected in *China's Peaceful Rise: Speeches of Zheng Bijian 1997–2005* (Washington, DC: Brookings Institution, 2005).

There has been a growing debate about the nature and extent of China's soft power assets and resources. It began with the publication of Joshua Cooper Ramo's *The Beijing Consensus* (London: Foreign Policy Centre, 2004). Other notable contributors have been Stefan Halper, *The Beijing Consensus: How China's Authoritarian Model Will Dominate the Twenty-First Century* (New York: Basic Books, 2010), and Joshua Kurlantzick, *Charm Offensive: How China's Soft Power is Transforming the World* (New Haven, CT: Yale University Press, 2007). Cogent scepticism is offered by Shaun Breslin in *The Soft Notion of China's 'Soft Power'* (London: Chatham House, 2011).

The balance of Western academic opinion has been moving towards the view that the Chinese government is increasingly accommodating itself to the norms and approaches of the US-centred international system. Useful articulations of such views can be found in Thomas Christensen, 'The advantages of an assertive China', *Foreign Affairs* 90/2 (2011); Bates Gill, *Rising Star: China's New Security Diplomacy* (Washington, DC: Brookings Institution, 2007); Alastair Iain Johnston, 'Is China a status quo power?', *International Security* 27/4 (2003); Evan Medeiros and M. Taylor Fravel, 'China's new diplomacy', *Foreign Affairs* 82/6 (2003); and Yong Deng and

Thomas Moore, 'China views globalization: toward a new great power politics?', *Washington Quarterly* 27/3 (2004). David Shambaugh has been an articulate dissenter from this emerging consensus, and has expressed his views, *inter alia*, in 'China or America: which is the revisionist power?', *Survival* 43/3 (2001), and 'Coping with a conflicted China', *Washington Quarterly* 34/1 (2011).

Index